A DAY AT THE RACES

The Horses, People and Races
that shaped the Sport of Kings

PETER MAY

MERLIN UNWIN BOOKS

First published in Great Britain by Merlin Unwin Books Ltd 2022

Merlin Unwin Books Ltd
Palmers House
7 Corve Street
Ludlow
Shropshire SY8 1DB
UK

www.merlinunwin.co.uk

ISBN 978-1-913159-35-1
Typeset in Minion Pro by Merlin Unwin Books
Printed and bound by CPI Group (UK) Ltd, Croydon

By the same author

In Search of the Winning System
Forecasting Methods for Horseracing
Horseracing: A Guide to Profitable Betting
Jumps Racing for Profit
Flat Racing for Profit

Contents

Weights, Distances, Currency

Many measurements given in this book are presented in imperial format. The following list possibly will make conversion to decimal easier, should that be necessary.

Weights

One imperial ton comprises twenty hundredweights (cwt)
One hundredweight is equivalent to eight stone (st)
One stone is fourteen pounds (lbs)
One pound weighs the same as 0.45 kilograms

Distances

There are eight furlongs to the mile
Each furlong is 220 yards in distance, making one mile 1760 yards
There are ten chains to the furlong, therefore 22 yards to a chain
One yard is equivalent to 0.91 metres
One yard is also three feet or thirty-six inches
A hand is four inches
One inch is the same as 2.54 centimetres

Currency

Pre-1971 there were twenty shillings (s) to a pound (£sterling)
One shilling was equal to twelve pence (d), making 240d equal to £1
A guinea was equivalent to twenty-one shillings, effectively £1.05 in decimal currency

Note: Figures in square brackets in the text throughout this book represent equivalent monetary values in 2020

Foreword by
Henrietta Knight
Racehorse Trainer

This is a fascinating book which chronologically traces the history of horseracing by way of highly informative sections relating to a variety of different aspects of the sport. From the first horserace ever run under rules in 1519 to the more familiar races and racehorses of the modern era, Peter May gives the reader in-depth information laced with facts and figures.

Flat racing was where horseracing began and many famous races were run in the 16th, 17th and 18th centuries but owners were not able to select their colours until 1762. In 1828 there was a dead heat for the Derby but the first recognized steeplechase did not take place until 1830 and thoroughbred racehorses were not given their January 1st birthdays until 1858. In Australia, the initial Melbourne Cup was run in 1861 but the first Sunday race meeting in Great Britain was not until 1992.

In addition to historical facts, Peter has selected horses and jockeys whose racing lives have significantly contributed to the sport. From Fred Archer, the brilliant champion jockey of the 19th century who tragically took his own life at the age of 29, to the successful careers of horses like Arkle, Best Mate, Desert Orchid, Enable, Galileo and Nijinsky, we are reminded of great names in racing's history.

A Day at the Races is a must for any horseracing enthusiast and should, without doubt, take its place on the bookshelves in the homes of all true students who will have their knowledge enriched by opening its pages. Peter May's enthusiasm is infectious. His research is phenomenal.

Preface

Horseracing has a fascinating history. In the beginning, it featured perhaps just a couple of faster than average colts ploughing their way across a mud-filled, open field; probably just a matter of a minor local rivalry and a small wager on the side.

Today, this global enterprise is very far removed from such a humble birth. It is lucrative and high-tech. It is fiercely competitive and has become the lifeblood of millions of avid followers, on the course, on television, on tablets, and on stream worldwide. The following chapters focus on a selection of critical days that served to shape the destiny of this sport of kings, as we now know it, at the start of the third millennium.

Since c.1500 (the starting line for this journey of discovery), not all the special days celebrated here are associated with landmark episodes that transformed the industry itself. Many are preserved to shine a light on extraordinary human and equine achievements that keep so many racing fans coming back for more.

Others mark key events in the evolution of the sport such as the introduction of the latest technology, the vagaries of dress codes, new races, and the countless tweaks to basic racing rules, which have all had an impact. References to the gambles won and lost are a reminder of horseracing's close association with, to some observers, the less desirable facet of the game. In an attempt to paint an even broader picture, these staging posts in racing's past are presented alongside other highly significant contemporaneous historical events in order to provide additional social context.

I have no doubt that some readers will not entirely agree with the list of horses, people, and races I have decided to include and will be surprised by some of the omissions. But a line has to be drawn somewhere and as much as I would have liked to include essays on Highflyer, Persimmon, Sadler's Wells, Danehill, Dancing Brave, Badsworth Boy, Remittance Man, Sprinter Sacre, Martin Pipe, Sir Henry Cecil, Aidan O'Brien, Fred Winter, and Henrietta Knight, unfortunately space prevented it. What is left is, hopefully, both entertaining and informative.

Peter May
January 2022

Timeline of Events

Early Years 1500-1799

Though races did take place in the sixteenth and seventeenth centuries, it was not until the emergence of a more rigorous structure, characterised by regular meetings, that interest in horseracing in Great Britain began to grow – and it did, rapidly. By the early years of the eighteenth century, racecourses were appearing all over the country and the sport had become so popular that legislation had to be passed to limit its expansion. Ascot racecourse was founded, suspended due to this new act of parliament, then reopened some years later.

As racing evolved, greater regulation was introduced to help manage the ever-expanding sport: by the end of the period, jockeys were required to wear the colours associated with their runners' owners, and James Weatherby, under the watchful eye of the Jockey Club, took over the publication of the racing calendar and introduced the stud book. Three Classics were added to the racing programme, and towards the end of the 1700s greater importance was attached to the Ascot June meeting. This era also saw one of the turf's most influential horses dominate races, a hugely successful jockey die in poverty, and more than one duel on Ascot Heath.

The First Horserace Run Under Rules   *20 March 1519*

Of course, the exact point in history when humans decided that riding horses was better than walking cannot be identified with total certainty. What can be asserted is that this newly found relationship bred in man an impulse to move at speed and a simultaneous urge to go faster than others. The competitive instinct to race was born.

The earliest registered accounts of horses competing against each other were during the reign of Henry II. With the exception of festival days, each Friday at Smithfield market, then named Smoothfield due to the smooth, level ground, horses were auctioned and also raced two or three at a time on occasion. These events attracted large crowds of London residents including earls, barons and knights, who no doubt made wagers on their fancies. One contemporary writer described the action thus: 'the grand point is, to prevent a competitor from getting before them. The horses tremble, are impatient and are continually in motion; and, at last, the signal once given, they strike, devour the course, hurrying along with unremitting velocity. The jockies... clap spurs to the willing horses, brandish their whips, and cheer them with their cries.' While these contests could be considered a very basic type of racing, there were no rules, no apparent regulation, and no recording of results.

Identifying the earliest race run under some form of rules, and accompanying regulations, is not something about which anyone can be definite. The most likely candidate, though, is the Kiplingcotes Derby. Documentary evidence exists that puts the inaugural running of this race in the year 1519, a time when Henry VIII was writing music, playing tennis, hunting, jousting, and having the occasional disagreement with his neighbours across the Channel.

The Founders of the contest, a body of Foxhunters, calculated that in order to attract public attention and put the race on a sound footing, a certain amount of regulation was required. They stipulated that:

A horse race to be observed and ridd yearly, on the third Thursday in March; open to horses of all ages, to carry horseman's weight, 10 stones, exclusive of the saddle, to enter at ye post, before eleven o'clock on the morning of ye race. The race to be run before two.

The designated course was four miles in length and traversed tracks, lanes, and fields. The site, near modern-day Market Weighton, was chosen because that particular part of Yorkshire most closely resembled the Downs of the southern counties. In accordance with the initial pronouncement the race had to be run every year, so even if conditions meant an event was unable to take place, a single horse was walked along the route. This is similar to walkovers in races under Jockey Club rules where the only declared runner is required to walk, or canter, past the Judge's box in order to be awarded the win.

By quirk of the rules, the runner-up in the Kiplingcotes Derby normally receives more money than the winner. Whilst a fixed amount is allocated to the race winner, the runner-up receives a proportion of each entry fee that can often exceed the winner's reward.

The Kiplingcotes Derby is still run every year, attracting spectators from around the world. The 2019 race marked its 500th anniversary and was won by Tracey Corrigan on her horse named Frog.

The Newmarket Plate   8 October 1665

Customs and traditions have played a role in shaping British culture for many hundreds of years. From cheese and tar-barrel rolling to Morris dancing, every part of the nation has its own traditions. Each Shrove Tuesday at Chester it was customary for a company of saddlers to present the Drapers with a wooden bell embellished with flowers. The ceremony, in which the bell was placed on the point of a lance, was attended by the Mayor and took place on the Roodee. In 1539 the wooden bell was replaced by one made of silver, valued at 3s 4d. The Mayor of Chester, Henry Gee, offered the newly named St George's Bell as a prize 'to be given to him who shall run the best and fastest on horseback'. The first race was run in February 1539. Supposedly, it was from the Mayor's surname that the phrase "gee-gees" was coined.

Running horses against each other for a prize gained interest amongst 'the noblemen and gentlemen, and the more opulent class of yeoman' during the reign of King James I, the monarch responsible for importing the Markham Arabian to England and building Palace House Stables in Newmarket. Initially, horseraces were simple affairs. There was no weighing of riders, who were either the owners or grooms; no racetrack, just a defined stretch of land over which to race; and few, if any, rules. However, towards the end of the first Stuart King of England's time in power, a more structured form of racing had been introduced, with rules governing the contests rigidly enforced.

During the reign of King Charles I, races continued to be held throughout the country with Hyde Park and Newmarket often used as racing venues. The English Civil War brought a halt to this ever-growing pastime, and horseracing was banned by Cromwell for periods in 1654 and 1658. Civil and military authorities were instructed to seize all racehorses and arrest any spectators who ignored these proclamations. With the Restoration, though, came King Charles II and the sport once again began to flourish with no little assistance from the monarch.

While the Great Plague ravaged the population of London, King Charles II, a keen equestrian, turned his attention to horseracing. At his insistence, bells were no longer offered as trophies and were replaced by more elaborate cups and plates often modelled on historical events. An sculpture of Boadicea standing in a chariot drawn by two horses, her injured daughter by her side, accompanied by a guard with sword, and a Roman standard bearer being trampled under hooves, formed the concept of the first Stewards' Cup. The original Goodwood Cup was a depiction of King Charles II, on horseback, presenting a cup to the winning jockey who is accompanied by a racehorse. Perhaps, even more significantly, the monarch declared that a horserace should be run at Newmarket 'on the second Thursday of October for ever'. The Newmarket Town Plate was thus inaugurated and has been run every year since.

A long list of rules accompanied the declaration of the race. These covered aspects of the contest such as which side of the flags to pass; the weight each horse had to carry (12st); entry fees; the time of the parade; and a regulation relating to who was, and more importantly, was not, allowed to ride. It would be natural to expect that such a rule would refer to riding ability, but not in this case. The focus was on employment status. The rule made it abundantly clear that the race organisers thought the holders of some jobs were not worthy to compete. It simply stated: 'No man is admitted to ride for the plate or prize that is either serving-man or groom.' A clear divide between the classes had been established and would be maintained in racing for many years.

King Charles II was not only a keen horseman but a very accomplished rider, and in the first few years of the Plate he won the race at least twice; possibly three times depending on which source of results is believed. Apart from the unique prize of a box of Newmarket sausages, the race also broke with convention by allowing women jockeys. Indeed, until 1972 it was the only race in Great Britain run under Jockey Club rules that allowed female riders.

First Race Meeting at Ascot   *11 August 1711*

With the death of William of Orange, Anne, the second daughter of James II became Queen of England in 1702. It was not an easy time for a new monarch to assume control. The military was engaged in a seemingly unending series of wars with France; the judiciary remained heavily influenced by the Church to the extent that trials for witchcraft were still routinely held; and parliament had descended into turmoil with the Whigs and Tories fighting to gain the upper hand. To alert an uninformed public to the difficulties the country was experiencing, the first daily newspaper was launched. The single-page *Daily Courant* was published by Elizabeth Mallet on Wednesday 11th March 1702. Fortunately, it was not quite all doom and gloom for the nation, and the paper was able to report many successes and advancements. Despite the conflict with France and the political chaos, in a number of ways, the country was flourishing especially with regard to agriculture, literature, and the sciences.

Queen Anne and her Consort, Prince George of Denmark, were patrons of Newmarket so it was no surprise that the sport of horseracing found favour. In 1711 the Queen purchased the Common at Ascot for a sum of £558 [£107,000] from William Lowen and, declaring it to be an ideal place for 'horses to gallop at full stretch', gave instructions for a course to be prepared.

Many men representing various trades were tasked with constructing the new racecourse and were rewarded well for their efforts considering the average rate of pay for skilled tradesmen was less than two shillings per day. As Cawthorne and Herod note in their history of the course, the carpenter, William Erlybrown, received the sum of £15 2s 8d [£2,900] for 'making and fixing the posts and other work'. Benjamin Cuthbert was paid £2 15s [£550] for painting those same posts; and a further £1 1s 6d [£200] was awarded to John Grape for 'engrossing the Articles for Her Majesty's Plate', enough to buy a stone of wool if he so desired.

The 12th July edition of the *London Gazette* included an announcement to the effect that 'Her Majesty's Plate of 100gns [£21,000] will be run on Ascot Common near Windsor on Tuesday 7th August.' The race was to be staged over three heats and was open to horses up to the age of six years, all of which had to carry 12st. Another race worth 50gns was subsequently declared for 6th August. However, due to the length of time it took to prepare the course, both races had to be postponed until the following week and it was not until Saturday 11th August 1711 that Queen Anne 'in a brilliant suite drove over from Windsor Castle' to enjoy the sport.

The following month Queen Anne was back at Ascot for a two-day meeting. These events were conducted at a leisurely pace with only one race scheduled for each day. The conditions attached to the races were very much the same as for some weight-for-age contests of today: entry was restricted to horses of a particular age that had not previously won a race to the value of £20.

For this second Ascot meeting the Queen was accompanied by the 'reigning beauty of the period' Miss Forester, a Maid of Honour. It was reported that Miss Forester was 'dressed like a man' with a 'long white riding coat, a full-flapped waistcoat, and a small cocked hat, three cornered, bound with broad gold lace, the point placed full in front over a white powdered long flowing periwig.' Ascot had not only taken the first tentative steps on the way to becoming one of the most prestigious racecourses in the country, but had already been noted for its patrons' fashionable attire.

Minimum Prize-Money Introduced   *24 June 1740*

In the early part of the eighteenth century, racing was evolving rapidly. The arrival of the Byerley Turk, the Darley Arabian, and the Godolphin Arabian who, apparently, was high on the withers, deformed by a hollow back and stood fifteen hands, established the foundations of the English Thoroughbred.

According to the racing analyst Admiral Rous, the first Arabian-Anglo crosses averaged fourteen hands two inches in height and had increased to fifteen hands by 1800. Rous calculated that their height was increasing year on year and by 1870 was fifteen hands two-and-a-half inches. Soon after the arrival of these stallions, bloodstock sales were taking place on a regular basis in London. One of the very first was staged at Hyde Park Corner by Richard Tattersall – a name associated with the sport ever since.

By 1740 horseracing was gaining in popularity with every sector of the population while other pastimes faded from the public gaze. Bear- and bull-baiting were such pursuits in which interest was lost. As one writer of the age noted 'The decline of demoralising pastimes and pursuits, must invariably be taken in proof of mental and social improvement.' However there was also a downside to this rapid expansion of horseracing. Minor unregulated meetings were springing up all over the country, which 'did nothing towards the advancement of the Turf' and, to some minds, cast discredit on the sport due to the high degree of lawlessness. Such unsavoury conduct was not restricted to the minor tracks though. The race for the Gold Cup at York in 1719 resulted in the disqualification of the winner 'for foul riding', a fight between the jockeys, a dispute of 'no very amiable character' between the runners' owners, and a court case, the outcome of which was a re-run of the contest.

Despite the evidence that all race meetings were subject to disagreements and occasional violent behaviour, the spotlight fell unfairly on the smaller meetings. The Duke of Bolton and his contemporaries outlined a bill with the specific intention of putting 'an end to the objectionable race meetings' by which they meant the minor meetings. This bill became an Act and, as summarised by James Whyte in *The History of the British Turf* (Vol. 1), stipulated:

Be it enacted by the authority aforesaid that from and after June 24th 1740, no person or persons whatsoever shall start or run in any match with or between any horse, mare, or gelding, for any sum of money, plate, or prize, or anything whatsoever, unless such match shall be started or run at Newmarket Heath, in the counties of Cambridge or Suffolk, or Black Hambleton, in the county of York, or the said sum of money, plate, or prize, or other thing be of the real intrinsic value of £50 or upwards.

Furthermore, the Act specified that runners could only be entered by their *bona fide* owners, and an owner could not enter more than one horse for a race. The penalty for illegally running a horse was not suspension for a short period of time, or even a cash fine, it was far more extreme. Any owner found to have breached these rules would have to forfeit the animal.

Parliament was keen to use horseracing as a way to 'improve and strengthen the breed' for military engagements where horses needed to be able to carry heavy weights over long distances. In an attempt to satisfy this objective the Act dictated the weights horses should carry: 10st for five-year-olds, 11st for six-year-olds and 12st for older runners. It was hoped that this stipulation would encourage breeders to focus on stronger more robust horses that would be better suited to the demands of the cavalry and provide an advantage in any future combat situation. The seriousness with which the Administration believed in this ill-considered plan was evident from the penalties imposed for failure to meet this new law. Weight-related infringements were exceptionally harshly penalised: forfeiture of the horse and a £200 [£40,000] fine. The early eighteenth century was not a good time to "weigh-in light".

Remarkably, Ascot racecourse became one of the casualties of the minimum prize regulation. Considering the Berkshire track's prominence in the hierarchy of modern day racecourses, it seems incredible that it could not satisfy the new financial conditions required of the Act. In 1740 the venue was poorly funded, despite being well supported by racegoers and, as a result, no further meetings were held at the course until 1744.

Owners Select Their Colours   *Mid October 1762*

Although in England the use of coloured silks by jockeys can be traced back to the early 1500s, the writings of the Roman poet Juvenal referred to chariot races in which distinguishing jackets coloured green and red were worn in Rome as early as the second century.

It was not until 1762 that colours were formally regularised and made compulsory in England. Before this date jockeys were allowed to wear any racing attire they chose. Most opted for a particular style that comprised of a black velvet cap with French peak, a white cambric cravat, long body coat, knee breeches, white cotton stockings, and black leather shoes. As well as being far from aerodynamic, the similarity of the clothing caused a great deal of confusion at the start and finish of races. Consequently the Jockey Club, which had been formed a few years earlier in 1750, took action and required jockeys to wear the owner's designated colours 'for the better convenience of distinguishing each horse during a race, and to avoid disputes that may arise from non-recognition of colours'. Owners chose sets of colours and, as of the second meeting in October, it was required of them to ensure their jockeys wore suitably coloured clothing. The colours registered for the Duke of Devonshire at the time were described simply as "straw", and they still are today some 250 years later.

Eclipse by a Distance   *1 April 1764*

Eclipse was so named because he was foaled during the solar eclipse on 1st April 1764 at the Cranbourne Lodge Stud owned by the Duke of Cumberland. As a yearling, Eclipse was of dubious temperament. In appearance he was on the large side, not particularly attractive, with a white blaze and one white sock on his off-hind. His owner-breeder, the youngest son of King George II, never fully recovered from a wound sustained at the Battle of Dettingen during the War of Austrian Succession and did not live to see Eclipse, a son of Marske, grow into the powerful horse that dominated racing for two seasons. At the dispersal sale of the Duke's bloodstock, after his death in 1765, Eclipse was purchased by William Wildman for around 80gns [£16,000].

Horses tended to start their racing careers later in life in the 1700s, so Eclipse was given time to grow fully into his frame before he started racing. Although he improved physically, his temperament did not, so Wildman sent him to a "nagsman" at Epsom to be broken. There he was 'ridden all day and occasionally all night' but, to the bewilderment of his riders, this did not appear to tire the animal. He just seemed able to keep running.

This approach to "training" may seem extreme, even verging on cruel, by modern standards. Similarly, running horses over distances of four miles three times in a single day may also be deemed excessive nowadays. The harshness of these methods was not intentional, there was no desire to effect some type of punishment on the animals. Horseracing was still in its infancy and a great deal of knowledge was yet to be gained regarding training, preparation and racing. In fact, horses had always been highly prized in Britain and, as a result, were well treated by their owners. As far back as the Anglo-Saxon era horses were revered, and in the hierarchy of animals were ranked second only to humans. Evidence for this exists in a document dated 1,000 A.D. in which the level of financial compensation for loss of various animals was delineated. Quoting this document, Admiral Rous explains in *Racing Past and Future*:

> *If a horse was destroyed or negligently lost, the compensation demanded was thirty shillings; for a mare or colt, twenty shillings... a cow, twenty-four pence; a pig, eight pence; and a man, an Anglo-Saxon pound, forty-eight shillings.*

The punishment for anyone convicted of deliberately injuring or killing racehorses was severe in the extreme. By way of an example, in 1811 Daniel Dawson was convicted of poisoning several horses 'by means of a crooked-syringe'. His penalty was execution by hanging.

Fortunately for all those involved, Eclipse survived his initial training and by the age of five had become a particularly impressive-looking horse, the 'object of universal comment'. According to one chronicler, 'His shoulders had great size, lowness, and obliquity; his fore-quarters were short, his quarters ample and finely proportioned, the muscles of his fore-arm and thigh greatly developed.' Wildman finally considered Eclipse ready to race and after some notable pre-dawn trials he finally made his racecourse debut at Epsom on 3rd May 1769. Word of his impressive performances in the trials had undoubtedly reached the ears of the betting public because he started as the 1/4 favourite. He won the first heat he contested easily, and as the myth goes, the trackside observer Dennis O'Kelly forecast the result of the second heat as "Eclipse first, the rest nowhere". In other words Eclipse to win by a distance (240 yards).

In the mid-1700s, it was not uncommon for racing at Epsom to start at 11am. After one or two heats, the racegoers returned to the town for a leisurely lunch before making their way back to the track for the next round of racing in the afternoon. This midday break also gave the horses a chance to recover from their morning's exertions. The rules of the time allowed for a certain amount of recuperative remedial treatment on the part of the trainer. Horses were rubbed down and any wounds treated, generally with solutions and poultices that contained alcohol. In fact, a great many recipes for healing and feeding thoroughbreds consisted of alcohol to a greater or lesser degree. To quote the advice proffered by Thomas Fairfax:

> If [the horse] is parched, he is to have a julep, made of gin, two quarts of barley water, and two ounces of syrup of lemons.

For eye infections, one recommendation was to use the 'gall of a pike or partridge, or the juice of celandine' mixed with gum tragacanth. Although this may sound more like an excerpt from a Shakespearean play, celandine is still sold as a treatment for warts and other skin ailments, and gum tragacanth is often incorporated into pharmaceutical products. Anglers will be relieved to know that the gall of a pike is no longer used as a cure for infections.

An alternative way of treating an infection of the eye was to create a funnel from a sheet of paper then 'set fire to the wide end and as it burns, a small quantity of oil will descend to the narrow part' which could be applied to the eye using a feather once it had been 'diluted with spittle'. Naturally alcohol also had a role to play with this treatment. After half an hour, it was suggested that the eye should be washed with water mixed with brandy. Based on the widespread use of the alcohol-based remedies that were so popular at the time, it is a wonder that any horse ran in a sober state.

O'Kelly's audacious claim regarding Eclipse's dominance would have remained uppermost in the thoughts of all those who had witnessed the morning contest, and would have been discussed at length on the journey back to the track. Due to the ease of his initial success, Eclipse did not require any form of "alcoholic healing" nor did the morning's exertions appear to have taxed his stamina to any great extent. The next race was over four miles, and for the first three miles he matched strides with his rivals, giving onlookers the impression that the race may unfold into a hard-fought finish. But in the final mile Eclipse powered away, and as he approached the winning post it was clear O'Kelly's prediction had been realised. No one was left unimpressed by the display, not least the Irishman who immediately purchased a half share for 650gns [£125,000]. It was an excellent investment, and much to O'Kelly's delight Eclipse raced a further eight times (including walkovers) in 1769, winning all eight contests. The following year O'Kelly purchased him outright.

Dennis O'Kelly was not a typical eighteenth century racehorse owner in that he was not a member of the aristocracy. In his early days, O'Kelly spent a short period of his life in the Fleet Prison where he had been confined for issues relating to debt. This jail-time had heightened his awareness of the many corrupt practices that were so successful in parting so many wealthy men from their money, especially those with an interest in gambling. After his release his luck turned and through various borderline-legal activities and shrewd investments, many of which were betting-related (no doubt a product of his newly acquired knowledge), he began to accumulate a substantial fortune which allowed him to expand his horseracing interests.

At that time in England the class system still reigned supreme. Even though O'Kelly owned one of the best racehorses ever to run, as well as a training estate near Epsom, many doors were still closed to him. The one he dearly wanted to open was that of the Jockey Club. O'Kelly was repeatedly refused admittance to the select institution, a decision that also deprived him from racing his horses in the more valuable Newmarket Stakes contests. He protested against this clear injustice any way he could, but to no avail.

Although the actions he took ultimately failed to achieve his objective of shaming the Jockey Club into granting his admission, they must have given him a degree of personal satisfaction. One such attempt at fighting back was to employ a stable jockey. This was nothing new, and many jockeys today are tied to particular owners, but O'Kelly's offer had a twist.

He approached a jockey and outlined the basic terms: for an annual stipend he could only ride for O'Kelly in races in which O'Kelly had runners. The jockey agreed to this, but then the owner offered to double the fee if the jockey further agreed never to ride for 'any of the black legged fraternity'. The jockey was confused and asked for clarification. O'Kelly replied '[what] I mean by the black legged fraternity [is] the Duke of Grafton, the Duke of Dorset...' and continued naming all the current members of the Jockey Club. He then added 'and all the set of *thaves* that belong to the humbug societies, and bug a boo clubs, where they can meet and rob one another without fear of detection.' Though taken aback by this rant, given the amount of money involved the jockey had no hesitation in accepting the offer.

A second year of racing brought more success for O'Kelly and Eclipse. Nine wins from nine races in 1770 took Eclipse's tally to seventeen straight victories. His undoubted dominance was, ultimately, to end his career. Eclipse was so superior to all other runners it was becoming difficult to find opponents to take him on. Five of his races in 1770 were walkovers including his final engagement that had promised to be an intriguing contest. In early October, Eclipse was declared for the King's Plate at Newmarket where he would face the unbeaten Goldfinder, winner of the second running of The Jockey Club Cup. Goldfinder 'possessed extraordinary speed and power' and many racing enthusiasts thought that he would be a match for Eclipse. Unfortunately, racegoers did not get the chance to see these two great horses compete against each other. On the morning of the race, Goldfinder broke down while exercising. He never raced again, and nor did Eclipse.

With the likelihood of few, if any, challengers in 1771, O'Kelly had no choice but to retire Eclipse to stud, although his racing career was over Eclipse's impact on British racing continued. He soon became one of the leading sires of the age producing over 160 winning horses, including four Derby winners, which between them won over 850 races according to *Baily's Sports and Pastimes*. Admiral Rous asserted that Eclispe was 'unequalled in those days as a racehorse, and equally celebrated as the sire of remarkable horses', adding that 'every good racehorse of the present day [1870] can boast of Eclipse blood'.

O'Kelly was never granted membership of the Jockey Club, but continued to accumulate money through shrewd investments and his partnership with Charlotte Hayes, an acquaintance from his time in the Fleet Prison, until his death in 1787.

Jockey Club Appoints James Weatherby *Sometime in 1770*

While Captain James Cook was trying to get sand from the newly discovered Botany Bay out of his shoes, Jockey Club members were persuading a solicitor to transfer his practice from Newcastle to Newmarket. After much discussion he finally agreed, and in 1770 James Weatherby became 'Keeper of the Match Book' and Secretary to the Jockey Club.

As racing's popularity rose, so did the amount of work required to both organise and regulate it, tasks which fell on the Jockey Club's secretariat.

Along with James, his elder brother John was recruited to a management role. Together the brothers formed a new enterprise from their base in Old Burlington Street, London. Within a few years the pair had made significant improvements to the way racing was administered. In 1773 James Weatherby incorporated the publication of the *Racing Calendar*, first published by John Cheny in 1727, into their portfolio of racing-related work. Eighteen years later Weatherbys published the first *Stud Book* now known as the *General Stud Book*. Weatherbys have been responsible for the maintenance of all records relating to thoroughbreds in Great Britain and Ireland ever since, with the *General Stud Book* updated every four years.

The First St Leger Stakes   *24 September 1776*

The late 1770s was a difficult time for the ruling classes of Great Britain, especially for those with an interest in the New World. Control was slipping from Britain's grasp, and by July 1776 the Thirteen Colonies, which constituted British North America, had declared independence from Great Britain. Whilst this had a serious impact on wealthy speculators who had considered America as a way to make easy money, those who had adopted a more cautious approach and kept their money in the homeland were breathing a sigh of relief. Anthony St Leger was one such person. Born in Ireland in 1731 and educated at Eton and Cambridge, St Leger settled in Yorkshire in 1763 where, after a short spell in the House of Commons, his focus shifted to horseracing.

Yorkshire was a hotbed for racing and, as expressed by one writer, 'there are no people so strongly imbued with a love of the "sport of kings" as the natives of the wide county of York.' Racing had taken place at Doncaster since the end of the sixteenth century. Maps of the area dated 1595 show the location of two courses. These meetings had always been well attended, and while the overwhelming majority of racegoers were reasonably well behaved, the lethal combination of swords and wine did cause a certain amount of unruly conduct. The Mayor and Aldermen both complained of 'quarrels, murders and bloodsheds' during the races. Keen to see racing continue for economic reasons, the Corporation of Doncaster was required to act and ensure good order at future meetings. Therefore, in 1614 they paid Anthony Hog the sum of 1s 6d [£20] for 'makinge the waye at the horse-race.' Over the coming years, with a more diligent approach to organisation, the popularity of racing in Yorkshire continued to expand. This encouraged greater investment in horseracing and, not wanting to miss out, in the early 1770s Anthony St Leger augmented his involvement in the burgeoning sport by building a racecourse on the Park Hill estate near to his stud.

Together with Charles Watson-Wentworth (2nd Marquess of Rockingham), a former First Lord and leading critic of Prime Minister Lord North's handling of the American affairs, St Leger devised a new race for three-year-old horses to be run in the Doncaster region over a distance of two miles. The first running was at Cantley Common on 24th September 1776 and the winner was Allabaculla owned by none other than Charles Watson-Wentworth. To mark the transfer of the race to Town Moor in 1778 it was given a new title. Originally the race was to be known as the Rockingham Stakes, however the Marquess insisted that it should be named in honour of its other Founder, Anthony St Leger.

First Running of the Oaks Stakes   14 May 1779

The discovery by Henry Wicker of a mineral spring between Ashstead and Epsom may not have benefitted his cattle herd that were grazing in its vicinity during a hot, dry summer, but in a short space of time it transformed the village of Epsom into a fashionable health resort. Londoners descended in their thousands to partake of the 'extremely disagreeable saline matter' named "Epsom Salts" in the hope of improving their health. Even the noted diarist Samuel Pepys was attracted by the promise of the spring's healing properties and on one occasion 'did drink four pints'.

As the fashions changed during the era, spas at Bath and Cheltenham were suddenly more in vogue, and the once flourishing town of Epsom began to decline. Fortunately for local businesses, the region had other key attractions that played host to the more appealing vices. Epsom was located close to one of the best racetracks in the country that had staged races in the spring and summer since the reign of King James I, another life-long devotee of racing. And for those who preferred drinking to betting, or drinking and betting, a number of alehouses were to be found the area.

In the eighteenth century, alehouses were increasing in popularity throughout the country. Many were simply residential properties that sold home-brewed ale, though towards the end of the 1700s custom built premises were appearing in the larger towns. One such alehouse was to be found on Banstead Downs, a short distance from Epsom racecourse. Located in what amounted to a 'plantation of oaks', "The Oaks" alehouse served the residents of Surrey with 'homebrewed [ale] of the most bucolic kind', and rapidly acquired a thriving trade.

General John Burgoyne, sometime politician, playwright and soldier (celebrated for his efforts in the American Revolutionary War), took a liking to The Oaks, most probably due to its location, and purchased it. Over the coming years Burgoyne 'added to the extent and elegance of the building, and fitted the place up for a hunting lodge'. Never a man to refuse a good deal, Burgoyne leased the property, along with the land, to his nephew Lord Derby (Edward Smith-Stanley, 12th Earl of Derby), who also enlarged the house and enclosed a large portion of the adjoining fields. The circumference of the extended property now stretched to approximately two miles.

At a dinner party at The Oaks, Lord Derby and Sir Charles Bunbury, whilst discussing the success of the St Leger, decided to instigate a race for three-year-old fillies over a shorter distance of one-and-a-half miles. The first running of this race, the Oaks Stakes, was in 1779. It attracted a field of twelve runners and was won by the 5/2 favourite, Bridget, owned by Lord Derby.

The following year Lord Derby and Bunbury introduced a similar race open to colts and fillies, this time over a mile though it was extended to twelve furlongs in 1874. Whereas Lord Derby named the Oaks Stakes after his property, this new race was given the name of his earldom. Whether it is true or not, the enduring myth surrounding the naming of the race declares that it was decided on the flip of a coin; had Bunbury won the toss then the race would have been named in his honour. Though he missed out on the naming, Bunbury gained a certain amount of satisfaction when his runner, Diomed, won the inaugural running of the race in 1780.

Three years later in 1783 the Oaks Stakes was won by Lord Grosvenor's Maid Of The Oaks named after one of General Burgoyne's more successful plays which he had written for the forthcoming marriage of Lord Derby and Lady Elizabeth Hamilton in 1774.

A Duel at Ascot   18 June 1784

As the popularity of Ascot races grew, so did the diversity of other entertainment that was on offer. Around a dozen marquees were to be found at each meeting, all devoted to gaming in one form or another. Everyone was welcome, and racegoers were encouraged to 'try their fortune with copper, silver or gold'. Naturally the gaming tables within these "betting booths" were heavily biased in favour of the proprietors who had paid a levy of as much as 12gns [£1,800] per table to be allowed to operate. As well as casino-style games, there were many other forms of entertainment such as cock-fighting, wrestling, and prize-fighting, all of which attracted significant sums on money in the form of wagers. On occasions, the visitors to the track provided their own entertainment. Such was the case on 18th June 1784 when a duel was fought between two racegoers.

Mr Richard England met William Peter Lee Rowlls, a man of considerable fortune and 'of character unimpeached, except by those of youth' at Ascot races in 1780. Rowlls was 'a little too fond of attending the races, plays, and those fashionable amusements to which young men are apt to devote their time' and after a series of transactions had quickly lost a considerable sum of money to England. Despite an apparent agreement being made between the two parties in which Rowlls would pay half the sum plus interest, a deep resentment festered within England. At a subsequent meeting at Ascot England was heard to claim that Rowlls could not be trusted to pay his debts. An argument ensued during which it was alleged Rowlls called England a 'rascal and a scoundrel' and threatened to strike him. A challenge was then proffered and accepted.

Duelling was not uncommon in Britain at the end of the eighteenth century. In the Sporting Intelligence section of *The Sporting Magazine* of 1795 three cases of duels were reported for November alone. Often a toss of a coin determined who took the first shot, the winner clearly had an advantage but such was the poor accuracy of the weapons used, more times than not, the first couple of rounds missed their intended targets. Seconds would then intervene in the hope that "honour had been satisfied" but, if not, new pistols were presented and a second round of firing would take place or the combatants would part with the disagreement unreconciled as was the case in Dublin when Pierce Power faced Lieutenant Hare on 22nd November 1795.

England and Rowlls, accompanied by their Seconds and a surgeon, met near Cranford Bridge where a brace of pistols was first presented and then, minutes later, discharged without result: in customary fashion, Rowlls fired into the ground and England into the air. At this point the Seconds attempted to intervene but the duellists were not to be deterred and the bout continued. According to John Sandiford, an eye witness, at this point Lady D'Arterie was heard to cry out "Gentlemen, is not three times enough to try your courage, or do you want to murder one another?" The two duellists then broke from the bout and conversed for a period of time before returning to their firing positions. Rowlls fired and missed, England's pistol misfired. With his next shot, England struck Rowlls in the right side of his groin, the lead shot penetrating his body to a depth of four inches. Rowlls fell to the ground, mortally wounded.

England immediately fled the country finally settling in France where he spent several years, but not all as a free man: he was committed to prison many times for a range of offences. On one occasion, England was sentenced to be guillotined, and even met the Executioner. A last minute pardon saved his life that time, allowing England to return to Britain in 1796 at which point he was indicted at the Old Bailey. According to one report, 'the prisoner deported himself with the utmost steadiness and composure, [he] was powdered, and dressed in a genteel suit of black,' and presented his evidence in the form of a written submission which was read aloud by an officer of the court. He claimed that he had no alternative but to duel with Rowlls; in his own words it was a case of 'duel or dishonour'. He further contended that Rowlls was seeking blood and only a death would end the dispute in his eyes. England was merely seeking to 'rescue his name and honour from the invidious reports which Mr. Rowlls had spread' and not the demise of his opponent.

A series of character witnesses then took the stand to attest to England's conduct as a Gentleman. These included the Marquis of Hertford who emphasised England's charity towards others; Mr Whitbread remarked that the prisoner was 'decent and gentlemanly'; Colonel Bishop said that he 'never saw Mr England have the least disposition to quarrelling' adding that he considered him to be 'well-behaved and well-bred'; Colonel Woolaston commented on his military service record; and finally Lord Derby gave his opinion that England was '[a] very civil, well-bred, polite gentleman, and on all occasions more studious to avoid quarrels than to seek them.'

These words would have come as a surprise to those aware of his many transgressions in Ireland, his homeland. England was a powerful man preferring to settle disputes with his fists and was a regular at court. On one such occasion he was indicted for fifteen cases of assault several of which resulted from disagreements and quarrels over sporting contests.

Murder was altogether more serious though and he nervously listened to the Judge's closing address after which the jury then spent about half-an-hour deliberating. Their verdict, when given was not guilty of murder but guilty of manslaughter. In sentencing, the Judge who was possibly a little vexed that the jury opted for the lesser charge, considered it 'proper to set you forth as an example in future, to let the world know, that they cannot commit even the crime of Manslaughter in a duel, without subjecting themselves to very considerable punishment': England was fined one shilling and sentenced to twelve months imprisonment.

Baronet Wins the Oatlands Stakes   *28 June 1791*

According to contemporary writers, the Oatlands Stakes of 1791 was one of the greatest races run at Ascot during the eighteenth century. Racegoers numbering 40,000 made their way to the track to watch the event which had attracted prize-money of 2,930gns [£110,000]. 'Rich and poor, high and low, made common cause in their endeavour to witness the contest' resulting in betting that was fast and furious. It was estimated that approaching one million pounds sterling changed hands over the race, roughly equivalent to £34 million today.

To accommodate such a vast throng, in excess of one hundred canvas booths were erected on the Heath to provide sustenance for the parched and ravenous racegoers. A further forty canvas-covered stands 'each seating from two to three hundred ladies, held the rank and beauty of the land.' Ten marquees were given over to the "Evens and Odds" tables (a simplified form of roulette) that supplemented a range of carnival-style games such as "hustling in the hat" and "pricking the garter" which were available to racegoers both on-course and along the roadsides on every approach to the track. Naturally, this form of gaming was not unique to Ascot. The *Gentleman's Magazine* of 1801 noted that:

> *It is an alarming fact that there is scarcely a fair, or a race, of the least celebrity, which is not infested with these villains, many of whom clear £500 annually by plundering the unsuspecting rustics, who attend such places, of their property.*

In 1791, the eyes of these so-called *sharpers* must have bulged as wide as the gentry's wallets as they surveyed such a potentially rich harvest.

The Oatlands Stakes, which was reproduced in oils by John Nost Sartorius, was a hard fought affair over the full two miles with an enthralling finish. At the line, victory was secured by Samuel Chifney on the Prince of Wales' Baronet by half-a-length from Mr Barton's Express, with Lord Barrymore's Chanticleer in third.

As well as receiving the huge purse, the Prince pocketed a further £17,000 [£2.5m] from his personal wagers.

After the result was announced, King George III congratulated his son and, as is widely quoted, he remarked 'your Baronets are more productive than mine. I made fourteen last week, but I get nothing from them. Your single Baronet is worth all mine put together.'

Disappointingly for racegoers in the Berkshire area, due to the lack of organisation by the track's authorities, there was to be no return of the Oatlands Stakes to Ascot, although a handicap of the same name was run in later years. Race officials had not anticipated such an immense crowd and the track was ill prepared for the vast number of racegoers. No effective crowd control measures had been put in place, which resulted in spectators impeding the runners with several seriously injured. This did not only happen at Ascot: at Epsom reports of pedestrians knocked down by carriages, and loose horses causing havoc amongst the racegoers were commonplace. However, the authorities decided that a change of venue was required and the race was transferred to Newmarket in 1792 where it was rescheduled for the spring. It remained a popular race with both owners and racegoers until the 1840s when shorter contests began to be favoured.

Samuel Chifney   *20 October 1791*

In the autumn of 1791, Samuel Chifney, by far the most talented jockey of the age, lost a race on Escape, a horse owned by the Prince of Wales. The following day Escape raced again and, with Chifney once more in the saddle, won easily, reversing the two-length defeat against the same opposition. To some observers this was suspicious, especially when they also believed the rumours that the jockey had 'laid it on thick in the right way'. Chifney was accused of stopping Escape from winning the first contest in order to inflate the odds when he ran twenty-four hours later. The Jockey Club upheld the decision despite Chifney's seemingly compelling explanation of the animal's failure and a sworn affidavit in which he stated that he did not bet against Escape on the day he lost. He did admit to placing 20gns on Escape when he won; hardly "laying it on thick" given the level of wagers accepted at the time, but still a significant sum. The Prince supported his jockey throughout the episode. However, he was warned that if he continued to allow Chifney to ride his horses then 'no gentleman would start against him'. The Prince railed against this affront and within a year had sold his bloodstock interests and ended his connection to the turf, although he did return to the sport in 1810. To demonstrate further his loyalty to his jockey the Prince continued to pay Chifney his annual retainer of 200gns [£32,000].

The Escape incident was a low point in an otherwise glittering racing career that had partnered Chifney with many of the wealthiest owners in the country. As well as transforming the way races were run from a 'slogging match to a mounted chess game', the muscular, lightly-built Chifney also demonstrated a better understanding of the ways a jockey can get the best from his horse. He rode with a slack rein, and sat differently from other jockeys, opting to position himself further back, as evidenced from the portrait by George Stubbs of the Oatlands Stakes winner Baronet. James Whyte asserted that 'he had a singular method of bringing his horse, when at full speed, to change his leg, which he accomplished in a quick and masterly manner'. Basically, Chifney was a class apart from his contemporaries and to one observer was 'the finest rider that ever threw his thigh over a racer.'

As a mentor, Chifney was instrumental in nurturing the talent of Frank Buckle who adopted a very similar riding style. Buckle, one of the most honest jockeys of any era, clearly benefited from Chifney's guidance and by the end of his career in 1831 he had ridden the winners of twenty-seven Classics, including a remarkable nine successes in the Oaks.

Later in life Chifney designed a new style of bit: the Chifney bit which is still in use today. Without financial support from the Jockey Club he was required to fund the development of this new piece of equipment himself. The cost was far more than Chifney expected and he became indebted to a saddler. Unable to reconcile the debt, the jockey was committed to Fleet Prison.

Fleet Prison, the former residence of Dennis O'Kelly, owner of Eclipse, was essentially a profit-making debtors' jail with the occupants required to pay for food and lodging. Throughout a controversial history it maintained a reputation as the most expensive prison in England. Initially built in 1197, Fleet Prison was destroyed by the followers of Wat Tyler during the Peasants' Revolt. Its next incarnation, on the same site, became a casualty of the Great Fire of London in 1666, and had to be rebuilt once again. Following the Gordon Riots of 1780 this substantial monument to "man's cold cruelty to man" was again burned to the ground and rebuilt.

Finally the Authorities began to appreciate quite how loathed this institution had become in the opinion of the public, and it was demolished sixty-five years later in 1845. The vast quantity of building materials was then sold at auction with the brickwork alone described by the Auctioneer as sufficient 'material for a small town'. By the time of its final demolition the number of inmates had dwindled to a comparative few. One of the remaining residents had been incarcerated there for over thirty very expensive years. Jeremiah Broad 'was a perfect character in his way, and from him a large sum of money was obtained under what was termed a vesting order from the Insolvent Debtor's Court.' Given the length of his stay at Fleet, Broad could conceivably have thought that he may have been released after the jail's demolition, but it was not to be. Instead, Broad was moved to the Queen's Prison to continue his stay at Her Majesty's pleasure.

As an act of generosity, inmates of the Fleet Prison were allowed to live outside the confines of the building's walls in specified locations as long as they compensated the Keeper for loss of earnings. It was in one of these dedicated areas, known as the "Rules of the Fleet", where Chifney, one of the greatest jockeys of any era, died 'without seeing the parson' in 1807.

1800-1849

The growth of racing continued and two more Classics were included in the programme of races. There were changes at Ascot's June meeting with the main cup race elevated to a "Gold Cup" then replaced by the "Emperor's Plate" before reverting to the original trophy.

Steeplechasing was established in Great Britain and began steadily to gain a following. The Jockey Club introduced more rule changes, and Nat Flatman became the first jockey to ride over one hundred winners in a season.

York staged the "race of the century" when The Flying Dutchman took on Voltigeur and at Liverpool a new race was introduced that later became known as the Grand National.

Sadly, fraud and corruption haunted the sport: a printing scandal resulted in multiple racecards published at Ascot's June meeting and, for the first time, the winner of the Derby was disqualified.

Eleanor's Classic Double   *21 May 1801*

Sir Charles Bunbury was a popular figure at British racecourses from the mid-1700s until his death in 1822. This popularity extended beyond the track and it helped him to retain his position as Member of Parliament for Suffolk for over fifty years. In character he was considered to possess an 'amiable temper' which matched his generous personality. Bunbury's association with horseracing was of paramount importance to the sport. The continued success and increasing popularity of racing was due in no small part to his influence.

In 1800 there were seventy-one tracks spread across England, Wales and Scotland and it seemed that horseracing festivals were being staged anywhere with sufficient room for a course. As an example, in 1817 the residents of Hammersmith and Fulham 'made preparations for the establishment of races annually on Wormwood Scrubs' a venue not particularly associated with racing.

Under Bunbury's guidance, and with his endorsement, two-year-old races were introduced. This was one area where he came in for criticism. Running juveniles necessitated a reduction in the length of races as well as the weight the horses carried. This was seen by some as a retrograde step in the development of the thoroughbred. It was feared that the breed would become weaker and lack stamina as a direct result of this policy, though there was no evidence to support this theory. Ultimately, the critics lost out and juvenile racing soon became an integral part of the racing programme.

Although Bunbury owned the first winner of the Derby amongst many other top class thoroughbreds, he had to wait twenty-one years before his colours, pink and white stripes, were carried to victory in the race again. On this occasion his winner was a filly named Eleanor. By the sire Whiskey out of a dam by Diomed, Eleanor made a winning debut at Newmarket on 20th April 1801. A month later on 21st May she lined up against one other filly and nine colts at Epsom where, under the jockey John Saunders, she became the first filly to win the Derby.

Just twenty-four hours later Eleanor was back at Epsom's mile-and-a-half start as the 4/7 favourite for the Oaks. She again made short work of her five opponents to win by a length and in so doing completed a notable Classic double. It was a further 56 years before a filly repeated this remarkable feat.

Eleanor was kept in training until the end of the 1805 season when she was retired to stand at Bunbury's Barton Hall stud. Sir Charles Bunbury won the Derby once more, in 1813, with Smolensko; Eleanor was his only Oaks winner.

Evolution of the Ascot Gold Cup   *11 June 1807*

Nowadays, the highlight of the Royal Ascot meeting for many racing enthusiasts is the Gold Cup. However, it was not until 1772 that a cup was offered as a prize at the meeting, which was then known as the "Windsor and Ascot Heath Races". In that year, the Duke of Cumberland instituted a race for five-year-olds over the four-mile course for which the owner of the winner, in addition to the usual prize-money, would receive a cup. Although there were several initial subscriptions for the first running of this race, subsequent withdrawals meant that the contest was a walkover for a horse named Marie. By remarkable coincidence, Marie was owned by the Duke of Cumberland.

In 1807 this cup became the "Gold Cup", and a trophy valued at a staggering 100gns [£10,000] was presented to the winning owner. As was customary in many races, the unfortunate owner of the runner-up would merely have his stake returned. The winner of this first running was a three-year-old named Master Jackey and the lucky owner was Mr Durrand.

To recognise the elevation of the race and the increasing importance of this meeting in the social calendar, an elaborate pavilion and two marquees had been built for Queen Charlotte and the Princesses, while opposite the Judge's box another was made available to the Prince of Wales. These developments naturally encouraged a greater attendance and, according to contemporaneous reports 'a very large concourse of people, and crowds of sociables, barouches, landaus, and landaulets with two, four or six horses in each' stretched across the heath.

Fashion was already playing a part at the meeting, and newspaper reports often focused more on the Royals' attire than the performances of the horses. In 1807 it was noted that 'Her Majesty was received by the Prince of Wales, dressed in bottle green, and his brothers – the Dukes of York, Cumberland, and Kent – in the Windsor uniform. Her Majesty and the three Princesses were dressed in white Spanish mantles – Princess Mary had on a black lace mantle, while Princess Amelia wore a white lace scarf lined with blue – and gipsy hats.' The clothes may have changed over the last two-hundred years, but it seems that the media was just as obsessed with what the Royal Family wore at Royal Ascot then as it is today.

Expansion of Betting Opportunities   *18 April 1809*

Under the reign of King George III, betting was fast becoming big business in Britain. Horseracing was one of the main drivers of this trend, but it appears that any activity could form the basis of a bet. Pigeon shooting, which was added to the roster of Olympic Sports in 1900, was one area that attracted wagers and it was not uncommon for £500 to change hands over a single shot. While the outcome of this type of bet was clearly understood by both betting parties, not all wagers were what they at first may have seemed. In early June 1800 a Naval Officer wagered that he could ride a blind horse around Sheerness racecourse without using his hands to guide the reins. Naturally, this attracted a large crowd of onlookers, and plenty of betting. Much to the amusement of those that had sided with the officer, and to the displeasure of those who had bet against him, he 'cut the reins asunder, and fastening the several parts to his feet' was able easily to guide the animal around the track.

Such disingenuous behaviour was prevalent in matters of betting at the time. For instance, a case was brought by an unnamed person against William Courtney at Kingston Lent Assizes. It was alleged that a wager of 100gns [£8,500] was agreed between the two parties on the basis that the plaintiff could procure three horses and run them for ninety miles in three hours. Courtney, the defendant, understood that the three horses would run thirty miles sequentially during the allotted time. In other words, the first horse would run thirty miles in the first hour, the second in the next, and so on. Instead, the wily plaintiff started all three horses at once giving them the opportunity to complete the thirty miles in the full three hours. Courtney refused to pay, stating that he had been cheated. After due consideration the jury found in his favour on the basis that the wording of the bet was unfair.

Endurance riding of this type was a popular medium for betting. On 6th October 1791, during a meeting at The Curragh, a Mr Wilde placed bets to the amount of 2,000gns on himself to ride '127 English miles in nine hours'. A circuit of two miles in circumference was marked out in a valley near the racecourse and an observer was employed to keep a record of the number of times it was traversed by horse and rider. At each interval, when Wilde changed horses, it was noted that he refreshed himself with 'a mouthful of brandy and water'. Remarkably, Wilde completed the 127 miles in six hours twenty-one minutes to win the bet. It was not noted whether, on completion of the task, he was in a sober state.

On 7th September 1780, Captain Hoare won a significant wager by riding three horses for thirty miles and drinking three bottles of claret all within three hours. In a similar challenge, Captain Newland won a 'considerable sum' by riding seven horses over a distance of 140 miles in seven hours thirty-four minutes at Longdown Hall near Chichester in 1801. He easily beat the allotted time of twelve hours to collect his winnings, despite a fall.

Not all betting challenges were undertaken on horseback. On 10th November 1801, Robert Bridges Barclay Allardice, more popularly known as Captain Barclay, won 5,000gns [£380,000] from a racehorse owner when completing ninety miles on foot in less than 'twenty-one and a half successive hours'. Dressed in flannel shirt, flannel trousers, lambs' wool stockings and thick-soled leather shoes, he completed the task with over an hour in hand.

Although famed for his inordinate strength, he once lifted an 18st [252lbs] man from floor to table top using just one hand placed under the man's feet, it was walking contests where Barclay excelled. After winning many wagers over varying distances, in 1809 Barclay proclaimed that he could walk one thousand miles in one thousand successive hours. Such a boast was scarcely believable and, as a consequence, the challenge attracted a great deal of interest – and bets. On a shorn and rolled Newmarket Heath over which a 'sixpence [would] roll a hundred yards', and in front of a vast audience, Barclay, weighing a little over 13st, took his first steps on 30th May. Throughout the marathon walk, his day commenced at 5am with a breakfast of cold meat, tea, and strong ale. A light lunch at noon generally consisted of roast or boiled beef and a pint of ale. Roast beef or mutton, two glasses of port, and a pint of ale constituted his evening meal at 6pm followed by roast meat and more strong ale at 11pm. During the day he quenched his thirst with Madeira and water. Despite a diet that consisted almost entirely of protein and alcohol, he completed the task with 'perfect ease and great spirit' to win the bet. His supporters who took the 2/1 and 5/2 offered in Tattersalls were also left smiling by his extraordinary achievement, but his tailor noted that Barclay's weight had dropped by over 2st [28lbs] and a range of adjustments to his clothes were required.

The stakes for some of these bets were enormous by today's standards. Whilst today many off-course bookmakers regularly refuse a bet of £50 on a 4/1 shot, bets in the thousands were commonplace in the early 1800s. Reputedly, on the day of the 1822 St Leger, a bet of 1000gns against a walking stick was agreed on Theodore, who went on to win the race at a price of 200/1, gaining the speculator who offered the walking stick for his part of the bet the equivalent of a little over £136,000 at today's rates.

In order to generate even more betting opportunities, additional high quality races were added to the racing calendar. Under the direction of Sir Charles Bunbury the 2,000 Guineas Stakes, for three-year-olds over a mile, was introduced on 18th April 1809. It was won by Christopher Wilson's 5/6 favourite, Wizard. Bunbury's runner, Fair Star, finished third. Irrespective of its title, the race was worth only 1,450gns.

Five years later an equivalent race for fillies was incorporated into the racing programme. The first 1,000 Guineas was run over a distance slightly short of a mile and was won by Charlotte, the 11/5 favourite who, like Wizard, was owned by Christopher Wilson.

Over the two hundred years since these two races were first run, their importance in the racing programme has grown significantly. As two of Britain's five Classics, they are now amongst the most prestigious contests of the racing year and attract a great deal of betting interest just as their Founder hoped.

Dead Heat in the Derby   *22 May 1828*

In the week in which London Zoo opened with the express purpose of scientifically studying animals, thoroughbreds, about which a great deal was already known, were racing across Newmarket Heath for a prize of 2,700gns [£310,000] in the 1828 2,000 Guineas. The winner was Cadland, a colt that was unraced as a juvenile and won his first race just twenty-four hours earlier when known as "The Sorcery Colt". After this Classic victory he was made 4/1 second favourite for the Derby, just behind The Colonel who was available at the unusual price of 15/4.

In contrast to Cadland, The Colonel was a successful juvenile winning several races, including the valuable Champagne Stakes at Doncaster. As a three-year-old, though, he remained unraced until the Epsom contest due to the logistics of transportation. Being trained in Malton, North Yorkshire, restricted racing opportunities for The Colonel. Walking was the most common way to get horses to the racetrack, so the frequency at which a horse could race depended on the number of meetings within a suitable distance from a runner's stable. A journey from Yorkshire to Surrey, for instance, could take two weeks, and although the runners travelled at a sedate pace to preserve energy, many were left exhausted and unfit to race by the time they reached the racecourse.

Trailers aided the transportation of horses to the track from as early as 1816, but only on rare occasions until the mid-1830s when one horse showed how beneficial their use could be to both horse and bettor. Elis, a runner from the John Day stable, was widely fancied for the 1836 St Leger as early as the previous autumn. He was backed in the subscription rooms throughout the year, but within days of the race remained in his box at Goodwood over 250 miles from Doncaster. To the majority of punters this meant he would not run, and yet he continued to be heavily supported. This apparent paradox was the basis of a betting coup organised by Lord George Bentinck. Only a privileged few were aware that a specially designed horse transporter had been built, which allowed Elis and a travelling companion to make the arduous trip in under three days. Elis arrived at Turf Moor in pristine condition, took the lead in the St Leger at the halfway point and was never challenged. Bentinck and his partners were said to have won over £24,000 [£2.8 million] an amount due in no small part to the greatly inflated prices they were able to take about their runner.

Although horseboxes were gaining in popularity, it was the expansion of the railway network in the mid-1800s that had the greatest impact on horse transportation. Trains provided a means for runners to travel much more widely than they had previously. These additional rail connections also improved the accessibility of horseracing to the public, but whether the racegoers arrived at their chosen destination feeling as well as the horses is open to debate. These early trains could travel at a speed of thirty miles per hour. This was thought to be excessive by some, including Queen Victoria, but would have been considered desperately slow for any rail passenger needing access to a toilet of which there was none available on board. In this regard, it is probably fortunate that the refreshments on offer were of notably poor quality and lacking any appeal to travellers. The novelist Anthony Trollope wrote 'the real disgrace of England is the railway sandwich, that whited sepulchre, fair enough outside, but so meagre, poor, and spiritless within'. Notwithstanding these travel issues, racecourse attendances increased along with betting turnover.

The Colonel made the arduous journey south in the spring of 1828 and met Cadland at Epsom on 22nd May, a day when it was either raining or about to rain. Much to the disappointment of the layers, the betting was not as frantic as hoped; bets in the thousands being replaced by those in the hundreds. Apparently many of the main players had learned expensive lessons from previous years and were aware that a single Levanter [someone who failed to honour his bets] could ruin a finely tuned book. Caution was now the watchword with *The Times* reporting that some layers were going to extreme lengths to discern the reliability of a fellow bettor. Phrenology was a popular area of study at the time and 'if a new face presents itself in the subscription-room, at Tattersall's, for the purpose of speculation, a leg, before entering into a bet with him, will scrutinize his physiognomy with all the earnestness and acumen of a professor, and all but say, "I should like to look at your bumps."'

Two false starts delayed the main event of the day, but once underway Cadland was in front, setting a strong pace at the head of a field that featured several runners that trackside observers had dismissed purely due to their appearance in the paddock. The Colonel, Omen, Alcaston and Zinganee, with Sam Chifney riding, completed a phalanx of runners on the heels of the second favourite. At the back of the trailing pack, Scipio was knocked over by another horse and his rider sustained a broken rib. Retaining the lead until the straight, Cadland was then joined by The Colonel. The two remained seemingly locked together regardless of their jockeys' attempts to gain an advantage. Zingaree was not far behind in third and looked a danger until the last fifty yards when he could give no more and began to weaken. Not so the leading pair. Cadland and The Colonel continued to battle to the finish, crossing the line simultaneously. The Judge had no option but to call a dead heat, the first such result in the history of Britain's premier Classic.

Following a period of intense discussion a second heat was announced. The Colonel was favoured by some racegoers because it was believed that he was the more stoutly bred of the two, and he was heavily backed at 5/6 and 4/5. By race time, the public found it difficult to separate the pair although The Colonel was marginally shorter than his rival in the market. Cadland's jockey, Jem Robinson, refreshed by a pinch of snuff before remounting, again decided to set the pace which, to some observers, was stronger than he had set in the first running of the race. The Colonel moved up to put the leader under some pressure in the closing stages, but Robinson had plenty in reserve and got Cadland home by half-a-length in a driving finish that was captured by artist James Pollard.

Despite the need for a second race to determine the Derby winner, it was subsequently reported that, in the Tattersall's subscription room, there were few if any complaints and only one significant defaulter. The vast majority of bettors considered the race to have been resolved fairly and bets were settled in a gentlemanly manner. After losing out at Epsom, The Colonel did gain some compensation. While initially available at 14/1, he was backed down to 7/1 third favourite for the St Leger due in no small part to the many bets from his Northern supporters. Much to their delight, the chestnut colt won the final Classic of the year by a comfortable three lengths as the 3/1 favourite.

One nineteenth century writer remarked that 'in the greatest of horse-races, the agony is quick, the excitement is condensed into a couple of minutes, and the recovery is proportionately rapid'. Whilst generally true, it was not the case with the 1828 Derby: the race started at 3pm and was not resolved until a little after 4:30pm.

First Recognised Steeplechase   8 March 1830

Although the origins of steeplechasing can be traced back to the 1700s, when horses were raced from church steeple to church steeple, these were very casual affairs lacking in any type of formalisation. The first recognised chase to take place in England was organised by Tommy Coleman, the owner of the Chequers Inn, St Albans, and took place 8th March 1830. It is fair to say that the contest was nothing like a modern steeplechase. The "course", as it was, maintained the chasing tradition and extended from Arlington Church to the Obelisk in Wrest Park near Silsoe, Bedfordshire, a distance of four miles. Sixteen runners took part in this first chase and the winner was Captain Macdowall on a horse named The Wonder.

The following spring the race attracted a significant crowd of onlookers and Coleman was required to exert a greater degree of control over the event. A horse named Moonraker was successful this time, with Wild Boar, ridden by Captain Martin Becher, an unlucky loser.

There was clearly a desire amongst racing fans for more jump racing, 'especially in the metropolis' according to *The New Sporting Magazine* where, in 1832, it was further reported with some added humour that 'it is now quite a mania – it would be well if the "church" was attractive as the "steeple"'. The same magazine included reviews of several races that had taken place in the weeks before its publication in late spring. One race was staged between Beachy Heath and Oxley Wood. This particularly stiff four-mile part of the country featured plenty of challenging fences and two wide brooks. Moonraker, carrying 12st, was again first home, on this occasion by 'upwards of one hundred yards' in a time of sixteen-and-a-half minutes. On the same afternoon Moonraker featured in a match for 100 sovereigns

[£11,800]. This time he made all from Scratch Wood near Barnet, to a field near Bushey Heath and finished alone. Around the same time, other races were staged from Washend Bridge near Greenford to the windmill at Hanwell; from Whittaker Mill to Thurlton Church; from Gissing Church to Thelton Church; and from Mr Booth's farm at Brixworth to the cottage on the hill opposite Blueberries Cover near Haslebeech. It can only be hoped that the Starter knew the exact location of Mr Booth's farm, and the Judge was aware of the hill opposite Blueberries Cover otherwise there may have been no little degree of confusion concerning this particular event.

Chasing was not restricted to England and was rapidly expanding to all corners of the British Isles. In Scotland, near Forfar, a race over four miles of ploughed fields and stiff fences took twenty minutes to complete. Unfortunately for the successful owner, the winner was adjudged to have carried insufficient weight, so the Silver Tankard trophy was presented to the rider of the second, Captain Douglas, who also took home many bruises and a broken rib from the several falls he endured.

It was clear from the locations of the races that National Hunt racing lacked for organisation, a more professional approach, and a consideration for health and safety. Fortunately there were plenty of riders willing to risk their lives in this most dangerous of pastimes. Serious and fatal injuries caused by falls in steeplechases were commonplace throughout the nineteenth century and were regularly reported in the sporting journals of the time. There is little doubt that such a high level of casualties amongst jockeys would cause the sport to be banned nowadays, but it seems that for those who spent much of their time hunting, this was simply part of the known risk associated with race-riding and was considered perfectly acceptable. The undergraduates from Oxford and Cambridge Universities did not appear too concerned with the dangers and an inter-university steeplechase was inaugurated in the early 1860s and staged at Aylesbury. Apparently Cambridge won the first race. Despite its popularity among spectators, it was not until the formation of the National Hunt Committee 1866 that the sport was conducted in a more organised fashion, but even that did little to stem the casualty rate.

Classic Glory for Nat Flatman   *7 May 1835*

Nat Flatman was one of the finest jockeys of the time. Born in 1810, Elnathan "Nat" Flatman made his first racecourse appearance at Newmarket's Craven Stakes meeting in 1829. Shortly after, he joined George Payne, trainer, owner and heavy gambler. Payne was based at Sulby Hall which he inherited when his father was shot in a duel. Success soon followed for Flatman, and on 7th May 1835 he won the first of his ten Classics when Preserve beat three rivals in the 1,000 Guineas. From 1840 to 1852 Nat Flatman was champion jockey. The highlight of this incredible run was 1848 when he became the first jockey to ride over one hundred winners in a season. He also secured the championship with just forty-two winners, the fewest recorded by a champion jockey until matched by Steve Donoghue in the war-ravaged programme of 1917.

Flatman was a workmanlike, reliable, and totally honest jockey. He was 'entirely without showy qualities' which may have been the reason he succumbed to few accidents throughout his career. Naturally there were falls, notably at the start of the 1845 Derby. The horse he was riding bolted after being 'savagely attacked by The Libel [another runner in the race]', throwing Flatman to the ground in the process; and in the Ascot Derby of 1852 when a dog raced onto the track causing his horse, Red Hind, to fall opposite the stands. Other than those two horrendous incidents, either of which could easily have had a worse outcome, he managed to avoid serious injury during his riding days. So it was particularly unfortunate that a racing accident led to his death.

On 29th September 1859, during Newmarket's First October Meeting, Flatman rode the Duke of Bedford's Golden Pippin in a match against Mr Robinson's Apollo. Though favourite, Golden Pippin ran poorly and was beaten three-quarters of a length. When dismounting from the unruly filly, Golden Pippin lashed out, kicking her jockey in the torso. According to *The Times*, 'Flatman was much injured.' However, the damage he sustained was not thought life-threatening and only basic medical treatment was provided. What neither Flatman nor his close companions knew was that one of his ribs had punctured a lung. This internal damage gave rise to an infection, which further developed into consumption. Almost a year later, after a prolonged illness, Nat Flatman died on 20th August 1860.

The First Grand National   26 February 1839

Who won the first Grand National? Most horseracing fans would know the answer, and in a Pub Quiz they would confidently answer "Lottery". In 1839 Lottery, who finished third on his chasing debut in the St Albans race a year earlier, did indeed win the Grand National under the guidance of jockey Jem Mason. The race was staged at Liverpool and famously featured Captain Becher who fell at the first brook, rolled into the water for safety, and so doing ensured that his name would be always associated with the race. However, there is evidence to support the claim that the first Grand National was actually run three years earlier.

The track at Aintree (a region that had historical links to the Anglo Saxon era as evidenced from its name, which is derived from the Anglo Saxon for "one tree" suggesting a distinct lack of forestation) was developed in 1829 by local businessman William Lynn and initially it staged flat races. After the success of the 1830 steeplechase run in Bedfordshire, Lynn decided to introduce a similar race at Aintree. The first such contest was held in 1836; the winner was The Duke, and the winning jockey was none other than Captain Martin Becher. However the race was not run over the now famous fences, or even over a regulation course. Horses started from a position in front of the Aintree Grand Stand, raced across a distance of country, and then returned to complete the contest opposite the stand. While this may appear to limit the viewing prospects of anyone attending the meeting, the configuration of the "course" was carefully plotted. Despite the race being run over approximately five miles, it was noted that spectators were afforded a good view of the contest throughout. Racegoers numbered in the thousands and according to *Bell's Life and Sporting Chronicle* 'The company was very numerous and highly respectable, the principal gentry from Liverpool, Manchester and Chester. A vast number of fashionable ladies graced the Stand.'

A year later, the second running of the "Grand Liverpool Steeplechase" gave The Duke back-to-back successes, though Becher was not this time in the plate. Sir William won the third running in 1838, however many of the details of this race are less than clear. Then we get back to Lottery in 1839. The name of the race was changed to "Liverpool and National Steeple Chase" in 1843, then finally to "Grand National Steeple Chase" in 1847 when it was won by Mathew, the 10/1 joint favourite.

Throughout its glorious history, the Grand National, as it is now known, has survived demonstrations by animal rights activists, bomb threats from IRA terrorists, and the possibility of the course being turned into a housing estate. It has also been associated with some of the greatest finishes, remarkable feats of human and equine achievement, and wonderful record-setting horses. When Andy Pandy over-jumped at Becher's Brook on the second circuit sending his jockey John Burke crashing to the Aintree turf, the likelihood that the 1977 Grand National would be a record-breaking race rose substantially. Red Rum was left in front with What A Buck, and at the next fence he was clear of the field, his biggest danger being the loose horses that were upsides him. Churchtown Boy mounted a challenge with two fences left, but a poor jump ended his chance. At the final fence the crowd knew they were about to witness an historic event and the cheers rang out from both sides of the course. From there to the winning post Red Rum's lead extended and, as Peter O'Sullevan said in commentary 'he's coming up to the line to win it like a fresh horse'. On 2nd April 1977, Red Rum became the first horse to win the great race three times and, for many, is the first horse that enters the mind when the term "Grand National" is mentioned, although hardened pub-quizzers may disagree.

Ascot Racecard Scandal   *13 June 1843*

In the same year that Charles Dickens wrote *A Christmas Carol*, a book that was quickly copied and sold illegally resulting in a criminal prosecution of *Parley's Illuminated Library*, Ascot was dealing with its own publishing scandal.

Printing racecards was as lucrative in the mid-1800s as it is today, so the contract to supply the racecards for the June Ascot meeting was extremely valuable. For many years the lucky printer was Richard Oxley of Windsor who was proprietor of the *Windsor and Eton Express*, official printer to the Queen and Royal Family, and a man with close connections to the Whig Committee. Oxley took great pride in his work even using carrier pigeons to convey the list of non-runners to the printers at Windsor in order to ensure the racecards were as complete as possible.

In 1843, Conservative Member of Parliament Lord Rosslyn, who managed the course on the monarch's behalf as the Master of the Buckhounds, gave the printing rights to a Mr Brown, an employee of the Conservative party. Oxley petitioned the Jockey Club highlighting the apparent conflict of interest. However, Lord Rosslyn was not a man to be dictated to by those of a lower social class and asserted his right to award the contract to whomever he chose. As a result, two racecards were in circulation at the meeting in 1843. Remarkably, as was the custom at the time, neither card featured a price on the cover. This allowed them to be sold for whatever the sales staff could get.

The following summer the conflict resumed with Oxley once again taking on Brown. As part of the battle, Brown who benefited from the support of Lord Rosslyn, circulated flyers freely to racegoers denouncing Oxley's racecards. Even Great Western Railway was on his side and prohibited the sale of Oxley's racecards at Slough station. Oxley, however, held a trump card: he enjoyed the support of the racing public who believed he had been mistreated. Brown's focus was on Oxley and he became so bound up in his attempts to win the argument that he let his production standards slip. In 1845 too few racecards were printed and those which were on sale were littered with errors. This was unacceptable even to Brown's most ardent supporters. The writing was on the wall, and in 1846 Oxley's company was reinstated as the official supplier.

Derby Day Fraud   22 May 1844

An examination of the record books will reveal that on 22nd May 1844 a horse named Orlando ridden by Nat Flatman won the Derby. But that's not how it appeared to the thousands of spectators who covered the Downs, gratefully occupying any vantage point on that typical spring day of sunshine and cloud. To the racegoers, Orlando was a clear second, beaten by almost a length by Running Rein.

Much to the disappointment of the vast crowd, on the previous Monday the Home Secretary, Sir James Graham, had issued an edict in which it was made clear that anyone found gambling in 'any booth or public place, at any table or instrument of gaming ... may be committed to the House of Correction, and there kept to hard labour for three months.' While the relatively new stand was a pleasant place to spend the afternoon, with space for 5,000 racegoers in the various rooms that provided refreshments, and room for a further 2,500 in the seated area on the roof, most people were at the track to bet, and not just on the races. In previous years, the hill was home to 'comic singers and dancers... shooting galleries, charlatans who by dint of eloquence palm off watch chains, games of skittles and sticks and musicians of all sorts' as well as the all-important betting booths. These booths would line each side of the track and stretch across the centre of the course towards the Derby start. In the view of one observer, they were 'innumerable ... and the vast majority which cover [the course] as far as the eye can reach, in every direction, is a sight of thrilling interest'.

In 1844 Graham had been taken at his word and the betting booths were empty: there were no games of chance, no cards, and no clubhouses. The overall effect was to engender a feeling of 'dullness' according to *The*

Times. Naturally this did not find favour amongst many in the crowd who were more accustomed to the riotous and intoxicating atmosphere created by the betting booths. One regular attendee made a direct, but not altogether serious, plea to Graham via the pages of *The Sportsman's Magazine*: 'Sir James, the thimble-rig* was, I may say, the life-blood of the Derby. I should like to know what harm it did.' The correspondent continued his entreaty with evidence from a more psychological perspective: 'Thimble-rigging, in some way, is part of what people call the human mind. They must have it in some way or other, or they give themselves up to solitary drinking.'

In that respect the fictional letter-writer was correct. Rather than enjoying an afternoon of sustained betting, and losing at rigged casino-style games, '...between the intervals of the races, eating and drinking were the business of the day'. The level of consumption was prodigious. Charles Dickens published a summary of the provisions consumed in the stand on a typical Derby Day in *Household Words*. Included in his menu of foodstuffs were 'rows of spits bearing rows of joints before blazing walls of fire; crates of boiled tongues, one hundred and thirty legs of lamb, saddles and shoulders in like proportion; a flock of lambs roasted, dished and garnished.' For those not keen on lamb there was 'beef, veal, ham, spring chickens, pigeon pies, lobsters, and a salad so large that it required a tub and birch broom for mixing.' Drinks were not in short supply either, with enough 'champagne, brandy and soda and bottle Bass' for everyone, winners or losers.

For those hoping for more excitement, the Derby itself was anything but dull, producing the first disqualification in the history of the race. Essentially, Running Rein and Leander were "ringers". Running Rein was in fact a four-year-old horse named Maccabeus and as an older horse had a substantial advantage in the race. In human terms, it would be comparable to racing a sixteen-year-old boy in an event against twelve-year-olds. Leander was possibly a five-year-old.

Whilst the conspirators were confident of success with one of their ringers, they looked for extra insurance. In an instance of extreme daring, the highly regarded Ratan was poisoned in his stable on the day of the race. This additional act of sabotage should have all but guaranteed them success.

---

* The thimble-rig game used three thimbles and a pea or other round object which was placed under one of the up-turned thimbles. The thimbles were switched around and the bettor simply had to identify under which thimble the object was to be found.

The conspiracy had been in play for a long time and every effort had been taken to disguise the identity of the two replacement runners. However, in a fraud of this magnitude keeping everyone onside and stopping leaks was almost impossible and rumours abounded before the start of the race. Furthermore, the horses had to pass the inspection of the public. After saddling, they were paraded around the paddock in front of vast numbers of race-watchers who had all paid a shilling for the privilege.

Although Running Rein was the easy winner, his success was met with 'howls and jeers from the crowd' many of whom were well aware of the skulduggery that had taken place. The fraud was unveiled when the owner of the farm where Maccabeus had been stabled for some time, Mr Worley, identified Running Rein as Maccabeus.

Colonel Jonathan Peel, owner of Orlando, immediately objected to the result, and the Jockey Club suspended all bets. An injunction was granted to prevent payment of the prize-money to the owners of Running Rein who themselves brought a civil action to recover the stake.

The court case did not go well for the conspirators. When Baron Alderson, presiding, asked to see Running Rein he was informed that the horse was missing. Furthermore, Leander, the other ringer had died suddenly and been disposed of, preventing any form of identification. Regarding the disappearance of Running Rein, Alderson announced that this could be a case of 'horse-stealing', which would result in a 'long term of penal servitude'. In light of this warning, the conspirators withdrew their claim and the race was awarded to Colonel Peel's Orlando.

Running Rein was probably not the first horse to run under the guise of another and he certainly wasn't the last. In 1974 a similar fraud was attempted involving two horses, Gay Future and Arctic Chevalier, in a far less prestigious race at the August Bank Holiday meeting at Cartmel; and in 1982 fraudsters replaced the two-year-old Flockton Grey with a three-year-old named Good Hand. In both instances the perpetrators were caught and convicted.

The Emperor's Plate   6 June 1844

By June 1844 the twenty-five-year-old Queen Victoria was into the seventh year of her reign, had survived an assassination attempt, given birth to three children, and was expecting a fourth. On a National level, George Williams founded the Young Men's Christian Association on the 6th June, and nine days later the "Factory Act" was passed by parliament. This Act restricted working hours for children, aged six to thirteen, to six hours per day, and set an upper limit of twelve hours for women. In racing, the highlight of the month was the meeting at Ascot, and in 1844 it was attended by Nicholas I, Emperor of Russia.

The Tsar's supporters would claim that he was a hard working member of the Royal Family with a strong sense of duty. His detractors, of which there were many more, would characterise the nervous, aggressive ruler as a 'stern despot and haughty autocrat'. Both factions would agree that he was a keen sportsman.

Naturally, the esteemed visitor gratefully accepted a place in the Royal procession alongside Queen Victoria, Prince Albert, and the King of Saxony. Whilst the Tsar may have been welcomed by the aristocracy, there were many who condemned his visit, mostly European émigrés now living in Britain. In order to provide a platform for them to air their views, a public meeting was held at Holborn with the 'purpose of ascertaining how far the people of England are prepared to welcome to their country the Russian Emperor Nicholas'. Over 1,000 people attended and many hundreds were turned away at the door due to pressure of space. The meeting lasted three hours with *The Times* reporting that it 'chiefly consisted of labouring men and mechanics, Chartists and Socialists... [it] was marked throughout by the most violent and rancorous language'. However, either by accident or design on the part of the organisers, the Emperor had already attended the races by the time this meeting took place, and was soon to depart the country, so there was no time for direct action had any been approved. Although many of the attendees had an enjoyable evening expressing their dislike of the Royal visitor, due to its poor timing nothing of note was achieved. The evening concluded with a collection to cover expenses and, given the number of people that attended, it is probable the organisers profited financially. For them the meeting was worthwhile, and for those in power who deigned to take any notice, it did suggest there existed a not insignificant level of disapproval regarding the visit and, possibly, a growing dissatisfaction with the concept of sovereign rule.

At Ascot, an unnamed chestnut colt owned by Lord Albemarle (Master of the Horse to the late William IV) took the honours in the Gold Cup when getting the better of Coranna by half-a-length. Immediately after the race the colt was named "The Emperor" out of respect for the august visitor. The Tsar then offered to present a trophy, to the winner of the race each year, to be known as the "Emperor's Plate". Describing the prize as a "plate" does it a distinct disservice, it was far more ornate than the word suggests. Fashioned by Hunt and Roskill of Bond Street, and based on a statue of Peter the Great, the trophy featured a rider on horseback, mounted on a rock that was raised on a three-cornered base around which were engraved views of Windsor Castle, the Kremlin and the Winter Palace. Figures of Russian soldiers also adorned the trophy which was valued at £500 [£60,000]. It was far from just a run-of-the-mill "plate".

This new trophy replaced the Gold Cup (the value of which was distributed to other races at the meeting) until 1853 when, at the outbreak of the Crimean War, its time was up. Ascot officials correctly reasoned that racing for a prize of Russian origin would no longer be considered acceptable by the British public and restored the original Gold Cup.

It now seems remarkable that horses were allowed to race without being named, especially in contests as important to the racing programme as the Ascot Gold Cup. It certainly did not make the interpretation of results and form any easier. *The Times* report of the race result was not the clearest of presentations (*see below*) and the lack of names only served to add confusion. Despite pressure from the sporting press throughout the second half of the nineteenth century, there was no requirement for owners to name their horses until 1913 and this was only for older runners; two-year-olds

---

THE GOLD CUP, value 360 sovs., by subscription of 20 sovs. Each, with 200 added from the fund; the second to receive 50 sovs. out of the stakes; 3-yrs-old. 6st 10lb. ; 4 yrs. 8st 6lb. ; 5 yrs, 9st. ; 6 yrs and aged, 9st. 3lb. Mares and geldings allowed 3lb. About two miles and a half.
(21 subscribers.)

Lord Abermarle's ch. c. by Defence, dam by Reveller out of
Design, 8yrs (Whitehouse) 1
Mr Townley's Corranna, 5yrs (Robinson) 2
Colonel Peel's Ionian, 3yrs. (Pettit) 3
Sir R. Blakeley's The Bishop of Romford's Cob, 4yrs
(Darling) 0
Sir G. Heathcote's Siricol, 4yrs. (Chapple) 0
Duke of Richmond's Lothario, 4yrs. (Rogers) 0
Mr. Ford's Poison, 4yrs. (Mann) 0
Colonel Anson's Attila, 5yrs, (Nat) 0

Betting:
5 to 2 agst Ionian.   8-1 ---------- Siricol.
3-1 ------- Lothario.   8-1 ---------- Poison.
4-1 ------- Corranna.   8-1 ---------- Attila.
6-1 ------- Bishop of Romford's Cob.   10-1 ---------the winner.

could race unnamed until a rule change 1946. One noteworthy example was Dorothy Paget's Chanter: although a leading juvenile of 1945, he was known as the "Lady Chantry colt".

The obstinate Paget refused to name her horses until compelled to do so. To make matters worse, at the time of The Emperor's win, owners who did opt to name their runners were perfectly entitled to give the same name to several horses. This led to an amount of misunderstanding, especially when identically-named runners were entered in the same race.

Naturally it also enabled nefarious schemes to be conducted with ease. In spring 1877 the Jockey Club amended the rules so that the name of a horse which had been used before had to be supplemented with a numerical suffix. It was hoped that this would 'close the door against any fraudulent practices which an unfettered licence in naming might bring into play.'

The Flying Dutchman   *23 May 1849*

After a prolonged period of rain, the going at Epsom was particularly soft when The Flying Dutchman lined up with twenty-five other runners to contest the 1849 Derby. Despite such an intriguing race, and the much-improved rail access between London and the track, the crowd numbered fewer than expected. The reduced turnout was attributed to the poor weather, although the relatively recent pricking of the *Railway Mania* bubble, which cost many thousands of the middle class a considerable sum and in many cases their entire savings, was also a key factor. Charlotte Bronte was one victim of the hundreds of rail schemes that gained assent from parliament but produced only losses. Investors were promised incredible returns on their money, but all too often the scheme in which they invested had insufficient financial support. Whilst it was claimed that a particular scheme had a large number of *subscribers*, thus enhancing the share price by implying a high level of liquidity, many of these investors simply did not exist. It was large-scale corruption and it produced large-scale losses. There was a silver lining, though, to this dark cloud of investment fraud: hundreds of lines were built before the bubble burst and these form the basis of the railway network that is still used today.

The Flying Dutchman, a dark-brown colt with a fiery eye standing a little over fifteen hands with a girth measuring five feet six inches, was unbeaten from five starts as a juvenile. This 'magnificent specimen of power' was made 2/1 joint favourite for the Derby and to many observers looked unbeatable.

Those looking to oppose The Flying Dutchman would cite the far from ideal underfoot conditions and the fact that he was making his seasonal debut: having not raced since his two-year-old campaign cast doubt over his likely level of fitness and whether he had "trained on".

As the race progressed The Flying Dutchman made stealthy progress, taking the lead as the runners entered the straight. Then, without warning, he appeared to falter, probably due to the soft surface, and was headed by the 50/1 outsider, Hotspur. Many in the crowd thought the conditions had the better of him and that his winning run was about to end. His jockey, Charles Marlow, was not giving up though. Marlow resorted to the whip and delivered two sharp blows at which point The Flying Dutchman responded, regained the advantage, and then drew further away to win by half-a-length.

The more astute racegoers who appreciated the importance of race times for assessing form were anticipating a slowly run race due to the ease in the ground, and they were proved correct. A time of three minutes was recorded by "Benson's Chronograph", the timepiece adopted by race officials since race timing began at the Derby meeting in 1846.

Although race timing had been in use for many years, its accuracy was subject to debate. It was claimed that Childers, also known as Flying Childers, was capable of running at a pace of eighty-two-and-a-half feet per second. This fanciful time equates to around 56 miles per hour, which is faster than the swiftest modern day quarter horses. At Newmarket, Flying Childers completed the four-mile course in six minutes forty seconds, equalling the time posted by Eclipse over a similar distance. Whilst an average speed of 36 mph does seem more realistic, it remains very unlikely that such a pace could be maintained by any horse over such a long distance. This raises doubts over both the timing process and the accuracy of the declared race distance, the latter being an issue that was still subject to error over the following 150 years.

Later in 1849, The Flying Dutchman added the St Leger to his growing list of successes, thus recording a Classic double. As a four-year-old he won the Emperor's Plate at Ascot by eight lengths and followed up with a ten-length win at Goodwood. At no point before or after the Derby, did a jockey need to use the whip when riding The Flying Dutchman, such was his superiority.

During the summer of 1850 the three-year-old, Voltigeur, was following a similar path to The Flying Dutchman by winning the Derby and St Leger. According to *The New Sporting Magazine*, he was of similar height to the older Champion and with the same deep girth. He may have had small ears and a light middle, but his muscular thighs and powerful quarters made him the best of his generation. It was inevitable that these two titans would meet: the battleground was Town Moor and the prize was the Doncaster Cup.

On race day, The Flying Dutchman was confidently expected to win and was installed as the 2/11 favourite for the two-runner affair. Whilst saddling, Charles Marlow, who was quite probably intoxicated at the time, took his instructions from The Flying Dutchman's trainer, John Fobert. In the race he completely ignored them, setting a blistering pace on the favourite. Voltigeur was given a more considerate ride and in the closing stages was able to pass the tiring Champion to win by half-a-length. The result was totally unexpected and a great *post mortem* ensued in which a range of excuses was suggested for The Flying Dutchman's defeat. The outcome was a rematch the following spring for a prize of 2,000gns [£300,000].

The two great horses met at York on 13th May 1851 where a crowd of 100,000 was waiting on a fine, dry day in anticipation of what was styled the "race of the century". Recent rain had softened the two-mile course over which they were to compete and, in order to eliminate any age advantage, Admiral Rous (creator of the weight-for-age scale) had assigned the runners different weights: Voltigeur would carry 8½ pounds less than his rival. The event could then be framed as the fairest contest possible between the two great horses.

At the off it was clear that Marlow had learned a valuable lesson from the Doncaster race and he let Nat Flatman take the lead on Voltigeur which steadily extended to three lengths. The order did not change throughout the majority of the race, with Marlow quite content to bide his time. With a furlong to go he gave The Flying Dutchman a kick with his heels and he easily drew alongside his younger rival; a few strides later he was clear and without recourse to the whip he secured a one-length victory.

The Flying Dutchman had gained revenge over his only conqueror and was immediately retired to stud. Voltigeur raced on for another season. Although he won his seasonal debut the following year, he was beaten at Ascot, and was then unable to concede 46lbs to the eventual winner of the Ebor Handicap. Incredibly, he was sent out again on the same afternoon to contest a five-furlong race, needless to say he didn't trouble the Judge in what was to be his last race in public.

1850-1899

||||||||||||||||||||||||||||||||||||||||||

Innovation dominated the second half of the nineteenth century. Alternative methods for starting races were investigated, the first Derby was committed to film, and both the *Sporting Life* and *Sporting Chronicle* published starting prices for the first time.

Horses were given new birthdays, and the first Melbourne Cup was staged in Australia. Danny Maher, part of the "American Invasion" set a new standard for jockeyship, and Fred Archer became the most successful rider in the sport.

The Triple Crown was won for the first time and a huge gamble on the Cambridgeshire Handicap was landed.

Tod Sloan went from hopeless to a champion in just a few years before being unfairly stopped in his tracks by a mean-spirited, and heavily-biased Jockey Club.

The great filly, Sceptre, was foaled, Alfred Lord Tennyson made a decent profit on the Derby and, of course, there was Ormonde.

West Australian's Triple Crown Bid   *14 September 1853*

On a crystal-clear day of brilliant blue skies and scintillating sunshine, thousands of men and women arrived at Doncaster by rail, by carriage, and on foot. As always the racing professionals were in attendance, yet their number was swamped by the 'human flood' of spectators who poured into the racecourse, shoehorning themselves into every conceivable vantage point along the track. The time-honoured motivation for such a vast assembly of people of every age demographic, every class, and every occupation would then have been a public hanging – especially the chance to jeer at the last throes of a convicted killer. But on this particular day, some tightly gathered local folks would have had you believe the stakes were even higher. Although not drawn by the carefully crafted language of a famous orator nor ready to marvel at the unveiling of a life-enhancing invention, the proud people of Yorkshire had amassed on Town Moor with a much more personal investment in the spectacle. They were there to witness a Yorkshire-trained horse win the Triple Crown.

As a juvenile West Australian was considered one of the finest of movers; he was also a late developer. His trainer, John Scott, finally took him to the racecourse at the end of October. At Newmarket that autumn day, the 5/2 shot was beaten into the runner-up position by Speed The Plough. Later in the week the two horses renewed their rivalry and this time the future champion came out best. This came as no surprise to the punters who were seemingly convinced that the Melbourne colt would improve on his debut effort and turnaround the form. They made him even-money favourite to do so. The North Yorkshire-trained juvenile clearly had many supporters: by Christmas he had been backed down to 12/1 favourite for the following year's Derby and was the 5/1 market leader for the 2,000 Guineas.

His return to the track in 1853 was delayed and he went straight to Newmarket to contest the 2,000 Guineas without a "prep" race. This lack of a recent run didn't dissuade the punters and the 'pick of the lot, to look at' was heavily supported. By race time he was being offered at 4/6. In the race the favourite backers had little to be concerned about, and as heavy rain soaked the lush spring grass of the Rowley Mile, West Australian comfortably recorded his first Classic success.

Scott was obviously wary of over-racing his stable star, so avoided the temptation of winning some easy money in lower grade stakes races. Instead he waited for the premier Classic. On a sunny Derby day at Epsom when clouds of dust constantly swept across the track, Frank Butler was last to leave the paddock on West Australian, but he was first back after the Guineas winner got the better of a protracted duel with Sittingbourne. With two Classics to his name, the chance of winning the Triple Crown in his home county was a distinct possibility.

On 14th September 1853 the ten runners declared for the St Leger cantered to the post. All eyes were on West Australian and Sittingbourne, the horse that had run the favourite so close in the Derby and considered by many to be his main threat. As the Starter raised his flag the level of excitement and anxiety amongst the crowd was fast approaching a feverish crescendo. Remarkably, in such a tense atmosphere, the horses and jockeys remained calm and 'at the very first signal, a beautiful start was effected.' Sittingbourne was soon at the head of affairs setting a good gallop. On the turn into the straight the front-runner weakened and Charles Marlow on The Reiver took over, much to the delight of a small section of the crowd who had plucked up sufficient courage to oppose the favourite. With just over a furlong to go, though, his supporters' cheers begin to fade as Frank Butler moved West Australian up to his quarters. Marlow may not have known it, but every racegoer on Town Moor did: the Derby winner was about to end his dreams of Classic glory for another year. As the runners passed the stands West Australian eased ahead of The Reiver and, with minimal encouragement from Butler, won by a very easy three lengths. The Yorkshire crowd had the Yorkshire win they wanted and the magical Triple Crown had been won for the first time in flat racing history.

As a four-year-old West Australian won his return race, then took the Ascot Gold Cup by a head before signing off his spectacular career with a twenty-length success at Goodwood. From ten starts, spread over three seasons, the great horse was only beaten once.

Two Handicaps in One Day   *6 April 1854*

Whilst war raged between British and Russian armies on the Crimean Peninsula, and members of the Light Cavalry were learning that charging on horseback towards banks of cannon is not the most effective way of achieving anything positive, many hundreds of surviving soldiers, as well as their horses, were suffering from injury and disease. There was only so much Florence Nightingale could do. Back home in England one particular thoroughbred was being especially well looked after and kept well clear of any possible injury or virus. The reason for the extra care and attention was to facilitate a carefully planned attack on some of the richest handicap races in the country.

Virago was a filly by Pyrrhus The First and as a two-year-old she raced only once, finishing well beaten in a stakes race at Shrewsbury racecourse. Based on this single performance she appeared to be a horse of limited ability and was handicapped as such for the following year's races. This was just what her astute trainer, former jockey "Honest John" Day, had planned. He had made sure Virago would not show her true form at Shrewsbury specifically to improve her chance of future success.

Stopping horses from winning to gain a financial advantage either immediately or in the future was not uncommon at the time. It seems that such practices were even condoned by the Jockey Club. In one classic case described in *The Sportsman's Magazine*, before his horse was about to start a race at Newmarket, General Scott was offered a bet by Mr Panton who called out to him 'General, I'll lay you a thousand pounds your horse is neither last nor first.'

The General accepted the bet, conversed with his jockey, then returned to the stands to watch his runner finish a remote last. Panton objected and refused to pay on the basis that General Scott had instructed his jockey to lose. Despite this apparent abuse of the rules, the Jockey Club sided with Scott concluding 'that the bet was laid not upon chance of the place in which the horse would come, if the rider was informed of it, but upon the opinion that he had not speed enough to be first, nor tractability enough to be brought in last.' Panton was required to settle the bet in full.

At the Epsom spring meeting on 6th April 1854 Virago made a return to racing in the City and Suburban Handicap for which she carried 6st 4lbs. Earlier in the year, in a private trial, she had comfortably beaten a stakes-winning five-year-old in receipt of just ten pounds, so her connections knew she was well-weighted for the ten-furlong handicap. And based on her starting price of just 2/1 they had made the most of the opportunity. Her twenty opponents had little chance of success, and Day's runner triumphed by a very easy three lengths. Incredibly, she turned out for the next non-juvenile race on the card, the Great Metropolitan Handicap. In the morning Virago had been available at 20/1 for this race, but while she waited at the post, enjoying the wonderfully sunny weather, her supporters had made her the clear market favourite. Under just 6st, which included a 5lbs penalty for her earlier win, Virago made good progress to join the leading group in the closing stages. Then, as they reached the stands, she eased away from her eighteen struggling rivals, winning the two-and-a-quarter mile contest by a comfortable length.

With the gamble landed, Virago was allowed to show her true ability. Over the summer more handicap success followed, as well as wins in the Goodwood Cup, a weight-for-age event, by fifteen lengths, the Nassau Stakes, the Yorkshire Oaks and the 1,000 Guineas at odds of 1/3. Many of her wins, like those at York and Doncaster, were secured in a canter. Her only defeat in the eleven races she contested in 1854 came over an inadequate six furlongs. Those who missed out on the Epsom gamble would have been more than just a little aggrieved to see the filly winning race after race. But there's always money to be made in handicap races by trainers willing to bend the rules to their advantage. For the lucky punters who had been aware of the Epsom gamble, the sight of Virago subsequently winning a Classic would no doubt have given them an intense feeling of satisfaction, and brought more than just a smile to their faces.

A New Birthday for Thoroughbreds   *1 January 1858*

On 25th April 1833 the Jockey Club decreed that the age of a horse would be calculated from 1st January as opposed to the previously used date of May Day. This was to reflect the changes in racing, specifically the introduction of national hunt races that were not confined to the summer months. Incredibly, this edict did not apply to all horses, just those based at Newmarket. Consequently, two dates were in use in the country, unless 'the Stewards of those races shall order otherwise', until 1858 when the January date was used for all thoroughbreds. A similar dual-date system applied in America with the northern states adopting 1st January to align with Britain, and the southern states opting to continue with the traditional date. It was not until the conclusion of the American Civil War that the use of just a single date was agreed. In Australia, and other southern hemisphere nations, 1st August is recognised as the birthday of all thoroughbreds.

Naturally, having a fixed birth date for all horses can cause issues, especially with premature births. A horse born in Britain in late December would be considered to be a yearling the following month, and twelve months later would be qualified for two-year-old races when, in fact, he or she was only just a year and a handful of days old. Such an animal would be at a huge disadvantage competing against those born in January or February, and in all probability would not be able to race competitively until a point was reached where the weight-for-age differences became negligible.

Though obviously crucial for owners and breeders, the foaling date is also important data for punters. When analysing two-year-old races, especially those in the early part of the year, the foaling date is always worth noting.

The other rules imposed by the Jockey Club at the time of the date change make even more interesting reading. They include several new regulations relating to races run in heats, and how the winner and runner-up should be determined. For instance, 'for the best of the plate, where three heats are run, the horse is second that wins one heat' and 'for the best of the heats, the horse is second that beats the other horses twice out of three times, though he do not win a heat' amongst many others that today read more like riddles than rules. "Give-and-take-plates" were becoming less fashionable at the time, but the rules governing their implementation were still in use and subject to modification. Along with a definition of weights and measures, 'four inches are a hand', 'fourteen pounds are a stone', the following rule determined the amount of weight each horse carried in these unique contests:

> Give-and-take-plates are, fourteen hands to carry stated weights, according to age; all above or under carry extra, or be allowed the proportion of seven pounds to an inch.

So rather than determining the weight carried by an analysis of previous results, the amount was purely related to the physical size of the runners thus allowing unraced horses to be handicapped. Given the modern day BHA's obsession with handicap races (80% of non-juvenile flat races run in Great Britain are handicaps), it is a little surprising that similar weight-to-height contests have not been added to the racing calendar in order to extend the coverage of weight-adjusted races still further.

Naturally there were rules relating to the basics of racing, such as how to deduce the winner of a race, and the disqualification of horses for "foul riding" or taking the wrong course. The bulk of the rules, though, related to betting, emphasising the level of importance it held within the sport.

As if there were not enough laws for racing and betting, an additional set was devised to regulate the access of members to the Jockey Club's "New Rooms" and "Coffee-Room". To gain access to the "New Rooms" a member would first have to be proposed by an existing Jockey Club member. His name and address, along with the details of the proposing member, had to be 'put up in the dining and card rooms at Newmarket'. The following day a ballot would take place in the 'morning between the hours of eleven and one or in the afternoon between the hours of four and six.' At least nine existing members of the Jockey Club had to vote and approval was given provided fewer than three votes were cast against admission. Fortunately for some members, there was an exception to this rule:

> A member of any of the clubs in St. James's Street, known by the names of White's, Brookes's, and Boodle's, may be admitted a member of the New Rooms without ballot.

Strangely, members of The Athenaeum Club, the Guard's Club and the MCC were not extended the same courtesy and their members were required to suffer the ignominy of the ballot.

Publication of the *Sporting Life*   24 March 1859

Priced at one penny [50p] and issued on Wednesdays and Saturdays, *Penny Bell's Life and Sporting News* was published for the first time on 24th March 1859. George Madden and Samuel Beeton guessed correctly that the burgeoning interest in sport meant there would be room in the market for a new sporting publication alongside the established *Bell's Life in London*. However, they reckoned without the problems their chosen name for the periodical would cause. A court injunction was issued and the original name of their new publication had to be changed. The new title chosen was *Sporting Life*.

Increasing sales resulted in the frequency of the paper's publication being upped to four days per week in 1881, and it became a daily in 1883 by which time it was covering a wide range of sports.

In 1871 the *Sporting Life* faced competition in the shape of the *Sporting Chronicle*. As a Manchester-based paper, the *Sporting Chronicle* tended to appeal more to racegoers in the north of England whereas the *Sporting Life* served those in the south.

Both made use of the electric telegraph and were able to publish stable reports, as well as lists of non-runners and other information punters needed. This helped to reduce the opacity of racing, making it more appealing to a wider range of the public. Historically, various methods had been used to get the results of races to the main cities. On at least one occasion, the result of the St Leger was transported to Manchester by dogs trained to hunt by trail. For greater distances, the pigeon express was often called upon with results flown from the north of the country to London. Generally, the birds had completed the journey by the morning after the race.

A further important innovation, introduced by the *Sporting Chronicle*, was the publication of starting prices. Bets could be placed "at starting price" which eliminated the potential for disputes between punters and the agents who placed the bets on their behalf.

In 1886 the *Sporting Life* incorporated *Bell's Life in London*. After merging with the *Sportsman* in 1924 it controlled a significant market share. The *Sporting Chronicle* continued until 1983 when its demise allowed the *Sporting Life* to dominate the sporting press until the *Racing Post* appeared in 1986.

A no less significant advancement in horseracing data was made in the mid-1940s. Founded by the mathematician Phil Bull and horseracing analyst Dick Whitford, Portway Press was the publishing arm of the *Timeform* organisation which became world famous for the accuracy of its ratings. The first book Portway Press published was *Racehorses of 1948*, an annual that quickly became essential reading for all serious punters.

Mayonaise Trounces Guineas Field   *12 May 1859*

Newmarket was never just a town with a racecourse nearby. From the very early days of the sport, the entire town was given over to the training and racing of thoroughbreds. The Heath, of course, afforded the area a distinct advantage when it came to preparing horses for racing. Many years before the track assumed its rightful position as the premier course of the nation, Philip Parsons in his *Essay on the Turf*, noted:

> *Here Nature, undebauched by art, spreads her ample bosom to receive*
> *her sons ambitious of renown; here no pillars of marble, no narrow*
> *and contracted limits, cramp the spirit of an Englishman. A wide*
> *and extensive carpet is spread indeed, but it is spread by the hand of*
> *Nature, as if on purpose to form a stage every way fit for the scenes that*
> *are acted upon it.*

Whereas Epsom cultivated a carnival atmosphere, racing at Newmarket was purely business. On racedays, no fortune-tellers were offering visions of what was yet to come, no musicians or acrobats entertained and annoyed racegoers in equal measure, and little by way of refreshment was generally available. Newmarket was all about the horses. Critical eyes of the townsfolk examined the runners in the parade ring, as they had done at every trial, the prospect for each was discussed in hushed tones, and bets made only after extensive analysis of their merits. If racegoers wanted a fun day out they went to Epsom, if they wanted to absorb themselves in the serious business of horseracing they made their way to Suffolk.

Despite this more diligent approach to betting and the absence of the "no-win" games of chance offered by the confidence-tricksters, at the end of a day's racing there were still plenty of losers amongst townsfolk and those who had visited from further afield. This was one characteristic shared by all racecourses and Newmarket was no different. After a challenging day, it was not uncommon to see racegoers attempting to negotiate the Devil's Dyke, the ancient divide between the kingdoms of East Anglia and Mercia, in order to evade the toll on the turnpike that they could no longer afford.

The thought of having to scale the dyke on their way home may have been in the minds of some of the racegoers who lined the rails for the 46th running of the 1,000 Guineas. But the magnetic draw of the sport was a force that many found impossible to resist. Those who made it to Newmarket for the first fillies' Classic on the 12th May 1859 (traditionally known as "rook shooting day"), were rewarded with a memorable race, one which has never been even remotely challenged since. Over the Ditch Mile the three-year-old filly, Mayonaise, ridden by champion jockey George Fordham put an astonishing twenty lengths between herself and the runner-up at the finishing line. Not even Frankel's Classic win in 2011 was that decisive.

On the back of this stunning performance Mayonaise was made 4/6 favourite for the Oaks but could only manage to run fourth to Summerside who was ridden by none other than George Fordham.

The First Melbourne Cup   *7 November 1861*

The earliest organised horseraces run in Australia were staged around the Sydney area of New South Wales in the 1790s with the first official meeting taking place at Hyde Park in 1810. By the 1850s the sport had migrated southwards and its popularity had increased significantly, especially in the newly formed state of Victoria. Keen to promote the sport, racing officials proposed a challenge match featuring the best horses of the two states. The race took place at Flemington racecourse, Melbourne, on 3rd October 1857, and it was estimated that over 20,000 spectators turned out to witness the three-mile contest.

Many of these racegoers would have taken up the offer of a "counter lunch" at Gregory's Tavern and Restaurant. By purchasing a pint of 'best Burton Brew or Yorkshire Ale', customers could enjoy a buffet style banquet where they could eat as much as they liked. Gregory's was the first establishment to offer counter lunches and no doubt had many takers willing to hand over a shilling [roughly £5 today] for the drink and a meal that, in summer, would have consisted of cold meat, sausage rolls, salad, bread, biscuits and cheese. Those with tastes that were more exotic may have visited Melbourne's first *Spanish Restaurant* which opened in 1857. Within just a few years this restaurant chain was expanding across the continent and as well as offering 'three courses for a shilling' it provided a 'private room for ladies' and 'beds for one shilling with hot and cold baths', ideal for racing fans that had travelled from far afield.

Realising the potential financial benefits that could accrue from races of this type, not least for the catering establishments in and around the racecourse, the Victorian Turf Club decided to stage an annual spring meeting featuring a two-mile handicap designed to attract the best horses in the country. Frederick Standish, a member of the Turf Club and former bankrupt gambler from England, suggested that the race should be named after the city, an idea that was accepted and implemented.

The first running of the Melbourne Cup was on 7th November 1861; the prize on offer was a gold watch. Seventeen runners lined-up but, despite being a flat race, only fourteen finished, with two of the three fallers dying at the course. Archer, a relatively unfancied runner from New South Wales, won the race easily, defeating the strongly favoured Victorian Champion racehorse, Mormon. This result was difficult for the "home" crowd to accept. Victoria had not long separated from New South Wales and, as an independent region, was desperate not to be seen as the poor relation. Recent gold finds in the Ballarat region may have put Victoria on an equal footing with its larger neighbour in financial terms, but recording sporting success was of equal importance to many of the state's residents. This interstate rivalry only served to make the 1862 running of the Melbourne Cup more competitive and many thousands of racegoers packed the stands at Flemington willing a homebred horse to win. However, much to their disappointment the result was the same as the previous year, another easy win for Archer.

Fortunately, the Victorians got the result they so craved when a Victoria-based runner won the following year. The victory was somewhat muted, though, because only seven runners were declared after many New

South Wales trainers staged a boycott because Archer was scratched from the race on a technicality: his trainer's declaration arrived a day late due to a public holiday in Victoria. To the home crowd a win was a win regardless of the circumstances.

Since those early days, the Melbourne Cup has grown in importance and now attracts runners from around the globe. Crowds of up 100,000 regularly attend, because not only is Cup day a public holiday for those working in the city, but it is an event of cultural significance in Australia. As the tagline goes, "it's the race that stops the nation".

Gladiateur's Derby   31 May 1865

The 86th anniversary of the Derby was a milestone in the history of the great race. For the first time the prize was taken by a French-owned, French-bred horse.

Gladiateur was bred at the stud owned by Count Frederic de Lagrange, yet despite these French roots, the son of Monarque was sent to Tom Jennings in Newmarket. Jennings was an astute trainer and immediately realised that the colt would need careful handling. The fact he suffered from an enlarged foreleg would not help his preparations for racing but, like his owner, Jennings was confident that Gladiateur would become a top class racehorse and entered him in the main races of the calendar: the English Classics and French Derby.

As a two-year-old, Gladiateur did not see a racecourse until the autumn of 1864 when he was successful in one of his three starts. Even that was better than could have been expected from a thoroughbred that, according to one critic, was 'a rough-looking, angular horse, without any quality.'

In early May 1865 Harry Grimshaw, Lagrange's jockey, who had moved from Yorkshire to Newmarket in order to improve his chances of Classic success, was in the saddle as Gladiateur joined seventeen other runners at the start for the 2,000 Guineas. After a delay of twenty-five minutes the flag was finally lowered. Tom Cannon, riding Pantaloon for the Marquess of Hastings had been instructed to set a strong gallop, possibly to improve the chances of the owner's other runner, Kangaroo (George Fordham). Cannon was not alone in trying to force the tempo, and several jockeys were keen to get to the front, which resulted in a furious early pace. Grimshaw was content to sit in the middle of the pack. At the Bushes [a marker approximately two furlongs from the winning post on the Rowley Mile course] Pantaloon dropped out, as expected, and as the runners met the rising ground it was clear that Kangaroo and Bedminster were also beaten. Gladiateur moved into contention but was joined by Archimedes, Liddington and Jack O'Lantern, 'thence ensued one of the finest races between the four witnessed for many years, the French representative winning in the last stride by a neck'. The "Avenger of Waterloo" as Gladiateur became affectionately known had one Classic to his name, and his owner was hungry for more.

The 1865 Derby attracted the biggest crowd in the history of the race. A new branch line extending towards Tattenham Corner had been built in order to improve the rail service from the south coast, and with longer and more frequent trains arriving in rapid succession, the course quickly filled with racegoers keen to see if Gladiateur could secure a second Classic. Whether this new rail service achieved its aim of reducing travelling times by easing road traffic was debatable. As travellers by road approached the course, 'innumerable vehicles from the four-in-hand drag to the humble donkey cart [converged] from every quarter of the compass.' To anyone seated in the stands the immediate impression from the briefest scan of the magnificent view was of carriages, carts, and other means of transportation. So numerous were these vehicles that they formed a 'triple barrier round the course' and were as 'nothing numerically compared with those... placed as the attendants consolingly urged "in a capital position for getting away again"'. For the vast majority, of course, there would be no quick getaway at the end of the day due to the unprecedented number of vehicles and the lack of any form of highway code.

The Prince of Wales arrived at the course just after 1pm having left London in his open, four-horse carriage at 11am. This was clearly thought to be the optimum time for arrival because, after the Prince made his way to the Royal Box, the stream of carriages that appeared at the back of the stands was 'incessant, and from among their occupants a full quorum of members of either branch of the Legislature might have been formed without difficulty.'

Such an immense influx of people needed accommodation and, for the duration of the meeting, the town of Epsom took on the appearance of a 'busy and crowded city'. Though most eagerly encouraged by the local farmers who could sell eggs, butter, poultry, and other farm produce at inflated prices, others were less welcoming of the tide of racegoers, and for good reason. In every significant assembly of people there will be an 'unprincipled proportion' as a member of the Surrey constabulary described them, intent of 'propagating vice, or robbing the bystanders.' Attendees were warned, in no uncertain terms, to be 'on their guard', just as they are when arriving at the Derby nowadays.

Shortly after the completion of the first race, the tiresome, thankless chore of clearing the course began - again. The strategy adopted by the constabulary followed the pattern used before the opening race: first remove the people, then the rubbish they left behind, and finally the untethered dogs that on many occasions in the past had caused serious injury to horses and riders. This may at first seem to be a straightforward task, but the sheer volume of people in attendance, and the scant regard they paid to the instructions given by the officials, made it even more time-consuming than usual.

At precisely 4pm the Starter signalled to the twenty-nine jockeys, whose coloured silks formed a 'rainbow-belt' stretching across the width of the track, and the Derby was underway - at the tenth attempt. As in the Guineas, Grimshaw sat "mid-division" in the early stages of the contest alongside the second favourite, Breadalbane. As they descended the hill, front-running Tilt gave way and rail-runner, Eltham, took the lead. With three-quarters of a mile to go, Wild Charley stumbled causing a collision between Archimedes, Audax and the steadily improving Gladiateur which 'completely knocked him off his stride'. Grimshaw needed to give the favourite time to regather his balance, not something that is easily achieved on the downhill stretch at Epsom. Many thought his chance had gone, but once back on an even keel Gladiateur moved smoothly up to the leaders as the runners entered the home straight. At the distance he showed what a good horse he was and powered away to win easily by two lengths. The crowd poured onto the track forming a 'dense, swarming, excited mass of humanity'. So great was the crush of spectators that the police struggled to clear a space for unsaddling, and the winner had to be surrounded by several mounted officers for protection.

After his Epsom success, Gladiateur returned to France to be greeted by a huge crowd of supporters. Whilst in Paris he won the Grand Prix de Paris in impressive style. A routine win at Goodwood and a walkover followed, before he won the St Leger, even though he appeared to be lame at the time. In so doing he became the second horse to complete the Triple Crown.

As a four-year-old Galdiateur won a three-runner Ascot Gold Cup by a remarkable forty lengths then returned to France and won several more contests, including one over four miles, after which he was retired to stud. This impressive catalogue of victories amassed over three seasons was not a bad return for a rough-looking horse that appeared to be devoid of quality.

Snow on Derby Day   *22 May 1867*

In the year in which Karl Marx finally completed *Das Capital* (Volume 1), Alfred Nobel applied for a patent for dynamite, Alaska was transferred from Russia to America, and Pierre Michaux had the idea of adding pedals to bicycles, in England the unseasonal weather was of considerable concern to a wider swathe of the population than just farmers, seafarers, and gardeners.

The British have often been accused of suffering from an irrational obsession with the weather. This may or may not have been true in the past, but what is unquestionable now is the existence of a global fixation with the weather. Climate Change is near the top of every nation's political agenda and is gaining prominence daily. The weather, even in the normally temperate south of England, does appear to be getting ever more erratic with violent storms now occurring on a regular basis. But many years before Climate Change became an ubiquitous phrase there were times when the weather was at variance with expectations. The early summer of 1867 was such a time.

The weather in May 1867 lurched from one end of the temperature scale to the other in a matter of days. The month started with such a remarkably warm spell that special reports found their way into media and a new word was added to the language. Reporting on the unusual meteorological conditions, the *Manchester Courier and Lancashire General Advertiser* printed a letter that included the term "heat-wave", the first time the phrase appeared in a British newspaper. This glorious weather was not to last though. On Derby day, 22nd May, it snowed: not just a light dusting, but heavy snow that produced blizzard-like conditions at Epsom. So poor was the weather that the Derby suffered from ten false starts. Eventually the thirty runners got off to a level break and after a sustained battle along the home straight the race was won by Hermit, one of the best juveniles of 1866 but unraced as a three-year-old. Lack of a recent run, and a report that he had broken a blood vessel shortly before the race, caused his price to drift and on the day he started at 1000/15. Consequently, Hermit's success was not welcomed by the betting public who had dismissed him as a no-hoper. Nor was it appreciated by Henry Hastings, 4th Marquess of Hastings who, for many years, had been a sporting rival of Hermit's owner, Henry Chaplin. Hastings lost in excess of £100,000 on the race as a result of his rash betting and hubris. Chaplin on the other hand won a small fortune including a substantial personal wager with Hastings.

Although, on their journey home, many racegoers would have been complaining about the cold weather and a long shot winning the big race, Henry Hastings had a great deal more to moan about: Derby Day had left him virtually bankrupt. In fact, he never fully recovered from the impact the losses inflicted on his mental state and his health deteriorated dramatically. Hastings died the following year aged just twenty-six.

As legend has it, his dying words were 'Hermit's Derby broke my heart, but I did not let it show, did I?'

Formosa's Four Classics   *9 September 1868*

Formosa made her racing debut at Bath in 1867, the same year the United States launched an attack on the island of Formosa, now known as Taiwan, in retaliation for the alleged massacre by the Paiwan warriors of the crew of an American merchant ship.

As debut runs go, Formosa's was not a particularly memorable display and gave no indication of what she would achieve a year later. Three runs at Ascot's Summer Meeting did produce one placed effort, a third in the Triennial Stakes, but again she did not seem to possess Classic-winning qualities. Described in *The Sporting Review* as standing a shade over fifteen hands high, and possessing a 'peculiar head... with small ears, but an intelligent, expressive eye... great depth of girth... but weak behind the saddle', Formosa finally got off the mark by winning a nursery at Stockbridge when carrying 7st 8lbs. This victory seemed to inspire her, because at Newmarket on her next start she won the valuable Chesterfield Stakes. After running third at Goodwood, the cleverly named Buccaneer filly (Formosa was home to Japanese pirates in the fourteenth century) won a minor contest at Abingdon before being well beaten by Green Sleeve in the Middle Park Stakes.

It would be fair to say that her juvenile profile did not even hint that Formosa would be challenging for Classic glory in 1868. However, on her seasonal reappearance in the 2,000 Guineas she was made 3/1 second favourite to win a race traditionally dominated by colts.

On a day when a cold wind raking across Newmarket Heath made for uncomfortable viewing, Tom Chaloner on Moslem decided to set the pace in the first Classic of the year. The fourteen runners remained tightly grouped until the *dip* [in the final two furlongs of the Rowley Mile the track descends, then rises forming a dip approximately one furlong from the finish] when Formosa joined Moslem at the head of affairs, with St Ronan in close attendance. With the others weakening, a battle then ensued with Formosa partnered by George Fordham gaining a slight lead over the front-runner and St Ronan dropping back seemingly beaten. Chaloner then managed to get Moslem back on terms, and the colt and filly matched strides to the line. A dead heat was called and a run-off was scheduled for later in the afternoon. However, the owners of the two runners agreed to share the prize. Furthermore, Moslem was granted a walkover in the run-off and, as a consequence, was designated the winner of the 2,000 Guineas.

Two days later, despite heavy support for Lady Coventry, Formosa was sent off the 10/11 favourite for the 1,000 Guineas. This was a much more straightforward race for Fordham who could afford to drop his hands on Formosa and canter to an easy victory. It was undoubtedly an impressive performance, with *The Times*, reporting that 'a much easier affair has scarcely been seen.'

Those who made it to Epsom on Oaks Day 1868 were greeted with a violent lunchtime storm of thunder, lightning, hail, and rain that descended in torrents. By 1pm a large portion of the road outside the course was flooded to a depth of three feet causing more than a little distress to many racegoers. Not all were displeased with the weather though; a flood to some was a money-making opportunity to others. With spectators desperate to get to the track and the relative sanctuary of the stands, 'a rich harvest was made by "roughs," who carried pedestrians across on their shoulders, and cabs plying over the temporary ferry demanded fabulous sums.' Other than costing a number of the higher echelons a few extra pennies, this raging storm blew in much graver consequences. It was so intense that, according to press reports, lives were lost, horses were killed, and the Keeper's cottage at the Warren was demolished. Although unsettled by the extreme atmospheric conditions, fortunately all of the runners preparing for the Oaks Stakes escaped injury.

It is interesting to note how Formosa appeared to the racing experts once she had Classic success to her name. To one trackside member of the press corps, Formosa was 'the best looking mare in the race... full of muscular power, she has a pleasing head and... a slightly crested neck.' There was no mention of a 'peculiar head' or being 'weak behind the saddle' this time. He added that, on leaving the ring, 'she walked away with Fordham a very picture, and even then it certainly looked to be all over. No animal has ever continued to improve more.' His assessment that the race was effectively over before it even began was, to a certain extent, quite accurate. George Fordham hit the front on Formosa with a mile to race, then simply cantered to the line to win unchallenged by ten lengths. The filly was by far the most impressive horse on show both in the paddock and on the track.

After two defeats by colts at the Ascot June meeting, Formosa was taken to Doncaster for the final Classic of the year. Her trainer, Henry Woolcott, had prepared the filly to perfection. She appeared physically stronger than in her last race, and in the parade she astounded the racegoers. As one writer eloquently noted 'her coat could not be equalled by any loom of Lyons, she walked before the stand as if conscious of her charms, and gladly waiting further opportunities of displaying them.' Although matched in the betting by King Alfred, the Derby runner-up who had beaten her at Ascot), the 100/30 joint favourite had no equal in the race. Tom Chaloner eased Formosa to the front at the furlong marker and she had the race in safekeeping some considerable distance before the pair crossed the winning line. *Baily's Magazine* noted that the 'telegraph-man took Formosa's name and number in his hand and hoisted it almost simultaneously with her passing the winning-post.' The margin of success was two lengths, but Formosa was unextended and could easily have doubled the distance.

With this victory, the Fillies' Triple Crown had been won for the first time and, with her dead-heat in the 2,000 Guineas, no horse had finished in front of her in four Classics.

Kinscem's Unbeaten Run Begins   *26 June 1876*

On 26th June 1876, the very day the lives of General Custer and the five companies under his command were lost at the Battle of the Little Big Horn, Kinscem made a winning start to her racing career in Berlin. The actual winning distance is not certain and varies from four to twelve lengths but what is known for definite is that it was an immensely impressive debut performance. Bred in Hungary, Kinscem, which translates as "My Treasure", was to race ten times in total as a juvenile over distances from four-and-a-half furlongs to a mile. Under the guidance of the English trainer Robert Hesp, she won all ten races, three of them by a distance.

Kinscem's sire, Cambuscan, was bred by Queen Victoria and won the July Stakes; her dam, Water Nymph, was a daughter of Cotswold (another Hungarian import from Great Britain) who had been runner-up in the Royal Hunt Cup. In terms of looks Kinscem was nothing to write home about. A liver chestnut standing just over sixteen hands, she was overly long, possessed a ewe neck [diminished muscle on top of the neck, and pronounced muscle underneath, which curves the neck in a downwards direction], and her ears would not have looked out of place on a mule. Kinscem also had a quirky nature: she was devoted to her groom and a cat named Csalogany. In fact she would often refuse to move if not accompanied by her two best friends and whilst this meant she regularly made slow starts to races, it did not stop her winning. Her three-year-old record was seventeen wins from seventeen races, and in the next two seasons she raced a further twenty-seven times without defeat, including her only race in Great Britain when she won the Goodwood Cup, again after a slow start.

Kinscem retired from racing at the end of the 1879 season having won all fifty-four of her races, the most wins ever recorded by an unbeaten thoroughbred. As a broodmare she produced five foals including the winners of the 1885 German Derby and 1886 Hungarian St Leger. Following an attack of colic, Kinscem died in 1887. As a mark of respect Hungarian newspapers were edged in black, and flags across the country were flown at half-mast.

A Cambridgeshire Gamble   *22 October 1878*

On the morning of 22nd October 1878 thousands of racegoers arrived in Newmarket, mostly by train and carriage, but also on horseback and on foot. The great attraction was the Cambridgeshire Handicap. So many had made their way to the market town that the High Street became host to a long, meandering procession of racing enthusiasts all anxious not to miss a moment of the drama yet to unfold. Intermingled with the jostling hordes were the costermongers, each one keen to sell their specialist wares. From succulent slices of the most exotic pineapples and oranges to the rather more humble apples and plums of more local origin, there was fruit enough to please the palate of every punter present that day. For those who preferred savoury snacks there were plenty of alternatives on offer. The market for nuts was particularly buoyant, especially for that famous harbinger of winter itself, the heart-warming roast chestnut.

The mass appeal of this race was difficult to justify in the minds of many racing folk. *The Times* racing correspondent was particularly bemused by the arrival of so many racegoers remarking 'it is curious that so many people are attracted here by the Cambridgeshire, because it is the one race above all others... that it is impossible to see anything of except the finish.'

Whether the majority of the crowd could see anything of the race or not, it did not stop them placing bets on its outcome. Changes to the betting laws seemed to have heightened the desire to bet whether legally on-course, or off-course via illegal Bookmakers' Runners who collected wagers on the streets of the major towns and cities. As one racing analyst accurately summarised:

The extermination of the betting-houses [by the 1853 Betting Act]... would seem only to have sharpened the appetite of the British public, who now hanker more keenly than ever after the forbidden fruit, and pour their monkeys, ponies, their quids and dollars, into the coffers of the commission agents, until the bookmaking clans have well-nigh become the dictators of the turf.

Given the Bookmakers' influence over the BHA in terms of race programming amongst other things, it could be argued that this position of dominance in the sport has been maintained until this very day.

In the race report it was claimed that 'nearly all of them [racegoers] have gone for Macbeth', a relatively unexposed horse that had been heavily backed by his trainer after running an impressive trial with Julius Caesar, a horse that had competed at the very highest level. Greenback also came in for support, along with Tallas and the American mare Start. As the thirty-eight runners made their way to post, the layers were offering 100/15 against Macbeth and Greenback. One horse that was struggling to attract money was Isonomy. This small, bay colt opened at 25/1 but was soon out to 40/1 and in the view of most trackside punters had little, if any, chance of success.

Two years earlier, in the summer of 1876, racehorse trainer John Porter visited Yardley stud near Birmingham to assess a selection of yearlings that were due to be sold at the upcoming sales. Around twenty were being encouraged to gallop around the paddock by members of the group 'rattling sticks in their hats' and of these Porter was most taken by the smallest of the bunch who was 'threading his way through the others as if determined to get to the front.' At the subsequent Doncaster Sales the small colt was purchased on behalf of Frederick Gretton and was named Isonomy, the meaning of which Porter thought exactly fitted the colt who was small but obviously 'felt... quite equal to the others and entitled to the same respect.'

As a two-year-old Isonomy did not race until August when he finished a poor third in a stakes race. Taken to Newmarket for a nursery stakes over four furlongs he managed to get his head in front, but was then beaten in a similar race. He ended the season with a win, a second and a third, from three starts. Though entered for both the 1878 Derby and St Leger, Isonomy's shrewd owner had other ideas.

The flamboyant, fearless gambler Frederick Gretton, whose family part owned the Bass Brewery, led what would be termed an "alternative" lifestyle. In 1873 he formed a relationship with Lucy Radmall, a teenage chorus girl who was 'a beautiful young coquette, with direct, impudent speech and a tiny waist'. She was also only half his age. In the eyes of the privileged class, conducting such a liaison in public was nothing short of disreputable and Gretton was shunned by the upper echelons of British Society. Consequently the couple moved to Paris where such arrangements were commonplace and attitudes were somewhat less conservative. Gretton would return to England on a regular basis to watch his horses run leaving Lucy, or 'Mrs Gretton as she became known' in France. On one of those visits he informed Porter of his racing plans for Isonomy which were as unconventional as his living arrangements. For the 1878 season, he decided to run the horse in just one race: the Cambridgeshire Handicap.

In early October 1878 Porter arranged a trial over the Cambridgeshire course. Four horses were involved: Ancient Pistol a winner of three races earlier in the season; Harbinger who had won over a mile and was then made second favourite for the Cesarewitch; Singleton who had victories in four races that summer; and Isonomy who was unraced since his defeat the previous season.

At the end of the trial, during which Porter had to hastily remove some unwanted "dolls" from the course just seconds before the horses reached them, the winner was declared to be Ancient Pistol by a neck from Isonomy; the four-year-old Harbinger was six lengths further away in third with Singleton fourth. Many people were on the Heath to witness the trial, so it was soon brought to the attention of the layers that Isonomy had been beaten and could be confidently opposed in the Cambridgeshire. Gretton and Porter knew otherwise. In the trial, Isonomy conceded 26lbs to Ancient Pistol and 19lbs to Singleton. Harbinger carried just 4lbs more than the runner-up but he was a year older. On that reading of the form, and with a mere 7st 1lb on his back, Isonomy looked far from a no-hoper in the Newmarket race.

The Cambridgeshire Handicap was scheduled for 3:20pm but due to delays to the earlier races the Starter's flag did not fall until 4pm. The autumnal light was already beginning to dim and the spire of Ely Cathedral had totally faded from view as the horses covered the first furlong of the race. Harry Morgan, a top class, lightweight jockey who could easily make the weight, kept Isonomy on the heels of the leaders through the early stages of the race. As the leading group came into the view of those in the stands he took the three-year-old to the front and drew clear. Isonomy won 'in a canter by two lengths' from Touchet and La Merveille. Much to the disappointment of on course punters, Macbeth, Greenback and Tallus were all well-beaten. Frederick Gretton, on the other hand, was counting his winnings that totalled well in excess of £40,000 [£4.8 million], a reasonable return for a horse that cost just 320gns.

With the plan perfectly executed and the gamble secured, Isonomy reverted to a more conventional racing programme. At Ascot the following June he won the Gold Vase and the Gold Cup (which he retained the following year) and for good measure he added the Goodwood Cup, Doncaster Cup and Ebor Handicap. This outstanding "Cup Treble" was not repeated until 1949, clearly illustrating how well Isonomy's true ability had been disguised to ensure a winning handicap mark and inflated odds at Newmarket.

Frederick Gretton died in 1882 and bequeathed a legacy of £6,000 per annum to Lucy who married Theodore Francis Brinckman a year later. The marriage was far from harmonious and the couple divorced in 1895. In 1901 Lucy married George Frederick William Byron, 9th Baron Byron, becoming Lady Byron. Although active in the suffragist movement, it was her work in the Great War that gained most recognition and in 1917, the year Lord Byron died, she was appointed Dame Commander, Order of the British Empire (DBE). Her third marriage was to Sir Robert Houston MP but this, too, was short-lived with Houston dying in 1926. As Lady Houston, the former chorus girl donated huge sums of money for the advancement of British aviation without which the aircraft manufacturer Supermarine would not have been able to compete, and win, the 1931 Schneider Trophy. By 1936 her physical and mental health were failing, and she was confined to bed for the best part of every day. On 29th December Lucy suffered a heart attack and died aged 79. Three years later the Supermarine Spitfire, the development of which she partly funded, was called into action as Britain faced its gravest crisis.

A Mythical Inspiration   *28 May 1879*

The 100th Derby was run on 28th May 1879 and was won by George Fordham on Sir Bevys. It was, in essence, a "double-first" for Fordham: his first ride of the year after a long illness and his first victory in Epsom's Blue Riband. The soft going had made the meeting a graveyard for punters and at 20/1 not many would have been on Sir Bevys. Yet the enthusiastic crowd, possibly more appreciating the return of the former champion jockey than the success of the horse, rapturously applauded the pair into the winner's enclosure.

One person who would have been cheering loudly for Sir Bevys was the poet laureate Alfred Lord Tennyson of *The Charge of the Light Brigade* fame. Tennyson has been quoted as saying that he had £5 on Sir Bevys to win the race because he was the 'hero of one of my early poems'. Quite which poem he was referring to remains elusive and it is more likely Tennyson was misquoted and the legendary Sir Bevys was a poetic hero of his early life as opposed to a character featured in a poem.

Sir Bevys of Hampton is a romantic narrative of the 1300s. The hero travels widely through Europe and the Near East where he encounters a range of character-defining tests, battles dragons and giants, acquires a magical horse named Hirondelle, is imprisoned, escapes, falls in love with the daughter of a King, is subsequently exiled, and finally reconciles with the mother of his two sons. So, it's quite remarkable that he also had the time to found Southampton. The tale has had a great deal of influence on poets, and modern-day film makers too, so it could possibly have influenced Tennyson as well. What is known for certain is that Alfred passed the betting gene to his grandson Lionel Tennyson.

Lionel Tennyson, 3rd Baron Tennyson, played cricket for Hampshire and England. He was also a lieutenant in the Rifle Brigade. Through the summer 1913 he was given leave to play for his county, but with the threat of war looming ever large, by 1914 it became clear that he would find it difficult to combine cricket with his army duties. Despite these military distractions, he still managed to turn out for Hampshire in the early summer and just as importantly found time to indulge in his second love: gambling. In the wonderful book, *The Final Over*, Christopher Sandford writes:

> [Tennyson] found the Southampton casino and the then thriving Tweseldown racecourse, near Aldershot, especially tempting. Tennyson always had a tip for a horse, a "sure thing" that would make everyone wealthy. A year earlier he managed to lose £12,000 in the course of a week at the races.

His cavalier approach to betting was reflected in the way he lived his life at home and on the front line. During the Great War he was wounded three times, reported killed in action twice, and was twice mentioned in despatches. Unlike his two younger brothers who were both killed in the conflict, Lionel Tennyson survived the war and returned home to continue his battle with the Bookmakers and play first class cricket as captain of his county until 1932.

Danny Maher   *29 October 1881*

Danny Maher formed part of the "American Invasion" of British Racing in the early years of the twentieth century. Born on 29th October 1881, Maher was riding winners as an apprentice jockey just fourteen years later, and at the age of seventeen was America's leading jockey. Riding for Bill Daly, amongst others, he won a host of major races from 1898 to 1900. However, his flourishing career in the States was cut short. The usual causes for the premature ending of a jockey's career, weight-gain, injury or suspension, were not, in this case, to blame. Instead, the reason was purely regulatory: the introduction of the Hart-Agnew law.

Enacted under pressure from activists, this new anti-gambling legislation had a major impact on horseracing in New York. Whilst racing did continue, it was severely curtailed due to the restrictions it imposed on betting. Only bets placed orally were permitted, and teams of law enforcement officials were instructed to arrest any person found to be writing potential bets on paper, racecards, or the proverbial back of a cigarette packet.

With New York's racing in such a poor state, jockeys and trainers crossed the Atlantic to ply their trade in England. Although many of the American jockeys were supremely talented, Danny Maher stood out. Of all the new arrivals he had the longest and most successful career. It was Maher's 'bright, warm-hearted character, and delightful personality' that first caught the attention of one-time Prime Minister Lord Rosebery, himself a talented sportsman, as well as a writer, historian, and book collector. The two friends formed a powerful racing partnership. This did mean that Maher missed potential Classic winners because his agreement required him always to ride a horse owned by Lord Rosebery if one had been declared to run. Maher was not one to complain though: when Rosebery offered to allow him to get off Prue in the 1913 Derby after Maher had been offered the ride on the favourite, Maher's response was to decline the offer, 'I am retained by Lord Rosebery and if Prue runs I shall certainly ride'.

During his time in England Maher won all five Classics plus a raft of other top races such as the Eclipse Stakes, Ascot Gold Cup, and the

Cambridgeshire Handicap. In 1908 and 1913 Maher claimed the Jockeys' championship, and by the time he retired had achieved a 25% win rate.

Years of fasting and smoking had an impact on Maher's health, and in 1916 he died of tuberculosis aged just 35. Lord Rosebery arranged the funeral, and sent a wreath with the simple, yet heartfelt message 'From his faithful friend'.

St Simon's Ascot Gold Cup   12 June 1884

In 1881 two assassinations rocked America: President James A Garfield was shot by Charles J Guiteau and Billy The Kid was gunned down by Pat Garrett. In Italy the first episode of *The Adventures of Pinocchio* was published, and on Tyneside, Stanley Cricket Club formed a football team that later became Newcastle Football Club. Near Newmarket, St Angela, a King Tom mare, gave birth to a brown foal who was destined to become one of the greatest horses of the age.

Sent to trainer John Dawson, the Galopin colt's prospects looked limited based on his pedigree, so his owner-breeder, the Hungarian nobleman Prince Batthyany, registered him for the 2,000 Guineas more in hope than expectation. However, this entry was declared void when the Prince died unexpectedly in 1883. In the subsequent dispersal sale the colt, now named St Simon, was purchased by the Duke of Portland for a reputed 1,600gns [£205,000] and sent to Mat Dawson's Heath House stables. Mat was the brother of John and started his career in Scotland before moving to Berkshire in the mid-1840s and then to Newmarket in 1866. He was the archetypal trainer of the time, sporting mutton-chop whiskers and stiff cravat. His expert eye for a yearling was unsurpassed along with his taste for whisky. Dawson was famed for his stable management and it served him well: by the end of his long career he had trained the winners of twenty-eight English Classics.

The Duke of Portland's immediate impression of St Simon when he first watched him work on the gallops was one of disappointment and he remarked to Dawson that St Simon could not 'stride over straw'. Whilst the Duke was far from an equine expert, he possessed 'beneath his fashionable vapid and foppish exterior a certain instinctive shrewdness where money was concerned'. When approached by Robert Peck and offered 2,000gns for the unimpressive colt he opted to forego the easy 400gns profit and decided to persevere with St Simon. It was one of his better decisions.

As a juvenile, the Galopin colt was unbeaten from five starts winning either by a significant margin or in a canter, or sometimes a combination of both. Towards the end of the season, St Simon's dominance prompted Dawson to invite a friend to watch the horse compete. Dawson added to the invite 'he is certainly the best two-year-old I have ever trained'.

The following season St Simon should have been contesting, and probably winning, the Triple Crown, but he was ineligible to run in the Classics. On the death of an owner all future nominations, such as entries for the Classics, were automatically voided. This rule remained in place until 1929. Consequently, the major cup races became his target. After some initial impressive trials, St Simon was declared for the Epsom Gold Cup. News of his stunning workouts had other owners running for cover, and in the Epsom race he was gifted a walkover. Two weeks later, in the Ascot Gold Cup, it was a different matter.

There was no Royal Procession for the 1884 Ascot races because of the death of the Duke of Albany; the Royal Stand was also closed out of respect. This did not dissuade the racegoers, and the attendance was 'prodigious... the number of coaches and vehicles on the course was considerably greater than had been seen for some seasons.' From an elevated position, the lawns and walkways appeared to the naked eye as a sea of top hats, intermingled with colourful silk dresses and bustles, and parasols aplenty.

On the 12th June 1884, the sky was clear and the temperature pleasantly warm as Iambic led the five runners in the parade for the Gold Cup. His stablemate St Simon followed him to post with Faugh-a-Ballagh, Friday, and the ill-tempered Tristan on their heels. Tristan's antics delayed the start by ten minutes, but once underway Iambic and Friday cut out the running with St Simon 'going leisurely enough' last of the five. At Swinley Bottom, a mile from home, Tristan took over from Friday, and was quickly joined by Faugh-a-Ballagh, the pair gaining a long lead over St Simon, which to most observers appeared insurmountable. Remarkably, though, by the final bend St Simon had closed the gap and was cruising effortlessly alongside the leading pair. To all in the stand it was clear that the race was effectively over and that they were witnessing a victory by a truly great racehorse. St Simon 'strode gaily to the front' then accelerated away to win by an easy twenty lengths in one of the most impressive Gold Cup wins in the history of the race.

St Simon dropped back to a mile for the Newcastle Cup and, on very hard going, easily disposed of his only rival, Chiselhurst, by eight lengths. Whilst he was as impressive as normal, the sun-baked going took its toll and although he beat the 1883 St Leger winner by twenty lengths in the Goodwood Cup he would not race again due to the injuries he had sustained.

In numerical terms, his racing career comprised of a mere nine wins from nine races, but the style of the victories, especially the Ascot Gold Cup win, marked him down as one of the very best racehorses to compete in Great Britain. At stud his 423 foals, which included Persimmon, St Frusquin and Diamond Jubilee, won over 500 races between them, including seventeen Classics.

A Champion Makes His Debut   *14 October 1885*

The crowd lining the rails on the Wednesday of Newmarket's Second October Meeting were hoping to get an answer to a question that had been mulled over for many weeks: which horse would be the winter favourite for the Derby? The main protagonists were Minting and Saraband who, along with The Bard, were the best two-year-olds of the year. The first named pair was to meet that afternoon in the Middle Park Stakes, the premier juvenile race of the meeting. A decisive win for either would ensure Derby favouritism. What the spectators were unaware of, as they cheered Minting home in a tight finish, was that they had not only watched the Derby favourite race that day. In the race preceding the Middle Park Stakes they had seen the following season's Derby winner, a horse that would later be proclaimed as one of the very best of the century. In years to come, these fortunate racegoers would be able to tell their children and grandchildren that they were at Newmarket the day Ormonde made his debut.

The opening race of the day was a match between the Duke of Portland's multiple winner Modwena and Helen Of Troy. The Duke's impeccably bred filly won at odds of 2/11 in a canter. But her work was not over for the day; in the Post Sweepstakes, staged just before the Middle Park Stakes, she faced two colts. Made 5/6 favourite to complete a quick double, Modwena's jockey decided to make all on the filly. It looked good for favourite backers until the trio reached the stands. Then, the previously unraced Ormonde, carrying the yellow and black colours of the Duke of Westminster, drew alongside her. A couple of strides later the powerful colt galloped clear to win by a very easy two lengths. Warbler, the only other runner, was a "bad third". Favourite backers had lost out, and more than just a few in the crowd were trying to evaluate precisely what they had just witnessed.

Ormonde was by the Derby winner Bend Or, and his dam was Lily Agnes a winner of twenty-one races including the Doncaster Cup. Owned and bred by Hugh Grosvenor, 1st Duke of Westminster, and trained by John Porter at Kingsclere, Ormonde raced twice more as a juvenile winning the Criterion Stakes and Dewhurst Plate, both at Newmarket. These victories represented a good return from a horse that, on arrival at Kingsclere, was ungainly in appearance and had splints under both knees. However, even greater success awaited the colt the following year.

On a cold, windy spring day in 1886, Ormonde was made third favourite for the 2,000 Guineas. Punters considered Minting (11/10) and Saraband (3/1) to be more likely to prevail in a race that had attracted heavy and sustained betting. Minting's trainer, Mat Dawson, would not hear of defeat for his unbeaten runner whom he firmly believed to be the best racehorse he had ever seen gallop – a view he shared with everyone he met. As so often happens, the result of the race did not match the order suggested by the odds on offer. In Porter's words 'From first to last [Ormonde] was master of the situation. A long way from home the issue rested between Ormonde and Minting and the latter was definitely and decisively beaten'. Ormonde strode away for an emphatic two-length win. Minting got closest to the Duke's runner, but there was then a ten-length gap back to the third, 33/1 shot Mephisto, whom Tom Cannon had ridden into 'the place for which he had been heavily backed'. Dawson found the defeat of Minting very difficult to take. Immediately after the race he left the racecourse and did not reappear for the remainder of the meeting.

The Derby was next on the agenda for the unbeaten Ormonde. Porter felt there was no need for a "prep" race because the three-year-old was progressing well and by that stage of the season it was already 'impossible to exaggerate his merits'. While the vast majority of racegoers were looking forward to seeing the Guineas winner challenge for a second Classic, writing after the contest, the race appeared to have made limited appeal to the racing correspondent of The Times:

> A less interesting race for the Derby than that run yesterday upon Epsom Downs has not been witnessed... for not only was the field the smallest which has contested the race since Pope won in 1809, but the nine competitors were, with the exception of Ormonde and The Bard, so moderate in quality that they would have been more in their place running for some insignificant handicap at Newmarket or Manchester.

The lack of quality was attributed to the proliferation of high value races scheduled in the racing calendar, giving owners more choice and a greater number of opportunities to run their better horses. These valuable races were not confined to Britain. Robert Vyner instructed Mat Dawson to run Minting in the Grand Prix de Paris rather than oppose Ormonde again. On this issue, *The Times* correspondent complained that 'we shall never again hear of an owner winning close upon £100,000 [£13 million] over the race'.

The 1886 Derby still attracted the public in their thousands though, with thirty-eight special trains despatched from Victoria station and nearly as many from both Waterloo and London Bridge, enabling Londoners to get to Epsom with the minimal of fuss. Rail travel had improved significantly through the Victoria era and by 1898 it was claimed that a party of six could complete a journey from Inverness to London in under fourteen hours at a cost of less than £25 [£3,200]. On the issue of transport in general *The Times* writer did find something positive to say about the day: 'the dust had been so effectually laid along the picturesque road which leads through Sutton to Epsom that the drive down was a very pleasant one.'

As had been the case since 1847 when Lord George Bentinck's proposal 'that the House on its rising do adjourn till Thursday', the House of Commons was adjourned so that the Honourable Members and those 'engaged in attendance upon the House' could enjoy the action, a policy which continued until 1893.

This time the layers and betting public got it right and, at a price of 4/9, Ormonde under Fred Archer won in a canter by a length-and-a-half from The Bard with St Mirren a "bad third".

Following his Derby success, Ormonde was taken to Ascot where he comfortably beat two opponents in the St James's Palace Stakes. Just three days later he faced stiffer opposition in the shape of Melton in the Hardwicke Stakes. There was almost 'universal desire to see Ormonde and Melton meet'. Melton had won the 1885 Derby and St Leger and, with the assistance of Fred Archer, it was thought by some that he could come out best of the two. While the horses matched strides throughout the majority of the contest, the hopes of those who believed the older horse would beat the young pretender were dashed halfway along the home straight when Ormonde strolled away to win with 'consummate ease'. The dual Classic winner was beginning to look all-powerful and defeat was not even remotely considered by his connections. Unfortunately, Nature can, and often does, intervene when least expected.

Shortly before the St Leger, John Porter noticed that Ormonde had contracted some type of breathing disorder. This worsened over the autumn, becoming progressively louder. It was a serious concern to the trainer, but not to the horse: the champion won the Doncaster Classic by four lengths, as well as the Champion Stakes, and a Newmarket handicap in which he conceded 28lbs to Mephisto.

During the winter of 1886/87 Arthur Conan Doyle and John Porter were both searching for solutions. Conan Doyle was lucky and found a publisher willing to accept *A Study In Scarlet*, his first work featuring Sherlock Holmes and Dr Watson; Porter did not enjoy such good fortune in his desperate hunt for a cure for Ormonde's breathing problems. With no tried and tested remedy available, on veterinary advice he agreed to allow a series of experimental treatments. As a result Ormonde did not reappear until the June Ascot meeting when he gave 25lbs and a beating to Kilwarin in the Rous Memorial Stakes. Later in the year Kilwarin won the St Leger.

Just seventy-two hours after that success, Ormonde was back on Ascot Heath for what was considered the highlight of the season. In the Hardwicke Stakes, he met Minting yet again and Bendigo, who had won the race in 1885 and the inaugural Eclipse Stakes in 1886. Minting's trainer, Mat Dawson, was confident his charge could reverse the Guineas form with Ormonde given the latter's breathing issues and John Porter was a little uneasy, fearing that his stable star may not be the horse he was before contracting the illness.

Having been successful in the Rous Memorial Stakes Tom Cannon was again booked to ride Ormonde. Cannon was a talented and determined jockey. He made his debut at the age of fourteen when he weighed just 3st 12lbs. His mount fell, but that did not deter the young jockey and later the same week he recorded his first success. During his career his achievements were over-shadowed by his contemporaries George Fordham and Fred Archer but that did not stop him winning thirteen Classics, though this did not quite match the record of his great-grandson, Lester Piggott.

As the flag fell, Minting was first away. No doubt his rider was instructed to make the race a true test of stamina and exploit any potential weakness the respiratory issue may have caused the favourite. Ormonde followed, and on the outside Phil held third place with Bendigo just behind. Turning into the straight Phil dropped out, Minting took the rails and Bendigo slipped past Ormonde to go a close second. Ormonde was switched to the outside. Although Bendigo did manage to get his head in front, at the distance he could no longer sustain the pace and the race was set to be a battle between the two main players. With fifty yards to race Minting held the lead and it appeared that Ormonde's unbeaten run could well come to an end. Cannon was not going to give in without a fight though, and he coaxed one last effort from the Triple Crown hero. Ormonde responded to his urgings, and at the line had a neck to spare over his rival.

It was the type of horserace that lifted hairs on necks, set nerves alight, and occasioned cheers and shrieks of euphoria from the most reserved racegoer. These reactions were not merely a product of the closeness of the finish. The race left no one at the track that afternoon in any doubt that they were surely in the presence of greatness. With this memorable performance Ormonde set the 'seal on his fame' as one noted writer claimed, a fame that has endured for well over one hundred years.

On his final start, Ormonde dropped back in trip to six furlongs but still won, ending his career unbeaten from sixteen starts. For many who witnessed Ormonde's races he was the greatest horse of the nineteenth century. Whilst remaining unbeaten was impressive in itself, when the quality of the opposition he faced was taken into account the true merit of his form becomes apparent. As Porter wrote, 'He was a giant among giants.'

Ormonde sired only a handful of foals in his two years at stud in England. He was then sent abroad. However he still had a impact on British bloodstock mainly through his offspring Orme and Goldfinch whose progeny won prestigious races in England and America.

The breathing issue that plagued his non-juvenile years on the track, and gained him the label of "a roarer", was thought to be hereditary. Ormonde's siblings and dam certainly supported that claim. Writing in *The Times*, the Duke of Westminster stated that he sold Ormonde because he 'had no wish to be the means of adding to the increase of a disease which affects far too many of our horses in this country.' Ormonde was purchased by Don Juan de Bocau for £12,000 and sent to Argentina. He did return to England for a brief spell, when owned by William Macdonough, then was sent to his owner's ranch in California where it was hoped the warmer climate would assist his breathing. Following his death in 1904, Macdonough donated the skeleton of Ormonde to the British Museum of Natural History.

Fred Archer   *8 November 1886*

Along with George Fordham, Fred Archer dominated flat racing in the second half of the nineteenth century. Between them, they won twenty-seven jockeys' championships from 1855 to 1886.

Archer was apprenticed to trainer Mat Dawson, one of the most successful trainers of the age, when he was ten-years-old. Three years later, in 1871, he won his first race on a juvenile named Athol Daisy, and the following year he won twenty-seven races in total. In 1873 he broke the one hundred barrier by recording 107 victories which took him to the runner-up position, behind Harry Constable, in the jockeys' championship. For the next thirteen years no jockey had a look-in, Archer scored 147 times in 1874 and peaked with 246 in 1885. During this amazing run, he won twenty-one Classics from sixty-two rides, a win rate that matched his incredible career average of 34%.

In contrast to his sparkling riding career, he suffered more than his fair share of tragedy in his personal life. Archer was devoted to his wife Nellie, but their marriage was destined to be very brief. In 1884 their son William died at birth, and just two years later Nellie was diagnosed with post-natal eclampsia after giving birth to a daughter. She died shortly after.

These tragedies and the years of wasting (Archer was 5ft 10ins tall and yet raced at weights of less than 9st) took their toll on "The Tin Man" and towards the end of the 1886 season he contracted a fever. He still rode though, which in retrospect was a poor decision. After losing on Tommy Tittlemouse at Lewes, Archer was in such a poor state of health that even he had to admit medical help was required. The trainer Martin Gurry was so concerned about Archer that he accompanied him on the train journey back to his home in Newmarket where Archer's sister, Mrs Coleman, and family friend Captain Bowling, were waiting for him.

The following day his condition had worsened and he was diagnosed with typhoid. Two nurses were engaged, and with their help his physical condition seemed to improve. Although he was lucid, he was possessed of the idea that he was about to die. Emotionally he was slipping into a deep depression. Despite his undeniable resilience and irrepressible determination to conquer any adverse circumstance he might encounter, the irrational, invisible and, all too often incurable illness was slowly gaining the upper hand.

On 8th November 1886, with Captain Bowling absent from the house, Archer asked his sister to send the nurse away claiming he had something to confide in her. With the nurse out of the room, Archer's sister turned to face him and realised that he was holding a revolver. She rushed to his side and attempted to wrestle the weapon from his grip. A short struggle ensued; then a shot rang out. Fred Archer, the most talented jockey of the era, lay dead on the floor. He was twenty-nine years old.

Sir Visto's Derby   *29 May 1895*

As the nineteenth century drew to a close, horseracing had become fully established as one of the principal pastimes of the privileged class. Flat racing was perfectly timed for those who spent their winters hunting and shooting. Staging the most prestigious races during the summer months allowed it to be enjoyed without affecting those two pillars of country pursuits that held sway in many households and sections of society. The importance of hunting and shooting could not be overstated as was evidenced by its regular appearance in a range of periodicals. The outcomes of shoots and hunts were reported in great detail as if they represented some type of significant sporting achievement.

Baily's Magazine of Sports and Pastimes was one such periodical that brought its readers up to date with the latest "scores" from the grouse moors of Scotland or hunting fields of Leicestershire and southern England. One report, from December 1898, celebrated a massive kill of birds. It was claimed that, in a two-day shoot at Lady Cardigan's coverts at Deene Park Northamptonshire, over three thousand six hundred head of game were shot by a party of just six guns. But this astonishing number of deaths paled into insignificance against the six thousand birds (mostly pheasants) killed at the Wood Norton shoot the following December. Such a kill rate would hardly have given the shooters time to refresh themselves from their hip flasks that were, almost without exception, made of solid silver, the cleansing properties of which apparently only served to improve the taste of the alcohol.

Further afield, at the Emperor's hunting party in the Royal Forest of Göhrde in Germany, the quarry was deer and wild boar. Three hundred of the former and two hundred of the latter were despatched in just two days. The same edition of the magazine also emphasised the hazards associated with these sports by covering the untimely death at the age of 39 of Captain Pryse Pryse Pryse (the family tended to use their surname also as a Christian name, and sometimes, as in this case, a middle name as well). While hunting, the son of Baronet Sir Pryse Pryse was bitten by a fox. Initially the wound to his hand was considered harmless, but by the following morning it was apparent that Captain Pryse was suffering from blood poisoning. His symptoms worsened over the coming days and the wound ultimately proved fatal. Sir Pryse commissioned a portrait of his late son that is currently housed at The National Library of Wales. On the back of the portrait there's a somewhat emotionless note from Pryse (snr):

My Son Pryse Pryse Pryse of Lodge Park painted by Miss Fourdain from a photograph in 1900. An excellent likeness. – Pryse Pryse

While those with a surplus of income and plenty of spare time for such pursuits as hunting and shooting could follow horseracing with ease by attending meetings and trials, for the vast majority of the population, the closest they came to a horserace was a brief summary published in the *Sporting Life* and *Sporting Chronicle*. However, this was about to change.

In equine terms the 1895 Derby was generally accepted to be a modest affair with the layers offering 5/1 the field. Despite the lack of any outstanding candidates, the crowds still flocked from London attracted by the appeal of a beautiful sunny day at the races. Many of them would have been intrigued to see a new item of equipment positioned near to the track. The object was seemingly a metal box supported by four wooden legs. Behind it stood Birt Acres in morning suit and top hat as the Epsom dress code required. What Acres' audience did not know was that the "box on legs" was in reality a camera, and for the first time the Derby would be committed to film.

Through clouds of blinding dust whipped up by the wind raking across the bone dry downs, Sir Visto won the Derby in a bunch finish for his owner, 5th Earl of Roseberry, the nation's Prime Minister and leader of the Liberal Party.

The Prime Minister's celebrations were to be short-lived though. Within a month Lord Roseberry along with his ministers tendered their resignations to the Queen who invited Lord Salisbury to form the next government. Lord Roseberry had been Prime Minister for just under fifteen months and whilst his tenure may not be viewed as an overwhelming success in political terms, during that time he did enjoy sporting success by winning the Derby twice. Moreover, in spite of the turmoil he faced in his work life, he still made the trip to Epsom to lead Sir Visto into the unsaddling enclosure to 'tremendous applause, sustained until after the Prime Minister had returned at the head of his horse'.

In 1895 the reproduction of images of any type was not a straightforward task. Newspapers required all photographs to be recreated as engravings in order to facilitate printing, an approach that was not simplified until 1904. Consequently, the filming of races marked not only an important breakthrough in the art of photography, but it made horseracing data, in visual rather than numerical form, more accessible. In the coming years, those who were not able to attend the races due to other commitments, or more likely the cost, were able to see the main contests as part of the *Pathé*

News shown in cinemas up and down the country from the early 1900s. A sport originally seen as a preserve of the elite was gradually being made more available to all sectors of the population.

Tod Sloan   *17 September 1897*

The treatment of Tod Sloan by the Jockey Club marks a low point in the authority's administration of the sport.

Sloan's early ventures in the world of horseracing did not go as well as he would have liked. Although he had a natural affinity with most animals, he was frightened of horses and it was clear to anyone who witnessed his attempts at riding that he would struggle to make it as a jockey. In fact, Sloan became so disheartened with riding that he even tried his hand at cooking for the stable staff. Somewhere deep in the back of his mind, though, was the thought, possibly more likely just a faint hope, that he had a future in the saddle.

After moving around the USA, Sloan ended up working for Johnny Campbell, a trainer in Kansas City. Campbell encouraged him to persevere with his riding, and through sheer hard work and a determination to succeed he was finally able to stay on a horse, at least for the duration of a short gallop. Not that he could yet be categorised as a competent rider. As he wrote in his autobiography, 'I wasn't thrown quite so often.' Despite his shortcomings he managed to get a ride in a race at New Orleans. The unlucky horse was named Lovelace and, much to everyone's surprise, Sloan managed to stay in the saddle and even scrape into third place. His other rides at the meeting did not fare so well and after a short while the view amongst the racing fraternity was that to stop a horse from winning 'all that had to be done was send for Sloan'. He kept working, though, and was later contracted to ride at the Bay District Track in San Francisco. Commenting on this appointment, one racing writer quipped that Sloan must have been engaged 'because of the loud clothes... instead of any merit as a rider.'

He continued to struggle and even considered another change of career, this time acting. But with help from Charlie Hanlon and George Rose, Sloan gained a better understanding of the thoroughbred. As a consequence, his confidence began to grow and the affinity he had with other animals was now apparent with horses, an invaluable trait for any rider. Thoughts of becoming a jockey were now at the forefront of his mind; maybe he could make a name for himself in the sport, and not one that was a byword for failure.

Being confident and having an understanding of horses is only part of the puzzle; the practicalities of riding are just as crucial. As so often happens, the major turning point in this respect came about by pure chance. Whilst riding on the gallops his horse bolted and the only way Sloan could pull him up was to get out of the saddle and onto the animal's neck. His riding partner was laughing at him, and Sloan, too, found the situation amusing, but crucially he also realised that when 'doing the neck crouch, the horse's stride seemed to be freer'. He had discovered the "monkey-on-the-stick seat", a unique riding technique that gave him an advantage over other jockeys who rode in a more traditional manner. Although most onlookers at first ridiculed his riding style they soon began to take notice when he started to win more and more races. By the summer of 1897 Sloan was winning one race out of every three he contested, an astounding ratio which caught the attention of racehorse owner James R. Keene. Keene had horses in training in England, notably St Cloud, who was entered in the Cambridgeshire and Cesarewitch handicaps, and he wanted Sloan to ride. On 17th September 1897 Sloan was on the *Majestic* bound for England.

After some initial doubts, and a period getting used to the "English way", the diminutive Sloan, he could ride at 6st and his shoes were size one-and-a-half (USA), got into full stride. At Manchester he rode four winners in an afternoon, an achievement he bettered at Newmarket when winning five consecutive races. Now he was getting attention from the English press for the right reasons, but not always for his riding. Sloan readily acknowledged that he 'was fanciful about shoes'. In interviews he was often teased about the amount of clothes he took when travelling, and the number of pairs of shoes. The interviewers always exaggerated but Sloan did admit that he packed 'three trunks of clothes [and] would carry a dozen or eighteen pairs [of shoes] on a journey of any length'.

By 1900 he was considered one of the most skilful jockeys riding in England, as well as the most stylish and flamboyant. Unknown to Sloan, though, dark clouds were gathering. He was an American dominating a British sport and that did not sit well with some of the more influential members of society.

For the most part, the Jockey Club was comprised of members of the aristocracy. They generally entertained the same disregard for their jockeys as they did their domestic staff. Plenty of evidence exists to support this characterisation of the relationship. One incident in particular, involving Sloan and his riding plans, seems to typify this quite perfectly. A member of the Jockey Club approached Sloan and asked him to ride one of his horses the following day. Sloan said that he would need to check his riding arrangements before agreeing, and asked the owner to wait until he had a chance to retrieve his diary from the jockeys' room. The owner took offence at this and, on turning away, simply said 'I wait for no jockey.' Despite Sloan's best attempts at an explanation, the Jockey Club member never spoke to him again. It was another black mark against his character in the eyes of the sport's ruling body.

Sloan's reluctance to acquiesce immediately to the demands of the Jockey Club elite was inevitably going to cause him problems and it ultimately ended his career. At a meeting with the Stewards in 1900 he was accused of betting against himself, which he strenuously denied, though he did admit to backing himself to win, something he had in common with most jockeys of the time. After consideration he was informed by the Jockey Club Officials that 'it was advisable for him not to apply for his licence' the following season. Sloan found the decision difficult to accept, and it could not have come at a worse time. Earlier in the year he had agreed to ride for the Prince of Wales the following season for a fee of 6,000gns [£780,000]; it was an agreement he could no longer fulfil.

Whilst Sloan was permitted to attend race meetings, and even ride on the gallops, he could not ride in races without a licence. Initially he thought the suspension would last just one year, so he applied for a licence in 1902. His application was rejected. He continued to apply each year but received the same negative response. Some fifteen years later, whilst working for the war effort, he was still applying annually, his requests still falling on deaf ears. The Jockey Club had stopped Sloan winning, they were not of a mind to allow him to return and once again dominate horseracing. Tod Sloan never raced again.

A Most Expensive Flying Fox · 31 May 1899

On 31st May 1899, as the crowds flocked to Epsom, at Trent Bridge W G Grace was making preparations for what turned out to be his final test appearance for England. Grace was 51 years old, and his ever-increasing bulk was not making his playing career any easier: the additional pounds were seriously impeding his fielding ability. Although he contributed twenty-eight runs to an opening partnership of seventy-five with C B Fry, in the second innings of the drawn match he could manage just a single. At the following selectors' meeting Grace stood down from the captaincy and retired from international cricket. As sensational as the post-Test consequences were, they could not match the Derby for drama.

The Duke of Westminster's Flying Fox, 'bright and bold in his eye' with a coat that shone like satin, had won the 2,000 Guineas five weeks earlier and was the clear favourite at 1/3 for the Epsom Classic. The French-trained Holocauste was next in the betting at 100/15. Holocauste would have started at a much shorter price had it not been for his less than impressive physical appearance. Apparently 'he made so unfavourable an impression that he went back several points in the betting.' His rather listless demeanour gave further credence to the rumour that he had suffered a recent shoulder injury and may not be fully sound.

Once the race was underway, racegoers who had chosen to ignore the rumours, and had taken what appeared to be a generous price about the second favourite, were encouraged to see him race up with the pace and safely negotiate the downhill turn. Flying Fox was there too, and moving easily as the leaders reached the straight. To the huge crowd it appeared that the main two protagonists were about to fight out a thrilling finish. But, completely unexpectedly, Holocauste began to falter. His action worsened, and a couple of strides later his rider had no choice but to pull up and dismount. The pre-race rumours clearly had substance. Flying Fox soon asserted his superiority and at the line had two lengths to spare over Damocles in second. The favourite had prevailed and it was reported that his jockey, Mornington Cannon (whose sister married Ernest Piggott, the grandfather of Lester) and trainer John Porter, who had just recorded his seventh Derby victory, received a great ovation as the colt was led back to the unsaddling area.

Later in the year Flying Fox added the St Leger to his 2,000 Guineas and Derby victories emulating his grandsire, Ormonde, by becoming a Triple Crown winner. Due mostly to these three Classic wins, the Duke of Westminster was the most successful owner of 1899 having won £43,965 [£5.7 million] and John Porter topped the trainers' table with £56,546 [£7.3 million] in prize money.

The Duke did not have time on his side, though, and died in December 1899. A dispersal sale was arranged for his bloodstock at which Flying Fox was sold for a record-breaking 37,500gns [£4.8 million] after sustained bidding from interested parties based in England, America, and France. The Frenchman Edmond Blanc was ultimately successful and Flying Fox was sent to stand at stud in France.

1900-1949

|||||||||||||||||||||||||||||||||||||

In a period dominated by two world wars, racing seemed to gain in popularity possibly because it provided a distraction from the horrors of the conflicts. Sceptre set a new Classic winning record, the Hermits of Salisbury Plain made the Bookmakers tremble in fear and someone stole the Ascot Gold Cup despite an armed guard.

The suffragettes increased their use of direct action and Martha Hennessy became the first female owner-breeder of a Classic winner.

In France, the racing authorities introduced the Prix de l'Arc de Triomphe, and in England the Cheltenham Gold Cup and Champion Hurdle were added to the jumps racing calendar.

Phar Lap and Man o' War broke records in Australia and America, and Golden Miller won five Gold Cups and a Grand National.

The result of the Derby was determined by photographic evidence for the first time, and the film National Velvet inspired girls to take up riding, but the Jockey Club still wouldn't allow them to compete in races.

A Royal 2,000 Guineas Victory   *2 May 1900*

The twentieth century heralded the era of aviation. At the forefront of this new branch of engineering, which promised much by way of discovery and innovation, was a former commander of the Prussian cavalry brigade who was determined to make his mark. After twenty-six years of research and development, Count Von Zeppelin finally completed his first powered airship capable of independent flight. On 2nd July 1900 the 420-feet long, cigar-shaped fusion of aluminium tubing, stretched cotton fabric, and seventeen bags of hydrogen gas, made its inaugural flight over Lake Constance in southern Germany. The enormous craft was powered by two sixteen horsepower Daimler engines attached to the gondolas suspended from its keel. Though this brief flight was seen as a successful achievement, further developments were hindered by the complexities associated with affecting a safe landing, and the rather pedestrian rate of travel. Zeppelin's creation was incapable of reaching speeds in excess of seventeen miles per hour while in flight, considerably slower than most horses, and less than half the speed of the more talented thoroughbreds of the age such as Diamond Jubilee.

In some ways the consecutive Triple Crown winners Flying Fox and the Prince of Wales' Diamond Jubilee were very different horses; in others they were quite similar. As two-year-olds, Flying Fox was much more successful, winning three of his five starts, whereas Diamond Jubilee was far less precocious managing just one win from six attempts. Both horses, though, had Galopin as a grandsire and both were highly-strung and difficult to train, Diamond Jubilee especially so.

The Prince's representative would have been no match for Flying Fox as a juvenile. On his debut in the 1899 Coventry Stakes at Ascot he kicked an onlooker whilst in the paddock then behaved roguishly at the start before running poorly behind the impressive Democrat. Taken to Newmarket for the July Stakes he repeated his pre-race antics. The even-money favourite caused a delay to the race of seven minutes 'by throwing his rider [the experienced stable jockey Jack Watts] and bolting to the stands.' His trainer, Richard Marsh, considered gelding the colt in an attempt to curb his increasingly wild temperament, but Diamond Jubilee was a rig and that made the operation too dangerous to risk, so he was spared the knife.

It was hoped a change of jockey would benefit the wayward colt, so Mornington Cannon replaced Watts. This did appear to have a positive impact; Diamond Jubilee finished second at Goodwood then was successful in one of his final three races of the season. He ended his two-year-old campaign by getting much closer to the top class Democrat in the Dewhurst Stakes than he had earlier in the season at Ascot, which was encouraging for his connections. Diamond Jubilee clearly had ability, he certainly had a Classic pedigree as a son of St Simon out of a Hampton mare (Perdita II), but it was of great concern to his connections that his ill-tempered ways might prevent him from showing his best the following season.

In sporting terms, 1900 was a memorable year. Despite several of their players serving in the military in South Africa, Yorkshire were unbeaten in the county Cricket Championship; Aston Villa won the Football League and Bury won the FA cup; Oxford won the first ice hockey varsity match (seven goals to six), although Cambridge gained revenge in the Boat Race; and in New York, James Corbett out-danced the younger, stronger, heavier World Heavyweight Boxing Champion James Jeffries for twenty-two rounds of a twenty-five round match, only to hit the canvas in round twenty-three. In horseracing, Mornington Cannon was booked to ride Diamond Jubilee in the 2,000 Guineas, but days before the race, whilst at exercise, the colt's temperament once again got the better of him.

On this occasion his antics were altogether more serious than refusing to race or trying to unship his rider: Diamond Jubilee knocked Cannon to the ground and then, with no small degree of ferocity, he savaged him. Not surprisingly the rider wanted nothing more to do with the apparently aggressive animal and his position was given to Diamond Jubilee's nineteen-year-old stable lad, Herbert Jones.

The weather was fine on 2nd May 1900 for the 92nd running of the 2,000 Guineas at Newmarket with sunshine aplenty and a cooling breeze. Conditions were further enhanced by the work of the Jockey Club and town officials, as reported in *The Times*: 'arrangement... for watering the streets and the roads leading to the heath are so good that the dust is not allowed to become the nuisance which it is at Epsom.'

Diamond Jubilee was almost unrecognizable from the violent two-year-old that ran so poorly. With a stablemate for a lead, he was on his best behaviour in the dust-free parade ring, and cantered smoothly to post for his young jockey. Thoughts of his recalcitrant nature rapidly ebbed away and his starting price began to shrink. At off time the impressive looking colt was down to 11/4, third best in the market. Throughout the race Jones kept Diamond Jubilee up with the pace, and after six furlongs 'it was pretty clear that the Prince would win', as one writer noted. In the final furlong Diamond Jubilee pulled away to score by a comfortable four lengths giving the Prince of Wales his first 2,000 Guineas win.

The ongoing Boer War, a conflict that brought to the public's attention the war correspondent for *The Morning Post*, the 24-year-old Winston Churchill, had a negative impact on racing in Britain at the turn of the century. In general, attendances dipped as people's thoughts were consumed by more weighty matters. However, the combination of fine weather and a 6/4 favourite for the Derby owned by the Prince of Wales, drew the crowds from London and the surrounding area in droves. For the first time, Epsom had erected a fully resourced medical room. At the spring meeting, five weeks earlier, a serious accident caused by one horse knocking another over near the end of the contest had highlighted how poorly courses were provisioned with respect to medical care. *The Times* correspondent had his own views on the matter and hoped that the 'Jockey Club will refuse in the future to license race meetings which have not made similar provision for first aid to injured riders.' In retrospect it is astonishing that courses had been allowed to function for so many years without paying such basic attention to the safety of the riders, stable staff, and spectators.

Partnered by Jones, Diamond Jubilee again behaved impeccably. In the race he was always in the first three with Jones waiting until the last four hundred yards before making his decisive move. Although Mornington Cannon mounted a challenge in the closing stages on the Duke of Portland's Simon Dale, Diamond Jubilee had sufficient stamina to maintain his lead. At the winning line he had half-a-length to spare with a further length back to Disguise ridden by Tod Sloan in third. The intractable colt now had two Classics to his name, in no small measure due to the efforts of his teenage jockey.

The Triple Crown was secured when Diamond Jubilee won the St Leger by a length-and-a-half from Mornington Cannon on Elopement. This was his easiest Classic victory but also the one in which his behaviour was poorest before the start. With this defeat, Mornington Cannon had been thwarted in two Classics by a horse that had viciously attacked him earlier in the year. It is probably safe to conclude that Diamond Jubilee was not his favourite horse.

As a four-year-old, the enigmatic colt was back to his worst, and after savaging another stable employee was retired to stud.

Democrat, the horse who got the better of Diamond Jubilee twice as a juvenile, failed to train on as a three-year-old winning just one minor contest from five attempts. After his owner's death, he was purchased by

Mr JB Joel (the successful diamond trader who was the father of Jim Joel, owner of Royal Palace and Maori Venture) at the dispersal sale, then at a later date by Richard Marsh, trainer of Diamond Jubilee, for 290gns. Marsh then presented him to General Lord Kitchener of Khartoum for use as a charger. As Griswold notes in his recollections, '[Democrat] had the proud honour of carrying that gallant soldier at the head of the British army in India at the Durbar of King Edward VII at Delhi'. In recognition of his achievements, a bronze statue of Lord Kitchener and Democrat was sculpted for display at the Maidan of Calcutta (now Kolkata).

First Use of Starting Gates in the Derby   *5 June 1901*

'How to start races evenly?' was a question repeatedly asked throughout the 1800s. In fact, for jumps racing, it was still on the lips of many commentators well into the 21st century. One solution was proposed by Admiral Rous.

Rous was essentially a naval man. He entered the service at thirteen years old, and during a distinguished career was involved in many actions on a number of different ships, narrowly escaping death on several occasions. He was also a keen horseman, no doubt influenced by his father who owned a stud farm and had won the 1815 2,000 Guineas with Tigris.

In 1838 the Admiral became a steward of the Jockey Club. A keen racing analyst, Rous devised and published the first weight-for-age scale, which included additional allowances for fillies. As a Handicapper he had no equal. Handicapping must have been a tortuous exercise in the 1800s with no electronic aids or race replays to watch. However, Rous was not only accurate in his assessments but also could rate races in hardly any time at all. According to *Baily's Magazine of Sports and Pastimes* 'his calculations of animals' performances must be something miraculous when it is considered that in the Second October and Houghton Meetings he is frequently called upon to handicap from forty to one hundred and twenty horses between a quarter-past six and dinner.'

Rous was active in the debate regarding the age at which horses should be allowed to start racing and was instrumental in establishing the 1870 rule change that limited the length of the flat racing season as follows:

No race meeting shall commence before the week which includes the 25th of March, nor continue beyond the week which includes the 15th of November.

But perhaps just as importantly he improved the method for starting races by flag. The Admiral proposed a system which involved the Starter and an additional flagman placed about one hundred yards down the track who could indicate whether the race had been started fairly or not. Although this system had certain advantages, it was far from perfect.

The new century saw the introduction of a starting gate at race meetings across the country. Modelled on those employed in Australia, it consisted of several strands of wire that were raised above the runners' heads by a spring mechanism when activated. Although mandatory for all juvenile races, use of the gate in 1900 was at the discretion of the Clerk of the Course for all other contests, though most made use of it following an initial test period. At Epsom, course officials ultimately decided against using the starting gate, and it was not for another twelve months that the new starting mechanism was used for the premier Classic. After two hundred years of experimentation, the sport had found the optimal way of starting races. Or so it was thought. In 1965 starting stalls were introduced providing a vastly superior method of getting races underway.

Sceptre's Spring   *18 March 1902*

Hugh Lupus Grosvenor, 1st Duke of Westminster, was one of the most successful owner-breeders of the closing years of the nineteenth century. He had inherited Eaton Stud, and through his careful management it became the racing powerhouse of its time. Both Triple Crown winners, Ormonde and Flying Fox, hailed from this most famous of establishments. When the Duke died on 22nd December 1899 his impressive stock of horses had to be sold. Of all the thoroughbreds that made their way to the Tattersalls July Sales, one of the most striking was a yearling filly. Her sire was Persimmon who had won the Derby and St Leger for the Prince of Wales, and while her dam Ornament had a less than impressive racing career, she was an excellent broodmare possessing the finest of bloodlines. Ornament was a full sister to the unbeaten Triple Crown winner Ormonde, and half sister to Farewell, winner of the 1,000 Guineas. The yearling, undoubtedly the best-bred filly of 1899, was named Sceptre.

Professional punter Robert Sievier, considered a rogue by many of his contemporaries, had experienced a remarkable run of good fortune at the end of 1899 and was intent on buying a good horse. The one he had set his sights on was Sceptre. At the Sales he paid 10,000gns [£1.3m] for the yearling, a record amount that was not to be exceeded for a further nineteen years. Sievier sent the filly to Charlie Morton at Wantage. In his care she easily won her first two races, and then finished third in her final race of the year, Doncaster's Champagne Stakes. It was a good start to her racing career, but Sievier had probably hoped for better. During the winter, Morton accepted a position as private trainer to Mr JB Joel. Left without a trainer, Sievier, a man not lacking in confidence in any sphere, made the decision to train Sceptre himself.

At the start of the 1902 season, Sceptre's new trainer made the astonishing announcement that his star filly would start her campaign in the Lincolnshire Handicap, a race that was to become the modern day Lincoln Handicap when transferred from Lincoln racecourse to Doncaster in 1965. This decision was driven purely by money: Sievier had backed Sceptre to win £30,000 [£3.7m] in the race. Despite having the best horse in the race running off a lenient handicap mark, his gamble came to nothing due to poor management. Sievier devised a plan of work for the filly that he left for his assistant to follow while he was out of the country. The assistant trainer applied his orders to the letter and the three-year-old was worked hard day after day. By the time Sievier returned, Sceptre was in a sorry state. To his credit Sievier made a great effort to repair the damage the punishing schedule had inflicted, but time was against him.

On Lincolnshire Handicap day Sceptre should not have raced but Sievier had too much at stake. From the off she ran freely, her apprentice jockey lacking both the strength and ability to keep her at a more appropriate pace. Though Sceptre was still in contention deep inside the final furlong, in a driving finish she lost out by a head to St Maclou. Robert Sievier's response to the defeat was in keeping with his brash, colourful ways: he announced that Sceptre would be taken to Newmarket to contest the 2,000 Guineas, adding that, for good measure, she would also run in the fillies' Classic.

At Newmarket on 2,000 Guineas day, Sceptre made her way to the starting line partnered by Herbert Randall. Robert Sievier wasn't taking chances with an inexperienced jockey this time. Randall was the son of the shoe manufacturer Sir Henry Randall and had ridden as an amateur before being granted a professional licence at the start of the 1902 season. He was both experienced and very competent. Sceptre was made 4/1 joint favourite with Mr G Faber's Duke Of Westminster for the race. Sievier unquestionably had money on his filly, and it was very soon apparent that his cash would be returned with interest. Sceptre won the race in a record time pulling two lengths clear of Pistol, with the highly regarded Ard Patrick another three lengths back in third.

The fillies' mile Classic was held just two days later. Many trainers would not have risked running such a valuable horse after such a short break, but Sievier was not a conventional trainer, and Sceptre took her place in the field. On this occasion it was the layers taking no risks, and at the off the filly was priced at 1/2. They were correct in their estimation; Sievier's star won by a length-and-a-half from St Windeline, with a four-length gap back to the third. Sceptre had two Classics under her belt and her owner was keen to make it four, so he entered her for both Epsom races.

Ard Patrick's Revenge   *4 June 1902*

King Edward VII and Queen Alexandra attended the Derby in 1902, their coronation year. The forecast heavy rainfall put a dampener on the Royals' day, and the weather outlook was sufficiently poor to dissuade many racegoers from making the trip to Epsom even though the race featured some top class thoroughbreds. The Epsom Classic brought Sceptre and Ard Patrick together again with connections of the latter keen to take revenge after their 2,000 Guineas defeat.

Ard Patrick had raced twice since Newmarket, finishing second when trying to concede 22lbs, and then being demoted to third in the Newmarket Stakes for "bumping and boring". For the big race he was partnered by the American jockey John "Skeets" Martin. A Pennsylvanian by birth, Martin made his way to Britain as part of the "American Invasion", arriving in 1899 after riding over 260 winners in the USA. His aggressive style may have been appreciated by racegoers, but was often frowned upon by the authorities earning the jockey several suspensions during his career in Europe which lasted until the early 1920s. Herbert Randall retained his position on Sceptre who, due to a remarkable gamble, started the even money favourite despite suffering from a bruised foot sustained a few days before the race.

Sceptre's race was effectively over in the first half mile. After a long delay at the start, she was slowly away and Randall desperately tried to make up ground. Effectively, he was just wasting his filly's stamina reserves. Although Secptre appeared to be travelling well as the field straightened up for home, she had little left to give. Martin had Ard Patrick against the running rail and, after matching strides with Sceptre, he established a lead as the filly weakened. From this position he was never going to be caught. At the winning post Ard Patrick was three lengths clear of the field giving trainer Sam Darling his second Derby success.

An exhausted Sceptre trailed in a disappointing fourth.

Despite the hard race, Sievier was in no mood to rest his filly. Sceptre was back on the racecourse two days later to contest the Oaks. The weather had not improved, if anything it had worsened, and a consistent fall of rain lasted the whole day. Starting at 5/2, an inflated price no doubt influenced by her recent loss, the only concern to her supporters was whether she would deign to take part but, after a great deal of cajoling, she finally joined the others at the starting gate. As the tapes went up Randall, who blamed himself for her Derby defeat, took a position just behind the leading group. As the runners reached the straight, Sceptre swooped on her rivals and, in an instant, the race was over. Her thirteen opponents were well beaten. At the finishing line the Champion filly had three lengths to spare over the runner-up and possibly three more gears to go through.

Sceptre's Triple Crown   *10 September 1902*

By the autumn of 1902 Sceptre's punishing schedule was drawing to a close. Since the Oaks she had run five times, including a trip to France for the Grand Prix de Paris in which Randall was not at his best. A dissatisfied Sievier decided to replace him with Fred Hardy for the Yorkshire Classic, a win in which would secure the Fillies' Triple Crown, a fourth Classic victory, and Sceptre's place in horseracing history.

At Town Moor, like the rain, the money poured onto Sceptre and she started the 100/30 favourite for the St Leger. The poor weather did little to discourage many thousands of racegoers from attending, but for the 'multitudes on the broad expanse of the moor there was little or no shelter' during one of the wettest St Leger days for many years. Despite having four runners in the race between them, the Dukes of Devonshire and Portland decided against making the journey to Doncaster. They were, no doubt, of the opinion that unless the Sceptre was in some way handicapped, either by the race conditions or by an inappropriate training schedule, their runners had little chance of success.

In the race Hardy kept Sceptre to the outside. It was a sound policy and enabled the great filly to avoid a three-horse collision, which could so easily have concluded her race much earlier than her supporters would have wished. Instead, from start to finish Sceptre enjoyed a relatively clear run to the line. Hardy sat tight and avoided making any type of significant forward move until reaching the home straight, at which point Sceptre was 'going so easily that there did not seem to be much doubt as to the result.' Amid a 'hurricane of applause' Sceptre ran out a comfortable three-length winner from Rising Glass with a further two lengths back to the third placed horse, Friar Tuck, ridden by her old partner Herbert Randall. Much to the chagrin of those observers who thought she was over-trained, and the others who believed she would not stay the trip, Sceptre was at her best on St Leger day and had never before been so dominant in a race. She had emulated Formosa by winning four Classics, and a place amongst racing's immortals was guaranteed.

In the years that followed, Robert Sievier, was to get to know the Old Bailey, and prominent barrister of the day Richard Muir, as well as he did the formbook. In 1908 he was called to defend himself against the accusation of bribery and extortion. The talented Muir, who in 1910 successfully prosecuted Hawley Harvey Crippen, acted for the defence and was again successful with Sievier found not guilty despite the wealth of evidence against him.

Sievier's luck finally ran out in March 1920 when he lost a six-day libel case at the Old Bailey to Richard Wootton. Sievier was branded a cheat at cards and billiards, and was accused of using the *Winning Post* newspaper as an instrument of bribery.

Over the course of his eventful life, Robert Standish Sievier was the self-proclaimed largest Bookmaker in Australia, until he lost his licence. He founded a newspaper, penned a successful play as well as several books, won and lost many fortunes, fought in South Africa and worked as an actor. Most significantly, he owned one of the best fillies ever to race in Great Britain.

A Filly to Rival Sceptre   *27 June 1903*

Pretty Polly may not have been as well bred as Sceptre but, arguably, she was every bit as good. This lack of blue-blood breeding may have been in the back of her trainer's thoughts when he first saw her because he later remarked: 'if anybody had told me the filly I was looking at was going to develop into a great racemare I should have laughed.'

Pretty Polly's owner-breeder was Major Eustace Loder who, given his success at the track, was soon nicknamed "Lucky Loder". He sent the filly to Peter Gilpin who trained at Clarehaven Lodge near Newmarket, a training centre he had custom built with the winnings from the bets he placed on his Cesarewitch winner of the same name.

Pretty Polly made her racecourse debut at Sandown on 27th June 1903. In the British Dominion Two-Year-Old Race the 6/1 fourth favourite made all to beat nine rivals, which included the colt John O' Gaunt, with consummate ease. *The Times* summarised the performance as 'Won in a canter by ten lengths'. Many observers considered the distance to be much further, not least the on-course photographers who were not able to get the winner and runner-up in the same shot. It was an excellent start to her racing career and by the end of her first campaign Pretty Polly had won nine races from nine starts, most without being fully extended.

As a three-year-old she won the 1,000 Guineas in a record time for the race by an easy three lengths. Her starting price just 1/4. The Oaks followed in early June. At the even shorter price of 8/100, she showed that the extra half-mile distance was of no significant inconvenience, winning the race by the same margin as the first Classic.

After two straightforward victories in Ascot's Coronation Stakes and the Naussau Stakes at Goodwood, Pretty Polly, 'in perfect condition', lined up against five opponents, including the Derby winner St Amant, in the St Leger. The day started grey and damp, but by race-time the weather had improved with the clouds swept away and the late summer sun making for a pleasant afternoon.

Starting at long odds-on, Pretty Polly broke quickly but was then restrained by her jockey Willie Lane. This left St Amant to set the pace, which he did for a mile. The favourite took over at this point and in the straight had the race at her mercy. Otto Madden, a supreme judge of pace and more capable than most in a finish, tried to make a race of it on Henry The First. It was to no avail, the filly was far superior and completed the Fillies' Triple Crown with an impressive victory. For good measure, two days later she won the Park Hill Stakes at the same meeting.

Whilst Pretty Polly's ability and temperament were not in question, she was a little quirky. Kinscem had a pet cat as a companion, and throughout her racing career Pretty Polly was accompanied to the races by a small brown cob which, according to reports, was always first to congratulate her when she returned to the winner's enclosure.

After fifteen straight victories, Pretty Polly was beginning to look unbeatable. Her next start, though, was on "heavy" going at Longchamp. The combination of a long season, unsuitable going, an energy sapping trip across a particularly rough English Channel, and a long train journey to Paris, was too much for the brilliant filly. In the race she struggled on the rain-soaked surface and could not get to the pace-setter Presto II. Pretty Polly tasted defeat for the first time in her career.

Loder kept Pretty Polly in training for two more seasons, finally retiring her after the second defeat of her career, the 1906 Ascot Gold Cup. In total she won twenty-two of her twenty-four races and fully deserves her position alongside Sceptre as one of the greatest fillies ever to race in Europe.

In Willie Lane's short career, Pretty Polly provided all three of his Classic wins. Towards the end of the 1904 season he was seriously injured in a fall and did not race again. The former Champion Jockey died in 1920 aged 37.

Hackler's Pride and the Confederates *28 October 1903*

It would be difficult to find a more remote setting in southern England than Salisbury Plain. Quite why our ancestors chose it as the site for the mystical Stonehenge remains a puzzle-unsolved; but for a racing yard founded upon absolute secrecy, no better location could ever have suited as well.

Druid's Lodge was a purpose-built racing stable in the control of Percy Cunliffe, Wilfred Purefoy, Frank Forester, and one of the shrewdest trainers of the time, Jack Fallon. Together they formed a syndicate nicknamed "The Hermits of Salisbury Plain" by one racing journalist, but were more commonly referred to as the Druid's Lodge Confederacy. At the start of the twentieth century 'they had the Bookmakers by the throat'.

Towards the end of the 1902 flat racing season the Confederates purchased a two-year-old Irish-bred filly. Hacker's Pride was a maiden that, crucially, had shown plenty of promise in her races. This made her the perfect horse for a gambling stable. By mid-November she was beating all comers at home, impressing her trainer to such an extent that she was entered in one of the richest end-of-season nursery races. Taken to Derby racecourse for the Chesterfield Nursery, she carried plenty of stable money which compressed her price from double figures down to 9/2. The huge sums bet on her included £180 [£22,000] from the stable lads who could ill-afford to lose such an amount. But they had confidence in the horse, underpinned by what they had witnessed on the gallops. It was confidence well placed. Under Ben Dillon, Hackler's Pride was first away and maintained a position in the front rank until the final furlong when she pulled clear to win by an easy four lengths. Naturally, the Confederates pocketed far more than the stable lads but more importantly the win convinced them that, with careful planning and no small amount of obfuscation, even greater returns could be achieved the following year.

By mid-June 1903, well into her three-year-old season, Hackler's Pride had only ever raced over the minimum distance. On a warm summer's day at Hurst Park she tackled a mile for the first time and stayed on well to take second place behind the useful yardstick Wild Oats. This performance impressed the Confederates and encouraged them to think along different lines for the filly. Her ability over a mile opened up new possibilities that had to be considered. A great deal of discussion ensued regarding potential races, with a focus on determining which ones would prove to be the most lucrative. Once an agreement was reached, they put in motion a series of carefully planned actions that would precede her new target for the season: the Cambridgeshire Handicap.

Essentially the approach the Confederacy adopted was one that is still used to defeat the Handicapper to this day. Over the summer, Hackler's Pride would race but would not show her true form. The Handicapper would react by lowering her rating, allowing her to compete in the Cambridgeshire off a weight that made her a virtual certainty. There was nothing illegal in this approach; the Confederates would be breaking no rules, just using the handicapping system to their advantage. Morally they would have questions to answer, but the profits would assuage any pangs of guilt they may have suffered.

Hackler's Pride contested some of the main summer handicaps without making the frame. The Confederates believed, and hoped, that on Cambridgeshire day the filly would be allocated a very low weight, in which case she would need to be ridden by a top-class lightweight jockey. Thinking long-term they decided that Jack Jarvis would be the best choice for the big autumn handicap, so in the Stewards Cup at Goodwood, Hackler's Pride was partnered with the fifteen-year-old for the first time. Jarvis was a very talented young jockey who could make lightweights. Just as importantly, he would be able to claim an apprentice's allowance, reducing any allotted weight still further. His ride on Hackler's Pride at the Sussex track was purely for him to gain some experience of the filly; she was never going to win, or even get near to winning Goodwood's most prestigious handicap.

Lightweight jockeys were often called upon when a gamble was planned in handicaps. One of the very lightest jockeys was John (Sam) Kitchenar. In 1840 the ten-year-old rode in a race off 3st 12lbs, his body weight was just 2st 7lbs. Four years later he was chosen to partner Red Deer in the Chester Cup. The horse had been allotted 4st, which was no problem to Kitchenar who scaled a meagre 3st 4lbs at the time. Off such a low weight, Red Deer was a near certainty and was backed accordingly, down to 7/2 favourite in a field of twenty-six. Despite starting in the second rank of thirteen runners (the track was too narrow to accommodate a field of so many horses in a single row), Kitchenar soon had the favourite clear of the opposition and won easily by six lengths landing some massive bets, the largest of which had been placed by Lord George Bentinck. After the announcement of the result, Red Deer's trainer, John Kent, released several homing pigeons to inform his stable staff at Goodwood of the result. It was a classic betting coup, which the Confederates were hoping to replicate.

Jarvis finished well-beaten in the Stewards Cup, as expected and planned. According to her stable lad she had been extremely lightly worked in the run up to the race and hadn't 'done a canter for a month.' The next time Jarvis was given the leg-up on Hackler's Pride was on Cambridgeshire day.

At home, Hackler's Pride was working with several different horses and their performances recorded in minute detail. Fallon even had a special nine-furlong gallop prepared to emulate the Cambridgeshire course. Nothing was left to chance and, of course, due to their remote location outsiders would know nothing of what happened on the gallops. When the weights for the Cambridgeshire Handicap were announced, Hackler's Pride was allotted 7st 1lb. The Confederates had four other runners in the race, and from an analysis of their respective weights, and gallops data, Fallon concluded that Hackler's Pride had 10lbs in hand. Purefoy was unsure this was sufficient and instructed his trainer to increase the advantage by any way he could.

By mid-October Hackler's Pride had improved further and was undeniably well handicapped. The Confederates could now focus on the other equally important part of their business: getting the money on. Having several runners in the race was part of the planning. It provided a means for them to disguise their main intentions and inflate the price of Hackler's Pride. By backing more than one of their horses they could throw the Bookmakers off the scent, as well as creating a market in which their main hope was available at even better odds. Over a period of time, enormous sums of money were placed with commission agents as far afield as South Africa; the Confederates used contacts in every country where bets were taken on British horseracing to facilitate their gambling aims.

The night before the race, rain fell in torrents. At one stage it was thought that the meeting might be abandoned such was the downpour. Fortunately, by the afternoon the sun was glinting through the clouds and it became a 'charming autumn day.' The Royalty were out in force including the

King, Prince Christian, Prince Soltykoff, Prince Oscar Wrede, the Duke of Cambridge, and the usual clutch of representatives of the British aristocracy. Around the course, betting continued apace with Burses heavily supported although, according to one report, he 'could not hold his own in the betting against Hackler's Pride and Kilglass'.

In total, twenty-seven runners went to post, of which only two carried more than 8st. Nine were ridden by claiming apprentices which caused one racing correspondent to conclude 'it cannot be said that the quality was equal to the quantity'. Hackler's Pride was number twenty-seven on the racecard, the high number corresponding to her low position in the weights.

As Jarvis entered the paddock Fallon snatched the whip from his hand, 'you won't need that', was all he said. So secretive were the preparations, even at that point Jarvis was unaware of the huge amount of money riding on his young shoulders, and that Hackler's Pride had been "laid out" for this one race.

Up with the pace throughout, Hackler's Pride poached a half-length lead at the Bushes, then in the Dip 'shot clear away from Burses, Kilgalss, Ballantrae and Simony'. She won easily, as the Confederates had calculated, and the three-length margin of success could have been much wider.

It is difficult to determine the exact amount won on this race by the Confederates, but conservative estimates would make it equivalent to around £20 million today.

Twelve months later Hackler's Pride and the Confederates were at it again. This time she started 7/2 joint favourite after being backed down from 33/1. Whilst the result was the same, the 1904 Cambridgeshire Handicap was a much harder-fought affair with Hackler's Pride winning by just a neck. Another momentous gamble had been landed and, for the first time in the history of the race, a horse had won the Cambridgeshire Handicap in consecutive seasons.

Development of Newbury Racecourse *26 September 1905*

The first annual two-day race meeting at Newbury took place in 1805; it was founded by a member of the Craven dynasty after whom the Craven Stakes at Newmarket is named. These meetings, along with the Wantage races that were staged on Craven-owned land near to the villages of Letcombe Bassett and Letcombe Regis, were very short-lived. It was not for another one hundred years that a racecourse was constructed at Newbury, and without one particularly fortuitous meeting it might never have happened.

The main Founder of Newbury Racecourse was the Kingsclere trainer John Porter who had prepared the Triple Crown winners Ormonde, Common, and Flying Fox. When travelling by train to London, Porter identified a 'level stretch of land immediately to the south of Newbury' as the ideal location for a racecourse. Convinced that its development would prove to be a successful enterprise, Porter purchased it from Mr Lloyd Baxendale of Greenham. Plans were outlined and Porter presented them to the Jockey Club. Much to his disbelief, and disappointment, his proposal was rejected on the grounds that there were already too many racecourses in Britain

On leaving the Jockey Club Rooms, where the meeting had taken place, by chance he met King Edward VII. A conversation then ensued in which Porter explained his reason for consulting the Jockey Club officials and their response. The monarch was impressed with Porter's proposal and requested to view the plans in more detail. With such a powerful ally on his side, Porter was not too surprised to find the next meeting with the Jockey Club was 'conducted in a very friendly atmosphere' and his licence was granted. The course at Greenham could then be prepared for use in the autumn of 1905.

The first race meeting at the new course was a two-day affair (possibly a nod to the historic meetings held there previously), and took place on 26th and 27th September. *The Times* reported that it had attracted a great deal of local support and given its location 'the sport should be good'. However, the correspondent added, 'the first day is made up of four handicaps, a selling plate, and a maiden plate, so... the class of the competitors is not likely to be high'.

Thankfully the quality of racing did improve over the coming years, and Newbury became associated with top class national hunt and flat racing. Golden Miller, Mill House and Borough Hill Lad were all seen clearing the unforgiving Newbury fences with ease, whilst flat racing fans were treated to displays by the great Bosra Sham, Derby winner Nashwan, and one of the best milers of all time, Brigadier Gerard. In recent times, though, the standard has slipped, as it has at many other tracks. Nowadays the main focus of British racing is handicap races which, as Admiral Rous claimed, are 'a positive boon to bad horses, and the chief inducement to keep a parcel of wretches in training.' Unfortunately, in the 21st century it is not uncommon for a low grade programme of races to be staged at Newbury, similar to those scheduled for its opening day over one hundred years ago.

Has Anyone Seen the Gold Cup? 18 June 1907

Whilst on display during the June Ascot meeting in 1907, the Gold Cup, valued at 500gns [£60,000], was stolen a mere two days before it would have been presented to the winning owner. According to *The Sydney Morning Herald* the cup was being exhibited behind the stands when the thieves pounced. In a classic case of distraction theft, while one or more of the culprits engaged the two guards (a police constable and an employee of the cup's manufacturers) in conversation, another member of the gang made off with the trophy. Despite the best efforts of the police, the cup was never found, and no one was apprehended in connection with the case that remains unsolved to this day.

A King's Derby 26 May 1909

While some horses are capable of performing at their best as juveniles, many need time to develop physically before reaching a stage when they can realise their full racing potential. Minoru was one of these late maturing horses.

As a juvenile Minoru did win first time out, but then ran poorly in several contests. Over the winter of 1908/09 he grew into his frame and strengthened; by Newbury's Greenham meeting in the spring he was looking fit and much stronger in the paddock. Even so, in attempting to give 5lbs to the highly rated Valens it was the considered opinion of the assembled racing experts that he would be beaten. Much to their surprise, after tracking the front-running rival he was asked for an effort with two hundred yards to go and sprinted away. Minoru's success was the first part of a double for King Edward VII who followed up with Oakmere in the Berkshire Three-Year-Old Handicap. When founding the course just four years earlier John Porter predicted that Newbury would be well supported by trainers due to its location. Any lingering doubts as to the accuracy of this claim were dispelled in the next race: the Beckhampton Two-Year-old Plate attracted a bumper field of thirty-seven runners.

Three weeks later racegoers filled every available space on Newmarket Heath. Unusually for the spring meeting, and probably due to the vast number that attended, they were allowed to watch the races from both sides of the track. Many were hoping to witness a Royal victory. To the form students, the 2,000 Guineas of 1909 was a two horse race between Bayardo, who was the champion juvenile of 1908, and Minoru. In the paddock the King's horse held the clear advantage being hard trained whereas Bayardo appeared less than fully fit. An injury, coupled with poor weather throughout the winter, prevented him from working as much as his trainer would have desired. Consequently, it was not too surprising when Bayardo faded in the closing stages of the race. In contrast, Minoru ran on strongly to score decisively from the 33/1 shot Phaleron.

Although absent from Newmarket, the King and Queen were in attendance at Epsom on Derby day and, as usual, they arrived in good time for the race. This particular year, more than any preceding year, it was apparent that the motor car was rapidly becoming the favoured means of transportation. Whereas in 1904 only 23,000 motor vehicles were on the roads of Great Britain, by 1909 the number had increased dramatically and a year later there were over 100,000 vehicle registrations despite a national speed limit of just 20mph. Cars had been imported from Europe mostly, but by 1909 American-made models were making a rare appearance in addition to British-built vehicles. It is possible that there were some early Fords at the track on 26th May, but more likely the regal Rolls Royce Silver Ghost would be competing for parking space beside Austin Landaulettes, a few six-cylinder Sheffield-Simplex Tourers, and the occasional Sears Model K Motor Buggy. *The Times* correspondent was confident this increased level of mechanisation would not have any lasting negative impact on horseracing:

Tastes in sport are less likely than most other habits of civilization to be transformed by the progress of mechanical science; and there is little good reason for apprehending that the popularity of the Derby will ever be annexed by that of the Brooklands racing track.

Of course, he was perfectly correct in his assertion. Other than its novelty value, how might the sight of metal boxes on four wheels even begin to compete with the transfixing vision of a horse forcing every fibre of its being in an attempt to beat the field? By comparison, automated effort was sterile and unseen. Cars may move like lightning, but racehorses will always move the soul.

Heavy rain at Epsom meant that many racegoers opted for shelter rather than making paddock-side observations. Those who braved the elements and made their way to the parade ring would have seen Minoru in excellent condition. In the race he ran as well as his looks suggested. With a furlong to go, Herbert Jones had Minoru racing alongside the long-time leader, Louviers. The pair had an advantage over Valens and William The

Fourth, and it was clear that one of the two leaders would prevail. In the desperate dash to the line, it first appeared that the crowd would be cheering home a Royal winner then, in an instant, Louviers had taken lead. And so it continued, the jockeys straining for every effort, urging their mounts for just that extra ounce of momentum which would secure victory in the most important race of their lives. In the last fifty yards they were locked together in battle, there was nothing between them, and this was still the case at the line. Only the Judge could decide which horse had won.

After a wait it was announced that Minoru had been given the verdict and the 'tumult of jubilation was overwhelming... acknowledging the plaudits of the multitude the King re-entered the enclosure holding his colt's leading rein, and then once more enthusiasm burst forth [with] cries of "Vive le Roi"'. For the first time, a reigning Sovereign had won the Derby. *The Times* considered it to be 'a spectacle never to be forgotten' and evidently believed that the celebrations would not be confined to the racecourse, asserting 'the congratulations showered upon His Majesty... will be re-echoed throughout the kingdom and empire'.

Whether the news did have an impact on those living in the far reaches of the Empire is uncertain, but for some the success lived long in the memory and for others it was an achievement worthy of note.

Many years later a reference was made to Minoru in the iconic 1970s television series *Upstairs Downstairs*. In the episode entitled "Guest Of Honour" King Edward VII dines at 165 Eton Place, the home of the Bellamy family. During the meal, whilst in conversation, he says 'Minoru... a well-bred colt but a late developer. Back him for the Derby Lady Marjorie.' Alfred Shaughnessy, who wrote the screenplay, was, perhaps, a horseracing fan.

Black Ascot   *15 June 1910*

Royal Ascot has been synonymous with fashion ever since 1807 when the "invitation only" Royal Enclosure was established and a dress code introduced. Whether this dress code was instigated to heighten the profile of the meeting, or to enable the less desirable attendees to be more easily segregated, is unclear. Whatever the reason, a code of sorts has been in place at the meeting ever since.

Historians tend to agree that the introduction of the dress code was due to the influence George "Beau" Brummell held over his close friend the Prince Regent. Apparently, Brummell declared that 'men of elegance should wear waisted black coats and white cravats'. His style advice duly formed the basis of the dress code. Over one hundred years later, a dress code is still applied although the rules have been relaxed a little in recent times to account for changing fashions.

In 1910 it was all-change at Ascot. Due to the continued Royal patronage it was finally agreed to name the meeting "Royal Ascot"; moreover there was a new Clerk of the Course, Sir Gordon Carter. Carter was fastidious in the extreme, a trait that not only dictated the way he managed the course, but also how he dressed. It is claimed that he had his shoelaces washed and ironed every night and would change his outfit up to five times per day during the June meeting.

Therefore, Carter must have been bitterly disappointed when, at the eleventh hour, it was decided that the meeting would not adopt the new name after all. And to make matters worse, all the colour was taken out of the fashionable attire on display rendering many of his numerous outfits unbefitting for the occasion. The reason for this abrupt change was difficult to argue against: the recent death of King Edward VII. An empty Royal Box was clearly visible to racegoers throughout the five days of the meeting which only went ahead because the late King was such an enthusiast for the sport. However, the colourful dresses, waistcoats, and handkerchiefs had to be kept for other occasions as all guests wore black as a mark of respect. For this reason the 1910 meeting became known as "Black Ascot" and it was the meeting in 1911 that was the first to be known as "Royal Ascot".

Turning Silver into Gold   *16 June 1910*

Bayardo was, quite simply, an outstanding racehorse, one of the very best to have raced in Great Britain.

The Bay Ronald colt was trained by Alec Taylor at Manton and made his debut in the five-furlong New Stakes at Ascot's June meeting in 1908. At home Bayardo had been working well, even getting the better of three-year-olds in some trials. At Ascot he faced two highly regarded juveniles in Perola and Perdiccas that had already produced top class performances on the track making his introduction to racing far from an easy task. This was not lost on the punters who didn't fancy the newcomer's chances and he was sent off at 7/1. Despite his generous starting price, jockey Bernard Dillon was confident; he knew Bayardo was a good horse in the making, and his judgement proved correct with his mount winning by an easy length-and-a-half. The two main dangers filled the places. After getting off the mark, and benefiting from the racing experience, Bayardo went on a winning spree recording wins in the majority of the top juvenile contests including the Middle Park Stakes and the Dewhurst Stakes. He ended the season as Champion Juvenile, unbeaten from seven races.

On the back of this sparkling first season, Bayardo was installed at odds-on for the first colts' Classic of 1909. However, the harshness of the Yorkshire winter severely restricted the opportunities for Taylor to work his runners. To make a testing situation even worse, Bayardo slipped on a frozen patch of ground and was lame for a good part of the off-season. Taylor was against running his stable star in the Guineas but his owner, Alfred Cox, was a determined man and he won the day. Bayardo would start at Newmarket regardless of his trainer's reservations.

As a much younger man, Alfred Cox failed to secure a place at The Royal Military Academy and was sent to Australia by his family and told to make his money in farming. Matters did not work out quite as planned, though. Cox may not have had any talent regarding military affairs, but he was skilled in other areas, particularly gambling. During the long voyage to the Antipodes he won a farm from a fellow passenger in a card game. Initially the derelict sheep farm in New South Wales, close to the border with South Australia, did not appear to offer any type of opportunity to turn a profit. His thoughts of making a quick fortune were evaporating more quickly than a rain puddle in the Australian outback. But the Englishman's luck had not entirely run out.

On a blisteringly hot day whilst Cox was surveying his empire and wondering what he could do to enhance his finances, he spotted something shining in the dust that coated every inch of the property. It was silver. Cox realised in an instant that while he was not metaphorically sitting on a gold mine, he was in reality sitting on a potential silver mine. His future was secured. After converting his miraculous discovery into cash, Cox returned to England with a determination to make his mark in the bloodstock industry. This he did, but not as Alfred Cox, instead, for some inexplicable reason, he chose to register his horses under the name "Mr Fairie".

As Taylor predicted, Bayardo was not at his best in the Guineas. Despite his very short starting price and the assistance of the great American jockey Danny Maher, he trailed in fourth, beaten over four lengths. The three-year-old was out to 9/2 for his next race, The Derby, even though in the paddock he appeared much fitter than at Newmarket. In the race he seemed to be moving well until the fall of the American colt St Martin badly hampered him, after which his jockey allowed him to coast home. Although there was an obvious reason for his failure, question marks were appearing over him with doubts cast about his staying ability and temperament.

By Ascot, Taylor was convinced the public would at last see the real Bayardo. The target race was the Prince of Wales Stakes, and the 4/1 shot did not let him down. At the finishing line he had just under a length to spare over Cattaro and the Oaks third, Verne, who were in receipt of 6lbs, and 19lbs respectively.

Taylor was correct in his assessment: Bayardo was back to his brilliant best, and over the coming weeks he proved it in no uncertain fashion by winning his next ten races including the Eclipse Stakes, St Leger, and Champion Stakes. Those commentators who had doubted Bayardo's will to win as well as his stamina credentials were left eating their words.

The main target for Bayardo's four-year-old season was the Ascot Gold Cup. He won his two "prep" races then, on 16th June 1910, lined up alongside a field of twelve top class opponents that featured the best staying horses from England, France, and America. The race had all the ingredients of a potentially outstanding encounter. In glorious sunshine Pure Gem delayed the start by initially refusing to approach the tape, but once in line the Starter released the gate and Southannan hit the front, setting a strong gallop. Bayardo was well off the lead, Maher riding a waiting race. These tactics had proved successful in the past but were not often employed by the American jockeys who preferred to dictate the tempo. At the halfway point the pace quickened further, exciting a feverish crowd that already knew they were witnessing a great contest. The change of pace was Maher's cue to let Bayardo stride on. The impact was immediate; Bayardo 'passed the others simply at his leisure'. As he swept into the Ascot straight, well clear of the talented, yet vastly inferior opposition, he was still travelling easily. At the line his advantage was four lengths, it could have been ten such was the ease of his success. This scintillating performance established Bayardo as the Champion racehorse of the season, for the third year in succession, an achievement that prompted *The Times* to note that 'Bayardo takes his place in the list of the great horses'.

Mr Fairie's Gold Cup winner was successful once more then was beaten in a close finish when trying to concede 36lbs to the three-year-old, Magic, in the Goodwood Cup. Danny Maher, so often the master at waiting tactics, was at fault for the defeat by allowing Magic to steal a lead that stretched to almost a furlong at one point. Even the great Bayardo could not give that much distance away whilst simultaneously conceding so much weight.

After the Goodwood race, Bayardo was retired to stud. His offspring included two Triple Crown winners: Gay Crusader and Gainsborough. There's no denying that Bayardo was one of the most brilliant horses of the last century. Not only did he win at the highest level, he also won championship races over distances ranging from six furlongs to two-and-a-half miles. Few horses can make such claims, but his failure to win the Guineas and Derby has meant that he is often, unfairly, passed over when a list of the "greatest horses" is compiled.

A Memorable Derby   *4 June 1913*

On page nine of *The Times* dated 5th June 1913, immediately below a portentous reference to the launch in Bremen of the German battleship *Ersatz Weissenburg*, a heading states simply *A Memorable Derby*. Whilst this headline is unquestionably accurate, it is the epitome of understatement. The 1913 Derby is arguably the most significant horserace in the nation's history. Over the last one hundred years it has been analysed in more detail than any other race run anywhere in the world. As well as being the catalyst for overdue radical change in British society, the race ensured, through its tragic circumstances, that Emily Davison was known to every man, woman and child in the country.

Born in 1872, Emily Davison studied for a BA (Honours) degree at Royal Holloway College, London, for two years. The death of her father in 1894 meant her family could no longer afford the termly fees of £30 [£4,000], and she had to end her studies early. Davison finally completed her degree after one further term at St Hugh's Hall Oxford the following year. Although Davison was an intelligent, talented, hard-working student, after she had completed the course there was no degree certificate for her to receive at a grand graduation ceremony. At that time Oxford did not award degrees to women. In fact, Britain's oldest university did not accede to equality in this matter until the 1920s; Cambridge University waited until after the Second World War.

Davison worked as a teacher for a while, but was gradually drawn into the suffragette movement. In 1906 the Liberal Party was returned to power and Davison joined the Women's Social and Political Union (WSPU) that had been founded by Emmeline and Christabel Pankhurst three years previously. These two events were not entirely unconnected. The fragile relationship between the new Liberal Administration and the suffragette movement deteriorated rapidly on their re-election, and the defeat of several suffrage bills gave rise to more direct action by the suffragettes which, in turn, increased the membership of the WSPU.

Also in 1906, jockey Herbert Jones recorded his sixth Classic victory on Gorgos, a 20/1 shot owned by Arthur James and trained by Richard Marsh at Newmarket. Jones came to prominence when, as a nineteen-year-old, he rode the Prince of Wales' seemingly intractable Diamond Jubilee to Triple Crown success in 1900. Further Classic victories followed with wins in the 2,000 Guineas and the Oaks in 1905 then his success at Newmarket in 1906. Three years later, in 1909, Jones reached the pinnacle of his career when he partnered the King's Minoru to Derby glory.

Two months before King Edward VII proudly led Minoru back to the winner's enclosure, Emily Davison was gaining her first taste of imprisonment. A series of short spells behind bars resulted from obstruction and stone throwing incidents. On one occasion she was arrested and imprisoned for throwing stones at the carriage of David Lloyd George. According to the Historian Maureen Howes, often the stones were wrapped in paper on which Davison had written her motto, "rebellion against tyrants is obedience to God" just to ensure the recipient fully appreciated the reason for the attack.

The following year, whilst Herbert Jones was enjoying more success in the Coronation Stakes and Sussex Stakes, Davison was arrested for breaking a window in the House of Commons. At roughly the same time, the newly crowned King George V sent a bay colt by Florizel II, who was a son of the imperious St Simon, to racehorse trainer Richard Marsh at Newmarket. The colt was named Anmer after a village on the Sandringham estate.

Suffragette activity increased over the next few years and the impact on public life became more pronounced as the nature of their attacks took a more destructive path. In December 1911 Davison was arrested for setting fire to a pillar box. For this act she received a sentence of six months' imprisonment, then in the late Autum of 1912 Davison was given a further ten days for assaulting a Baptist Minister she mistook for David Lloyd George. Davison really did not like the "Welsh Wizard".

In the spring of 1913 it was clear to Marsh that Anmer was not going to emulate his illustrious grandsire, but he was still declared for the Derby and Herbert Jones was booked to ride. Ninety miles away in Kent a group of suffragettes perpetrated one of their most audacious crimes to date.

The Royal Tunbridge Wells Cricket Club possessed one of the most picturesque grounds in the land. Lined with rhododendron bushes, it was described as 'the most delectable English cricket ground'. Named after William Nevill, the 1st Marquess of Abergavenny, the *Nevill Ground* was first used by Kent County Cricket Club in 1901. The players were so impressed by the ground that the construction of a pavilion was commissioned. Designed by a local architect, CH Strange, it was completed in 1903. Ten years later it lay in charred ruins as a result of an arson attack by suffragette extremists. It was not just the building that was destroyed; all it housed including cricket equipment, nets, and, most importantly, valuable archives were reduced to ashes. Although no arrests were made, there was an angry backlash against the activists not least from cricket-fan Sir Arthur Conan Doyle who was a member of the club.

By way of justification, it was later claimed that this particular building was targeted because of a comment made by one of the Kent Officials. Apparently, he was heard to say 'It is not true that women are banned from the pavilion. Who do you think makes the tea?' In 1913 though, women were not banned from the pavilion, so it is doubtful whether this remark was ever made. As daring as that raid was, and despite the negative publicity it garnered for the suffragette movement, Davison had a far more shocking act in mind.

Herbert Jones did not give Anmer much chance in the Derby on 4th June 1913, nor did the betting public, and the King's colt started at 50/1. In front of an estimated crowd of 500,000, which included the King and Queen, Anmer was already struggling by the time the leaders rounded Tattenham Corner. Jones already knew it was not going to be his year, but what he hadn't counted on was Emily Davison rushing from the inner rail and attempting to grab his reins as he rounded the bend at a speed exceeding thirty miles an hour. Davison was knocked to the ground and Anmer 'turned a complete somersault' as he was brought down, landing on Jones in the process. According to one police report, Jones was stretchered to the Jockeys' Room where he was treated for concussion. Davison received medical treatment on the track by a doctor who was attending the races as a spectator. She was then taken to Epsom Cottage Hospital by car. Tragically, the injuries Davison received in the incident were fatal.

While it was clear that Davison was making a suffragist protest, her exact intentions have never been established. Was she trying to attach one of the suffragette movement's flags she carried to the bridle of the horse as some claim? Or, more disturbingly, had she decided to martyr herself in order to gain more recognition for the cause she felt so deeply about? The fact she had in her possession a return rail ticket casts doubt on the martyrdom theory, although it could easily have been purchased in error by way of habit. *The Times* correspondent thought it was a 'desperate act', and questioned whether Davison had 'some mad notion that she could spoil the race'. He surmised rather unsympathetically:

> *Reckless fanaticism is not regarded by [the public] as a qualification for the franchise. They are disposed to look upon manifestations of that temper with contempt and with disgust. When these manifestations are attended by indifference to human life, they begin to suspect that they are not altogether sane.*

Whatever her reasons, the act certainly had an impact on Jones. Fifteen years after this momentous race, Jones laid a wreath at the funeral of Emmeline Pankhurst 'to do honour to the memory of Mrs Pankhurst and Miss Emily Davison.'

Amazingly the drama did not end with the horses passing the winning post in one of the closest finishes in the Derby. The Stewards took it upon themselves to hold an enquiry and decided to disqualify the winner, 6/4 favourite Craganour, in favour of 100/1 shot Aboyeur. And even that didn't go to plan. The crowd were aware of the enquiry, but the "all right" signal was raised by 'an irresponsible person without official instructions.' Bookmakers started to pay out on Craganour and the result was 'at once telegraphed all over the world, there must have been many men in many lands yesterday who for a brief spell rejoiced in the glad illusion' claimed one racing correspondent. A while later it was announced that due to interference caused by the American jockey Johnny Reiff (brother of Lester Reiff who was warned off in 1901 for rough riding), and his failure to keep the horse running in a straight line, the winner was disqualified.

While most Bookmakers were celebrating the success of the relatively unbacked winner, some were counting their losses. Aboyeur hailed from the infamous Druid's Lodge stable, and many bets were placed in the last fifteen minutes before the "off". One commission agent acting for Confederate Percy Cunliffe managed to get £250 [£29,000] each way on Aboyeur at 100/1 with Ladbrokes. His account was promptly closed. It is fair to say that Aboyeur was not the best Derby winner of the century: later that summer he was exported to Russia, where he probably became a victim of the 1917 Revolution.

So, all things considered, the 1913 Epsom Classic was, as *The Times* stated, a memorable Derby.

The German battleship mentioned on the same page as the Derby report was commissioned on 1st October 1914. In 1916 it was involved in the Battle of Jutland where, as a front line attack vessel, it was hit several times. Ultimately, the *Ersatz Weissenburg* surrendered to the British and was interned at Scapa Flow where it remained until scuttled in 1919. It is now a deep diving attraction.

The Ultimate Sacrifice   *4 August 1914*

With Germany refusing to remove its troops from Belgium by midnight on 3rd August 1914, the deadline specified by Prime Minister Herbert Asquith, Great Britain officially declared war on its continental neighbour. In order to avoid total capitulation in the forthcoming conflict, Britain needed rapidly to expand the size of its military. Within days a recruitment drive went into full force endeavouring to enlist as many men as possible from every walk of life. Sportsmen were not immune from this request and thousands rushed to join the armed forces. Modest village green cricketers stood in line at the recruitment office alongside amateur and professional players from every sporting discipline. Not to be left out, the elite sports stars of the era, including such luminaries as Leslie Cheape an internationally renowned polo player, and Laurence Doherty who had won five consecutive Wimbledon titles from 1902 to 1906, also willingly accepted the King's Shilling.

The Government viewed football as a particularly fertile ground for recruiting potential troops. At matches, thousands of mainly young men filled the terraces, so advertising, in the form of posters either stuck to walls or carried by men with sandwich boards, were visible from every vantage point. Pledge cards to join the military were foisted upon the fans and respected figures from the community delivered rousing speeches at half time. As well as recruiting individuals, teams enlisted *en masse* in "Pals' battalions", a term first coined by Lord Derby. Clapton Orient, now known as Leyton Orient Football Club, were the first English team to enlist in this fashion with forty players and staff joining on a single day.

Horseracing and hunting were not left untouched by the conflict. Although it is often described as the "first mechanized war", horses still had a major role to play in the transportation of munitions and supplies to the front line. The proximity of the main area of combat meant that transporting the animals was far easier than it had been in the Boer War, the last major conflict. Moving horses from all parts of the British Empire to South Africa had been a logistical problem on an altogether more complex level. Troop ships were used mainly, with horses retained in stalls that were, in most cases, no more than thirty inches wide. While the horse deck was covered with coconut matting to help prevent horses slipping whilst exercising, just as importantly it had to be watertight. The troop deck, on many ships, was located directly below the horse deck, so any leakage would have made for an even more uncomfortable time for the men. During the South African campaign, over 360,000 horses were transported in this fashion to Port Elizabeth where the harsh climate, an astonishing 60% combat attrition rate, and disease, such as horse-sickness and sand-colic, meant that over 300,000 did not survive.

By the end of the Great War, less that twenty years later, Britain had lost a further 480,000 horses, according to statisticians. Therefore, across the two conflicts over three-quarters of a million horses were sacrificed, a significant proportion of which were steeplechasers supplied by the many hunts that were active in almost every county of England at the time.

As well as horses there were many casualties amongst racing's four hundred jockeys (one hundred and ninety licensed riders and two hundred and ten apprentices) during the 1914-18 conflict. Frederick Allfrey, a successful point-to-point rider and polo player, was involved in the last "lance-on-lance" charge of the war when serving with the 9th Queen's Royal Lancers. At the head of the charge against a battery of eleven heavy guns secreted in a wooded area, was another successful jockey, Lieutenant Colonel David Campbell, who had ridden The Soarer to success in the 1896 Grand National (hence his regimental nickname: "Soarer Campbell"). According to *The Times*, 'near Provins on 6th September 1914 thirty Lancers charged and routed 150 of the enemy's cavalry... Lieutenant Allfrey dismounted to extract a lance from the body of a comrade, and while he was doing this he was shot by a wounded German'. Allfrey was just twenty-two years old at the time of his death. Despite being wounded in his leg, arm, and shoulder, Campbell remarkably survived the charge, and the war. The 9th Queen's Royal Lancers was one of the first regiments to take up polo and their team had won every Regimental Polo Cup up to the start of the conflict. By the end of November 1914 six team members had been killed, and a further five were wounded.

A week earlier, Claude Norman de Crespigny, a Lieutenant in the 2nd Dragoon Guards (Queen's Bays) was killed in action near Compiegne. In thick fog the regiment was gradually being outflanked, which would have led to its utter annihilation. To prevent this happening, Lieutenant Crespigny, who was a brilliant all-round sportsman and rider, attacked a tactically vital position on the regiment's right flank. Ultimately the barrage of shells and rifle fire was too great and every man who stood alongside the Lieutenant that day was either killed or wounded. Despite the loss of life, this action was not in vain. According to Captain Springfield this successful sortie saved many hundreds of lives. When found, Lieutenant Crespigny had a broken right arm, which had been bound, and two other more serious wounds to the abdomen. He was clutching his sword in his left hand suggesting he was prepared to fight until the very end. In writing to Crespigny's parents, General Allenby who commanded the Cavalry Brigade of which the "Bays" were part, emphasised the Lieutenant's bravery stating 'I must tell you that he died a hero's death.' Crespigny was twenty-six years old and was married to Miss Rose Gordon.

Herbert William "Jack" Tyrrwhitt-Drake was a very talented horseman riding sixty-one winners in the 1911 season, the most of any amateur and enough to rank him second in the jockeys' championship. Two of his wins came at the Cheltenham Festival and two years later he managed to ride into a place in the Grand National. Tyrrwhitt-Drake was one of the first to enlist in the "Jockeys' regiment", the 19th Hussars. However, his time with the Hussars lasted less than a year; Tyrrwhitt-Drake contracted pneumonia and died in France on 11th March 1915. Had hostilities not broken out between the nations he would have been riding at the Festival the very day he died.

Fred Lester Rickaby was born in 1894 to a racing family. By the time he joined the Veterinary Corps in 1916 he had already won multiple Classics. In 1918 Rickaby was wounded whilst serving with the Tank Corps and died at Doingt, France, exactly one month before Armistice Day. He was twenty-four years old. His sister Iris, herself a talented horsewoman married into the Piggott dynasty and on 5th November 1935 had a son whom she named Lester.

George Butchers had notched one hundred career wins before enlisting. Whilst fighting at Roeux in May 1917 he was attempting to get help for a wounded companion when he was killed. Charles Beatty was a successful jumps jockey who guided Filbert to the runner-up position in the 1897 Grand National. After working as assistant trainer to Colonel McCalmont he assumed control of the stables on his employer's death in 1901 and began training horses for Lord Howard de Walden. In 1916, while on duty with the Mounted Infantry, he was severely injured and his left arm had to be amputated. This caused concern at the very highest level. Charles Wigram, the King's Private Secretary wrote to Beatty's commanding officer expressing the monarch's sorrow:

> *His Majesty noticed his name in the Casualty List two days ago, and*
> *instructed me to enquire about his wound... His Majesty was only*
> *yesterday recalling the incident when he [Beatty] cantered alongside the*
> *King's motor on a very handsome horse. Should you see Beatty, will you*
> *please tell him from the King how truly His Majesty sympathises with*
> *him on his misfortune.*

A year later Beatty died of his wounds after aggravating the injury by falling from his horse.

Not all riders entered the Army. Rear-Admiral Sir Christopher Craddock was an accomplished rider, making the frame in the Grand Military Gold Cup in 1906 at the age of forty-three. Just three months into the war he was killed, together with a crew of nine hundred, at the Battle of Coronel when HMS *Good Hope* was sunk. The fact that this battle was fought off the coast of Chile illustrates how global the conflict had become in such a short space of time.

Of course, many jockeys and other stable staff survived the Great War. Frank Wise lost a leg and three fingers during the fighting but still managed to win the 1929 Irish Grand National on Alike.

So many of the Great War pilots seemed to be utterly devoid of fear. Jack Wilson was such a man. Before gaining his pilot's licence in June 1914, Wilson played county cricket for Yorkshire. At the outbreak of the conflict he was commissioned into the Royal Naval Air Service and had been promoted to Flight Lieutenant by the end of the year. In an aeroplane that would need a strong tailwind to break modern day motorway speed limits, he successfully attacked two German submarines at Zeebrugge. In the early hours of 7th June 1915, at roughly the same time as a Zeppelin was dropping incendiary and explosive devices on the residents long the east coast of England, Wilson piloted a plane that bombed an airship hangar at Evere, also in Belgium, destroying the building and everything within. This was at a time when dropping bombs meant leaning over the side of the plane, bomb in hand, and releasing it at the appropriate instant whilst ducking to avoid the hostile anti-aircraft fire. For this daring raid Wilson, and his co-pilot Flight Sub-Lieutenant John Mills, were awarded the Distinguished Service Cross. After the war, he began a new career as an amateur jockey, riding over two hundred winners including the 1925 Grand National winner, Double Chance. Wilson lived until 1959.

George Arthur Boyd-Rochfort (known as Arthur) rode over jumps and owned the Tally Ho Stud in Ireland. After joining the First Battalion of the Scots Guards, he was engaged in hostilities between Cambrin and La Brasse in August 1915. Amid ferocious fighting, a German mortar bomb landed close to where he was organising a small working party. Without considering his own safety, Boyd-Rochfort immediately picked the device up and threw into a safe zone, where it exploded. His quick thinking, and bravery, saved the lives of several men and he was awarded the Victoria Cross. Arthur Boyd-Rochfort survived the war along with his two brothers, Cecil (Henry Cecil's stepfather, who won the Croix de Guerre) and Lieutenant Colonel Boyd-Rochfort of the 21st Lancers.

The conflict is first, and rightly, remembered for the millions of heroic servicemen who paid the ultimate price. However, the loss of entire sporting careers is a factual footnote that is sometimes forgotten. Countless numbers, in all sports, were forced to sacrifice the fame and fortune that their glittering talents so richly deserved in what, at the time, was believed to be the war to end all wars.

All Flat Races Transferred to Newmarket   *24 May 1915*

At the start of the Great War the generally accepted opinion, especially amongst those from the upper echelons of society including a young Harold MacMillan, was that the conflict would be over before Christmas. This view was also held on the other side of the English Channel. When addressing troops who were departing for the front in August 1914, Kaiser Wilhelm II assured them that they would 'be home before the leaves fall from the trees.'

By the spring of 1915 minds were beginning to change. The death toll from the Western Front was increasing every day and the sinking of the passenger liner *Lusitania* crystallised the fear that the nation's crucial food supply routes were vulnerable to Germany's rampant submarine fleet. Britain's prospects looked bleak and many began to question whether such frivolities as horseracing should continue. The Jockey Club were in favour of maintaining the full racing programme emphasising its importance as a vital industry that provided employment and livelihoods for thousands of people. The Government took a different view and on 19th May 1915 Walter

Runciman, the President of the Board of Trade, made a formal request to the Jockey Club to suspend all racing with the exception of meetings at Newmarket. Reluctantly racing's rulers acquiesced and it was decreed that from 24th May all races were to be held at the Suffolk course. Naturally, this move increased the number of races staged at Newmarket as well as the field sizes, but horseracing survived, albeit in a diminished fashion.

Martha Hennessy's Classic Success   *1 May 1918*

Had the bidding for a Bayardo-Rosedrop yearling at the 1916 Newmarket Sales not fallen ten percent short of the reserve of 2,000gns, then Lady James Douglas would not have become the first lady owner of a Classic winner.

Born Martha Lucy Hennessy, Lady James Douglas married Lord James Douglas in 1888 three years after her first husband, Richard Hennessy (her cousin), had died. Lord James Douglas was the son of Lord Queensbury. His brother, John Douglas, initiated the rules of boxing known the world over as the "Queensbury Rules"; he was also an adversary of Oscar Wilde and a key player in the famous trial of 1895. His older brother, Francis Douglas, was killed in tragic circumstances when descending from the Matterhorn after completing the first successful ascent of the Swiss mountain. The misfortune associated with this family did not end there. In 1891, James, by then an alcoholic, committed suicide leaving Martha twice widowed in the space of six years.

The new century brought with it some overdue good fortune for Martha. In 1910 she purchased farmland in Hampshire and created the Harwood Stud. One of her first purchases was Rosedrop, winner of the 1910 Oaks.

On 24th January 1915 a Bayardo-Rosedrop colt, later named Gainsborough, was foaled at Harwood. After failing to make the reserve at the sales in 1916, he was sent to trainer Alec Taylor and prepared for racing. Although he was successful in one race as a juvenile, Gainsborough's three-year-old season did not start too well with a defeat over an inadequate five furlongs at Newmarket. Just two weeks later on 1st May 1918, he started 4/1 third favourite for the 2,000 Guineas. His relatively short price was no doubt influenced by the fact that the step up to a mile would be in his favour given that his brilliant sire won the St Leger in 1909 and the Gold Cup. This confidence was well placed, Gainsborough won the Guineas by a length-and-a-half. Lady James Douglas thus became the first female owner-breeder of a Classic winner.

In June Gainsborough won the Derby, run at Newmarket, in comfortable fashion. Later in the summer he added the St Leger which had been renamed the September Stakes and was also run at the Suffolk course. By doing so, Gainsborough became one of a select trio of horses (the other two were stable companion Gay Crusader and Pommern) to win the "substitute Triple Crown".

Royal Hunt Cup Record 14 June 1919

The Great War ended in November 1918 and the huge task of demobilisation began soon after. At the end of the conflict the British Army numbered around four million soldiers, within a year this figure was reduced to under one million in a massive logistical exercise conducted with classic military precision – at least it would have been had politicians not become involved. Tortuous debates ensued regarding the order in which the troops should return. Demobilisation on a "first in, first out" approach was proposed, though MPs with an eye on the ecomony suggested bringing home those with more valuable skills first. An age-based selection criterior was favoured by a few, with others opting for the return to be "batallion by batallion". All the while the morale of the men overseas was sinking to new levels and dissention was rising.

Getting the troops home from Europe was the first step in a complex post-war rebuilding process; the second was reintegration into society. These servicemen had been promised a better life after the war but on returning to Britain they soon realised that, if anything, their quality of life would be much poorer than it was the day they joined up. The war had had a withering impact on almost every aspect of society. The economy was in a parlous state, unemployment was rising fast, and there was an acute housing shortage facing those returning from the front line.

In social terms, the war had blurred the lines between the classes. Although the social order was still evident, from 1914 to 1918 working class men stood shoulder to shoulder with their titled compatriots in the trenches. This led to a less deferential attitude, and the Edwardian era's class hierarchy was fast diminishing. Moreover the *Representation of the People Act* gave the vote to all men over the age of twenty-one and women over the age of thirty (subject to residency conditions); one seismic electoral instant 'trebled the franchise' giving a voice to a much wider range of the population.

Those dissatisfied with their lot were far more inclined to protest. Police and troops were instructed to break-up a mass rally in Glasgow which the Government thought may ultimately lead to anarchy on the scale witnessed during the 1917 Russian Revolution. Such unrest had been anticipated, and as early as 1916 radical plans for a post-war Britain were being discussed in parliament. Education was at the centre of these ideas with a better-educated population considered to be more productive. Proposals included increasing the school leaving age from thirteen to fourteen, 'something to which the trades unions put up enormous resistance', and the introduction of compulsory post-school education for those in work but under sixteen. Provision of new housing was another area that needed to be overhauled with some estimates suggesting that over a million additional homes were required. Lack of manpower through the war years, and a stagnation in house-building pre-war, had compounded this problem. A Government fearful of a revolt ignited by prominent members of the Labour Party who had celebrated the Russian revolution and believed such action was the only path to a better world, was desperate to get the country back to pre-war normality. Addressing these key issues was considered an essential step in their bid to restore the confidence and loyalty of a discontented population.

Racing was at least beginning to restore the fixture list to its 1913 order and racecourses once again began to flourish across the nation. The Derby returned to Epsom and was won by Grand Parade owned by the 1st Baron Glanely, known by his friends as William Tatem, the self-made shipping magnate from Devon. There was also good news awaiting those who enjoyed the splendour and pageantry of Royal Ascot; the June meeting, complete with Royal Procession, would return to Berkshire following a four-year absence.

After operating under extreme geographical restrictions since the outbreak of the conflict, racing was gradually returning to all parts of the country. On the Saturday before the 1919 Royal meeting, the four-year-old chestnut colt Irish Elegance was parading before racegoers at Manchester racecourse prior to running in the Salford Borough Handicap. At the same time, over 2,300 miles away, two British aviators were preparing their aircraft for a flight that would make history. Irish Elegance won in good style at Manchester, much to the disappointment of *The Times* racing correspondent who was looking forward to seeing the July Cup winner running at the Royal meeting four days later. The victory would undoubtedly mean that Irish Elegance would have to carry more weight than any horse had ever carried to victory in the Royal Ascot contest which would surely dissuade his connections him from running. Or so the reporter believed.

As the racegoers at Manchester began to make their way home after the six-race programme, some counting their winnings, others ruing their bad luck, an overloaded modified Vickers Vimy bomber took off from St John's in Newfoundland in an attempt to complete a non-stop flight across the Atlantic.

Pilot John Alcock and navigator Arthur Brown were trusting their two Rolls-Royce Eagle engines to carry them safely to Ireland and secure the £10,000 prize offered by the *Daily Mail* for the first continuous transatlantic flight completed within seventy-two hours. Plagued by technical problems, including a blown exhaust system and generator failure, which deprived them of radio contact, the pair battled through dense fog and snowstorms to finally land in Ireland on the morning of 15th June sixteen hours after take off. Alcock and Brown had demonstrated that transatlantic flight was a possibility and set a benchmark for all aviators who followed them.

Though not fully realised at the time, this remarkable accomplishment would have a lasting impact on horseracing. In the same way that the advent of the railways revolutionised horse transportation within Great Britain, transatlantic travel by air would open up many opportunities for owners: their horses would soon be able to race in continental Europe, the United States, and even Australia, without first undergoing an arduous sea voyage.

When the runners for Royal Ascot were declared, *The Times* correspondent was no doubt delighted to see Irish Elegance listed for the Royal Hunt Cup. He would not have been so impressed by the burden his fancy had to carry: 9st 11lbs.

Twenty-six runners lined up for the Royal Hunt Cup on the Wednesday of the Royal Meeting. The King's Jutland, carrying just 7st 5lbs and ridden by Champion Jockey Steve Donoghue, and Irish Elegance were morning favourites with 10/1 available about each in a race where upwards of a dozen horses were well fancied. In the paddock the two market leaders stood out from the rest: Irish Elegance's chestnut coat gleamed in the summer sun, while Jutland looked trained to the minute. By post time, they were down to 7/1, and still could not be separated; that would be decided only by the race.

From the start, Irish Elegance matched strides with fellow front-runner Arion, who shouldered just 7st 13lbs, the pair setting a solid pace. As the race progressed, the 7/1 joint favourite pulled clear, but it was not over according to one vocal member in the stands. "Arion will catch him," he cried at the top of his voice, "the weight must tell." But Arion couldn't catch him no matter how he tried. When jockey Fred Templeman asked for more, Irish

Elegance obliged. Try as he might, Arion could not match the 'marvel' as one reporter referred to the colt, and at the line was a length-and-a-half behind. In winning, Irish Elegance set a new weight-carrying record for the race and achieved 'one of the most magnificent performances in the record of handicaps.' Jutland did not match his outstanding appearance and finished well beaten. It was not all bad news for the monarch though, his Pesaro ran second in the Ascot Derby Stakes, and the day ended with a Royal winner when the King's Viceroy took the Waterford Stakes.

Alcock and Brown's flight would no doubt have given the more patriotic members of the country a considerable lift, and a winning favourite in the Royal Hunt Cup is always welcome amongst racegoers. However, it is doubtful that even triumphs such as these would have much compensated the many thousands trying to come to terms with the horrors that had so recently scourged their lives. The thoughts now uppermost in people's minds were finding new homes and new jobs in a starkly different post-war Britain.

Man o' War's Record-Breaking Win   *12 June 1920*

By the end of 1919, two names were on the lips of every sports-loving American: Babe Ruth and Man o' War. George Herman "Babe" Ruth had been hitting the ball out of the park for the Boston Red Sox since joining them five years earlier. In 1919 he broke the record for the number of home runs scored in a season, but even that heroic effort was not enough to qualify the Red Sox for the World Series against the Cincinnati Reds. An even greater disappointment awaited the Red Sox fans though. On Boxing Day, the Red Sox stunned the world of baseball by accepting an offer for Ruth from the New York Yankees. At his new club, much was expected of the former pitcher turned hitter in 1920.

Man o' War's first public appearance came at Belmont Park on 6th June 1919. Starting at odds-on the juvenile, who had cost his owner $5,000 at the yearling sales the previous autumn, made short work of his opponents winning by an impressive six lengths. Another three wins followed in June, then a single win in each of July and early August before a disastrous race at Saratoga on 13th August.

It looked like being another regulation odds-on success for the unbeaten two-year-old, but the combination of a terrible start, a poor run, and a significant weight differential brought about his first career defeat. According to some observers, after several false starts, Man o' War was still circling at the back of the field when the gate was released. After making up the lost ground, he was boxed in and impeded by runners falling back in the field at a crucial stage of the race. In the last half-furlong he was finally able to stride on without impediment and both horse and jockey made a determined effort to get to the winning line in front. But on this occasion it was not to be. Upset – the horse Man o' War had beaten comfortably by two lengths on their last meeting – took advantage of the circumstances and the 15lbs he was receiving from the favourite, to record an unexpected neck victory.

Back at Saratoga ten days later, Man o' War gained revenge on Upset. An eighth win followed in late August, and he rounded off the season with a win at Belmont Park, the track where he had made his debut three months previously. Much was expected of this potentially great racehorse in 1920.

Man o' War was sired by Fair Play whose racing career was adversely affected by the Hart-Agnew anti-gambling legislation. However, he still enjoyed considerable success on the track over distances up to fourteen furlongs, so there was every chance Man o' War would be able to emulate Sir Barton who, in 1919, became the first horse to win the Kentucky Derby, Preakness Stakes, and Belmont Stakes - the Triple Crown as it was christened some years later and awarded retrospectively. This notion was quickly dispelled when Samuel Riddle, Man o' War's owner, decided against declaring him for the 1920 Kentucky Derby believing that it was too early for the young horse to race over ten furlongs. He obviously thought a nine-furlong race was acceptable because in mid-May, ten days after the Derby, Man o' War won the Preakness Stakes by a length-and-a-half from his old foe, Upset. At the end of the month, Man o' War set an American record for the mile when winning the Withers Stakes in a time of 1m 35.8s despite being eased down in the closing stages of the contest.

On 12th June 1920 as Man o' War was being paraded before the third leg of the Triple Crown, the Belmont Stakes, the huge crowd at the track were unaware they were about to witness one the most memorable racing performances of the era. In the parade ring Louis Feustel turned to jockey Clarence Kummer, "The crowd want to see this fellow do something", he said "let him race and we'll get a record". Kummer nodded, knowing what his trainer wanted. Man o' War was first away from the gate and first past the finishing post, his single rival, the highly regarded Donnaconna who was widely considered to be the second best colt in the country, effectively never in the race. The jockey eased the 1/20 favourite in the last furlong but still had twenty lengths to spare at the line. Beating a single opponent is not a particularly notable achievement, but what made this race special was the race time. By completing the course in a time of 2m 14.2s Man o' War set a new record for races over eleven furlongs, a record that remained unmatched until 1961.

Man o' War added another eight wins to his tally including a handicap at odds of 1/100, a thirteen-furlong match at Belmont Park for which his winning margin was reported to be a quarter of a mile in a new record time of 2m 40s, and the Jockey Club Gold Cup. At the end of his racing career, Man o' War had lost just once in twenty-one starts and had set five American time records.

Babe Ruth didn't do too badly in 1920 either. By mid-summer he had equalled his 1919 record of twenty-nine home runs, and by the end of the season he had amassed an astonishing fifty-four. Ruth improved on this figure in 1921, and hit a career best total of sixty in 1927 setting a new record that stood until 1961, the same year in which Man o' War's Belmont Stakes record was broken, bringing the two sporting greats of 1920 together again in the minds of sports fans.

The First Prix de l'Arc de Triomphe   3 October 1920

The first Prix de l'Arc de Triomphe was run on 3rd October 1920. Unlike the Grand Prix de Paris, which was established in 1863 and quickly became the most prestigious race for three-year-olds, the "Arc" was open to all non-juveniles. Even so, eight of the first ten winners were from the younger age group.

Nowadays, the "Arc" attracts the best middle distance horses from every corner of Europe. This is not an entirely new phenomenon, though. The first race had a distinctly international feel as exemplified by the winner and his connections. Comrade was owned by Evremond de Saint-Alary, a leading owner-breeder in France and was trained at Newmarket by Peter Gilpin who, a few years earlier, had Pretty Polly in his care. On "Arc" day, Comrade was ridden by Frank Bullock who was Australian by birth and had ridden winners in England, Germany, France, America and, of course, Australia.

Bullock enjoyed more "Arc" success two years later when riding Ksar to glory. He retired in 1925 and took up training in which sphere he enjoyed more success in many of the countries in which he had ridden winners, and one he hadn't, India.

First Cheltenham Gold Cup   *12 March 1924*

The post-war era was one of significant change in every aspect of British life. The Great War had crippled the country economically and had set in motion the gradual break up of the British Empire. Technological advancements, several developed during the conflict, changed the way people travelled, worked, and lived their lives.

By 1924 the pace of change had increased rapidly and many "firsts" were achieved in the year. In the political sphere, Ramsay MacDonald became the nation's first Labour Prime Minister after the collapse of Stanley Baldwin's minority government. His tenure did not last long though, and the Conservatives were back in power by the autumn. The first Shipping Forecast was broadcast to New Year's Day listeners on BBC Radio, and a fortnight later the first ever "listening play" thrilled audiences across the country. And for fans of linguistic puzzling, the Sunday Express published the first crossword.

For racing enthusiasts a new race was added to the National Hunt calendar. On the 12th March 1924 a sum of £700 [£43,000] would be presented to the owner of the horse which won that day's Cheltenham Gold Cup. Despite the significant prize on offer, the Gold Cup was not the most valuable race of Cheltenham's spring meeting: both the National Hunt Handicap Steeplechase and County Handicap Hurdle promised greater returns for the lucky connections.

The 1924 Gold Cup was an exciting affair with three horses in close contention as they raced up the hill to the finishing line. The winner was Red Splash by a head from Conjuror II who was only a neck in front of Gerald I. It was a thrilling finish to a race that has continued to enthral racing enthusiasts throughout its long history.

Though considered the most prestigious Festival race nowadays, in its early years the Gold Cup was treated as a trial race for the Grand National. One racing correspondent wrote of the inaugural Gold Cup: 'I cannot believe that the winner at Aintree on March 28 was in this race yesterday.' The hierarchy was clear, and while rating a handicap above the Gold Cup may seem a bizarre evaluation of the merits of the two events, in 1924 the prize for the Grand National was worth £5,000 [£300,000] giving the Cheltenham Gold Cup a great deal of catching-up to do.

That momentous Cheltenham card also featured an intergalactic winner. The National Hunt Juvenile Steeplechase, run thirty minutes before the first Gold Cup, was won by Mount Rivers. As *Star Trek* fans are probably aware, Mount Rivers was trained by Captain Kirk.

Twelve months later Ballinode became the second winner of the Gold Cup and the first mare to win the race; it would not be until 1958 that a mare repeated the feat and won what has now become arguably the most prestigious race in the jumps calendar.

First Champion Hurdle   *9 March 1927*

Three years after the first Gold Cup was contested at Cheltenham, a hurdle equivalent was added to the programme of races. The first Champion Hurdle Challenge Cup was run on the 9th March 1927 for total prize-money of £500 [£31,000] of which the winner would get £375 [£24,000].

Despite a brief rain shower, the weather was perfect and a record crowd, keen to witness this first running of this great race, enjoyed a fine afternoon of racing. The most popular contest of the day, the National Hunt Steeplechase, attracted forty-three runners the largest field of its history, and yet not one of them had won previously under Jockey Club rules. Only sixteen completed the course, in a race won by Fine Yarn at 33/1.

In contrast to the National Hunt Steeplechase, the Champion Hurdle Challenge Cup featured just four horses. Blaris started as the 11/10 favourite. He had been declared for an alternative race earlier in the week but was withdrawn suggesting that connections preferred his chances in the new hurdle race. Prior to Cheltenham, Blaris had been competing in chases, which it was thought might have taken the edge off his speed. It was soon clear that it hadn't: he raced alongside Harpist for much of the contest then, two hurdles from home, sprinted away to win easily, his owner collecting £375 and the trophy. *The Times* correspondent was certainly impressed with the performance concluding that 'Blaris has established sound claims to be considered the best hurdler in training, just as he is, in all probability, the best young steeplechaser.'

The following year the race was won by the remarkable Brown Jack who then added the Goodwood Cup, Doncaster Cup, Chester Cup, Ebor Handicap and six wins in the Queen Alexandra Stakes to his long list of victories.

Twelve years passed before a mare was successful in the contest. On the eve of the Second World War, African Sister, ridden by Keith Piggott, won the race at a price of 10/1 in extremely fortunate circumstances. A long way off the pace, African Sister was seemingly well beaten as the runners approached the closing stages of the race. However, a melee at the last hurdle ended the chances of all runners that were in front of her. The fortunate African Sister was left in the lead and came home the three-length winner. Without that particular last hurdle incident a mare would not have won the Champion Hurdle until Dawn Run in 1984.

Fewest Finishers in the National   30 March 1928

Heavy overnight rain before the Grand National is always of concern to the runners' connections because the resultant soft going increases the severity of the test and generally produces a higher ratio of casualties. Such was the case in 1928, but even the most experienced Grand National observers would not have suspected that only two of the forty-two starters would cross the finishing line, and one of those only made it after being remounted.

Tipperary Tim, ridden by William Dutton, an amateur jockey and full time solicitor, started at odds of 100/1, a price that reasonably reflected his chance of success before the race started. After the first circuit of the 1928 Aintree showpiece his odds would have been much closer to 2/1.

Following two false starts the runners charged towards the first fence in front of a crowd that left no room in the stands for latecomers. All partnerships remained intact after the first, but the next few fences claimed their customary number of fallers. It was the open ditch at the Canal Turn that caused the most fallers, though. More than twenty horses were taken out of the race by this single obstacle. And by the time the field had cleared it for a second time only three remained on their feet: Great Span, Billy Barton, and Tipperary Tim. Great Span fell two fences from home and Billy Barton fell at the last, though his jockey remounted. That left the 100/1 shot to come home at his leisure, and in so doing he became the first "tubed" winner of the Grand National.

Introduction of the Tote   2 July 1929

There's no doubting the sound economic principle that underpinned the introduction of the Tote in 1929. Rather than lining the pockets of wealthy Bookmakers, the guaranteed profits generated on every race could be invested in the sport once the expenses of running the service had been deducted. Other countries that staged racing had for some years realised the potential of Tote-style betting and had benefited considerably after its introduction. Some even went a step further and allowed the Tote to operate as a monopoly. In Britain it was thought that the introduction of the Tote would ultimately lead to the eradication of illegal gambling by providing an alternative that punters would consider safer than dealing directly with unregulated Bookmakers.

The Tote first appeared at Carlisle and Newmarket on 2nd July 1929. The two 'brown bungalow-like' buildings, as *The Times* described them, which housed the Tote employees and their equipment were situated between the main betting rings. They were quickly nicknamed the "Hencoops" and although the *Daily Mail* claimed that 'women like the Tote' it was generally shunned by the majority of punters. Like so many large-scale Government projects, good intentions were not supported by sound planning.

In France and Australia the Tote-style machines were powered by electricity making the process of accepting bets less time-consuming. This also facilitated the calculation of payout dividends within seconds. Anyone lucky enough to pick a winner would be made aware of the payout as soon as the jockey had weighed-in. The British machines were manual in design, and had to be worked by hand, significantly slowing the transaction process and delaying the payout. They were also subject to error; on the very first race in which the Tote was used the 'figures went wrong on the total board' according to one on-course observer. There was a nice bonus for winning punters though. The winner, Huncoat, paid 39/1 on the Tote compared to an official starting price of 33/1. Unfortunately for those in favour of the Tote the second race was won by the King's horse which had attracted a great deal of small bets. The Tote price of 5/1 compared poorly to a ring price of 100/15. Despite the teething problems and variable payout, The Times racing correspondent seemed quite impressed, concluding his article with 'Quite a lot of money went through the machine, which, I venture to prophesy, has come to stay.'

To a certain extent he was correct, the Tote is still with us. But the sale to BetFred was a major mistake by the authorities. Profits no longer stayed in racing, so those who wanted to support the sport through their bets no longer had a reason to bet with the Tote. Moreover, the margins were increased, reducing the amount returned to punters making Tote betting even less attractive. With the exchanges offering better prices and accepting bets via smartphones, it is now difficult to see a positive long-term future for the Tote.

The Rise of Phar Lap   *21 September 1929*

Very few racehorses make an impact outside of the tight-knit racing community. Even fewer are the subject of a film and a PhD thesis. Phar Lap was one of those select horses. On the announcement of his tragic death the whole Australasian continent mourned such was the affection with which he was held. According to *The Mercury* 'Tears were shed silently in many a home.'

Foaled in New Zealand, Phar Lap was purchased on behalf of the successful businessman David Davis for 160gns. His pedigree was far from impressive, and when he arrived in Australia his appearance matched his breeding. The horse was thin, over-grown and had an awkward gait. To make him even less appealing there were several warts on his face. His new owner took an immediate dislike to the colt and it took much persuasion on the part of his prospective trainer for Davis not to send the horse straight back. Finally an agreement was reached whereby his trainer, the Sydney-based Harry Telford, would lease the animal from Davis.

As a two-year-old Phar Lap, which is Thai for lightning, achieved little. He was unplaced on his first four starts before finally gaining a success in a nursery (a juvenile handicap) race. His three-year-old campaign started in the same fashion with four straight defeats, then a glimmer of hope raised the spirits of his trainer. At Randwick racecourse in mid-September 1929 Phar Lap ran second to Mollison in the valuable Chelmsford Stakes classified as a "Principal" race at the time, and a Group 2 nowadays. A week later on 21st September, Phar Lap won the nine-furlong Rosehill Guineas at Rosehill Gardens racecourse. The huge, backward gelding had simply needed time to mature and grow into his massive frame. Phar Lap may have been a 'pathetic-looking' juvenile, but now he was a powerful, long-striding winner who would only fail to make the frame in one subsequent race in his entire career.

Following his win at Rosehill Gardens, Phar Lap won twelve of his next fourteen races including the Derby and St Leger. His most notable failure was in the Melbourne Cup where, trying to make all on his first attempt at two miles, he was caught close home and finished third.

In the early months of 1930 Phar Lap put together a winning run of nine races. After running second in the Warwick Stakes in August, another long winning run began. During this period of dominance which lasted throughout the Southern Hemisphere's spring, Nightmarch who won the 1929 Melbourne Cup, finished runner-up to Phar Lap in four consecutive races. That was more than enough for his owner who realised that attempting to retain the crown would be a pointless exercise with Phar Lap in opposition. Instead, he opted to race his horse overseas.

Harry Telford's main aim had always been the Melbourne Cup to the extent that it had almost become an obsession. Phar Lap provided him with an outstanding chance of realising his long-held dream so, in the weeks leading up to the contest, every care was taken with his training regime. Even so there were some things outside Telford's control. As part of Phar Lap's preparation he was scheduled to run in the Melbourne Stakes three days before the big handicap. A quick-fire double looked a near certainty until, on the morning of the "prep" race, a car drew alongside the champion who was being led by his jockey on a small pony, and a shotgun was discharged in their direction. Miraculously neither of the horses, nor the rider, was injured, but it was a close call. Later that day the unflappable Phar Lap duly won the Melbourne Stakes. Three days later Telford was proudly holding the Melbourne Cup aloft after Phar Lap, carrying 9st 12lbs, had won Australia's premier race by an easy three lengths. Two more victories brought 1930 to a close with Phar Lap recording nineteen wins from twenty-one races during the calendar year.

After a break, he returned to the track with a win on 14th February 1931, the first of twelve victories from thirteen starts prior to his third "Cup" run. Unfortunately for Telford and Davis, the Handicapper gave their star thoroughbred no chance of successfully defending his crown by allotting the champion 10st 10lbs. Not surprisingly Phar Lap, undeniably the best horse in more than a generation, was well-beaten in the race.

Taken to North America for his next race, in spite of his trainer's objections, Phar Lap won the Agua Cliente Handicap, the most valuable race in the world, in a record time. It was to be his last race. Phar Lap was transferred to a ranch in California where, in early April 1932 just sixteen days after his final stunning success, he died under mysterious circumstances. Naturally many conspiracy theories then emerged, including the involvement of Mafia-style gangs acting on behalf of Bookmakers. The cause of his death remained a problem-unsolved until Associate Professor Ivan Kempson and Dermot Henry from *Museum Victoria* were given access to hair samples for testing. On examination they found a high level of arsenic and concluded that Phar Lap was poisoned either accidentally or with malicious intent.

It was a sad end to the career of a horse that inspired several books and a film. Phar Lap, who featured on a postage stamp in the 1970s, was inducted into the Australian and New Zealand Halls of Fame and is now considered a national icon. His hide, skeleton, and heart have been exhibited in museums since his death, and a life-size bronze sculpture has been created in his honour and is displayed near his place of birth at Timaru. The Melbourne Cup may be the race that stops a nation; Phar Lap was a horse that enthralled a continent.

Stormy Times for Ascot and England   *18 June 1930*

In the summer of 1930 a small band of Australian sportsmen arrived in England with one aim: to win a small ash-filled urn. While it may not be the most glamorous trophy in the world of sport, since the diminutive vase was first presented in the early 1880s it has become the most coveted prize in cricket and has engendered an intense sporting rivalry between England and Australia.

Among the tourists that summer was a twenty-one-year-old estate agent from Cootamundra, New South Wales, who was taking part in his first overseas tour. He possessed an unorthodox style but played with absolute focus and a half-smile that hinted at utter self-belief. And by all accounts, he could bat a bit. On the scorecard he appeared as DG Bradman, later in life he was more simply known as "The Don".

Inexplicably the first test match clashed with Royal Ascot causing a great deal of consternation amongst those who liked to be seen at such important events in the social calendar. At least the weather was fine and dry, and with Jack Hobbs making 78 and 74 runs England started the series with a comfortable 93-run victory. The estate agent was out for a paltry eight in the first innings but, worryingly for England, he put together 131 in the second.

As racegoers made their way along the well-worn path that provided the shortest route from the railway station to Ascot's Royal Enclosure, thoughts would have been about horses, betting, and the pleasant weather that made the opening day of the meeting so much more enjoyable. None of the attendees could have imagined what was about to happen that June day.

Partway through the afternoon the weather suddenly took a dramatic turn; the second day of the Royal meeting would not be as benign as the first. Ascot then suffered one of the worst thunderstorms in its two-hundred-year history. *The Sydney Morning Herald* reported that 'women parading on the lawn rushed pell mell for shelter. Their frocks were ruined in the deluge.' The rain continued for almost an hour causing the enclosure and paddock to flood. Any wooden items of racecourse furniture that were not fixed to either the building or the ground began to float as the water levels rose. Spectators were compelled to wade, ankle deep, when making their way to the stands.

The loss of an expensive outfit may have been the cause of much distress to some members, but for one person the impact of the storm was altogether more serious. As the thunder continued, several racegoers witnessed lightning strikes in and around the course. While sheltering from the storm, Bookmaker Walter Holbein was struck and knocked to the ground by lightning that had been attracted to the metal of the umbrella he was holding. Carried to the first aid room, Mr Holbein was witnessed struggling for breath in a desperate fight to survival. Sadly, it was to no avail. The day's programme was then brought to an abrupt halt as flooding and poor visibility made it unsafe for the horses to run. Only two races had been completed, The Coronation Stakes, won by Qurrat-al-Ain, and The Royal Hunt Cup in which The MacNab made all against the stands' rail. Quite remarkably, the flood receded almost as quickly as it formed and the track had dried out by day three, so the final two days of the meeting went ahead as scheduled with the addition of the abandoned races from the second day. It was a stark warning to course officials, one they should possibly have heeded more than they did.

In the Lord's test match the following week 'Bradman's Brilliance' as *The Times* called it secured an Australian win. In the first innings he hit 254 runs with a range of shots that sent the ball to every corner of the ground. On a bright and cool day at Headingly two weeks later, he went out to bat after eleven balls had been bowled. After a couple of shaky shots, he started to dominate the bowling, scoring fifty in his first forty-five minutes at the crease. At lunch, Bradman was into three figures, one observer remarking that 'there had never been a more audacious, care-free hundred.' By tea he had made 200, and at close of play he had amassed 309 not out, a record for the number of test runs scored by a player in a single day. It was an impeccable innings that precipitated a considerable amount of praise from the cricketing press. As one writer noted, 'he pulverized the English bowling by a display of batsmanship which... was beyond all criticism.' Under the headline 'Hurricane display demoralises bowling' *The Toowoomba Chronicle* asserted that Bradman 'treated every ball... as only could be done by a batting genius.' Incredibly, England managed to escape with a draw.

The fourth test was also drawn, but by winning at the Oval the Australians could return home with the Ashes due in no small part to the efforts of the most talented player ever to pick up a cricket bat.

Dorothy Paget and Golden Miller   *20 January 1931*

The two-mile Wigston Steeplechase at Leicester was selected as part of Easter Hero's preparations for the forthcoming Gold Cup. The eleven-year-old had triumphed in the Championship race in 1929 and 1930 and the hat-trick looked more likely than ever after he disposed of his eight opponents to win the Leicester contest by twelve lengths and a distance. However, on the same card that mild January day, the short-priced winner of the two-mile maiden hurdle race would have more impact on Cheltenham's Blue Riband than Easter Hero or any other horse over the next decade.

Golden Miller had run well in his previous race at Newbury but, in the view of one racing correspondent, 'scarcely such form as to warrant such short odds'. His backers were never in any doubt that their money was safe though. Golden Miller took up the running with six furlongs to go and won the two-mile contest as he pleased by a very easy five lengths prompting *The Times* reporter to consider him to be 'a very useful young hurdler, although probably nothing like so good as his owner's other four-year-old hurdler Insurance'. The Leicester gamble on Golden Miller had been landed, and it would not be the last in the career of this incredible horse.

The owner of Golden Miller and Insurance, Dorothy Paget, was born in 1905, the daughter of the Conservative Member of Parliament Lord Queenborough and American heiress Pauline Payne Whitney. Paget was somewhat unconventional. By all accounts she despised men, not just one or two select individuals, but all men. The colour green also made it onto her list of "dislikes". Her staff at Hermit's Wood in Chalfont St Giles, Buckinghamshire, were given colours in place of names, and the only male allowed onto the property was an odd-job man who received his instructions from one of Paget's many secretaries, possibly Blue one week and Yellow the next.

Paget had a proclivity to sleep during the day and work at night. In her case, work was mostly playing cards, studying horseracing form, and betting. Remarkably, some Bookmakers allowed her to bet with them during the night, after racing, when the results were known. Her integrity was beyond reproach, and all of her selections were honoured in full whether they had won or lost earlier that day. Such a degree of trust between bettor and layer harks back to the Victorian era when bets were placed orally with no money changing hands until "settling-day". Eagerly awaited by winners, and met with trepidation by losers, "settling-day" was the day of reckoning for those with an interest in betting. The "Subscription Room", found in the celebrated Hyde Park Corner establishment of Messers Tattersalls and Son, was the location where many betting transactions were made. Though spacious, the room lacked any form of adornment except for a "painted libel" of Eclipse over the fireplace. A painted libel was essentially a caricature. In this instance it was probably the 1773 image of Dennis O'Kelly, presented as a macaroni (someone who dresses or speaks in an outlandish fashion) and riding Eclipse. A narrow lounge-desk was positioned in the centre of the room around which bets were settled. These transactions were described in some detail in *The Sportsman's Magazine*:

What most strikes a person present for the first time on the great settling day, is the business-like regularity with which large sums change hands; books involving the payment and receipt of thousands of pounds are balanced with a few strokes of a pen or pencil, and yet for none of these large sums does the creditor hold either bill or bond, nor can he by any legal means recover them.

Bets were honoured, with only a few exceptions, apparently far fewer than in the commercial world. Whilst some less principled bettors did fail to honour their bets, the threat of loss of reputation by becoming *levanters* was sufficient to compel the overwhelming majority to make good their wagers.

After a spell bankrolling a Motor Racing team, Paget turned her attention to horseracing and in 1931 purchased Golden Miller and Insurance for a reported £12,000 [£824,000] after their trainer, Basil Briscoe, promised her that the two would win the Champion Hurdle and Gold Cup. For once, a trainer's forecast about the prospects of his horses proved correct: Insurance won the Champion Hurdle in 1932 and 1933, and Golden Miller won five Gold Cups, an achievement that has yet to be equalled, and for good measure he also won the 1934 Grand National under 12st 2lbs in a record time. For many jumps racing fans, these achievements put Golden Miller at the head of the list of greatest chasers. Connections of Arkle, Kauto Star, Best Mate, and Desert Orchid may choose to disagree.

Dorothy Paget's unconventional lifestyle unfortunately did not lead to a long life; at the age of fifty-four she died of heart-failure.

A Good Day to be on a Battleship   *25 March 1938*

During his career on the flat, the diminutive Battleship won ten of his twenty-two races, a reasonable return for any horse, but the son of Man o' War was to make an even greater impact over fences. His first season as a steeplechaser brought three wins from four runs; then, in 1934, he showed that he was still on the upgrade by winning the American Grand National.

Two years later Battleship was on his way to England, specifically to the Reg Hobbs stables in Lambourn. He made an immediate impact in his new home by winning several jumps races and naturally thoughts turned to the Grand National. To many observers this was simply not an option. Battleship was not overly big, and the *Sporting Life* doubted whether such a small horse would be up to the demands of the Aintree course. Hobbs also had his doubts and, according to some, he convinced Battleship's owner, Ms. Marion DuPont, to withdraw the horse from the 1937 race.

Twelve months later Battleship's name appeared on the list of entries for the National, and this time his owner was determined he would run. The trainer's son, Bruce Hobbs, then only seventeen years old was booked to ride.

Bruce Hobbs was born in New York in 1920. Two years later his family moved back to England and at the age of thirteen he made his racing debut. His first winner came at Wolverhampton two years later, and by the age of sixteen Hobbs had been successful in ten races. The Aintree National would pose an altogether different test for the teenager though.

With Nazi Germany annexing Austria just a week before the National, putting nations across Europe on the brink of another war, there could have been no better named horse for the most prestigious steeplechase in the world than Battleship. So it was particularly surprising that he failed to attract the pin-stickers' and name-followers' cash and started at a generous 40/1.

After a wet morning, the race itself was run in brilliant sunshine which found favour amongst the huge crowd. Only thirteen of the thirty-six runners were destined to complete the course, and in the closing stages the race became a desperate affair. Battleship was behind Royal Danieli at the last but soon made up the lost ground to draw upsides. A two-way battle then ensued with the runners neck and neck along the 465-yard finishing straight. At the line it seemed almost impossible for the Judge to determine who had won. The crowd waited in anticipation as the race officials attempted to discern the finishing order. Finally the result was announced. The last pre-war Grand National had set a new record. By winning the Aintree contest,

Battleship, the horse considered too small for the uniquely demanding fences became the first chaser to win Grand Nationals on both sides of the Atlantic.

Although he was already established as a jockey of considerable potential, and was well known to racegoers, it was the Grand National of 1938 that brought Hobbs to the attention of the non-racing public. His success at Aintree came just three months after his seventeenth birthday and he remains the youngest jockey to win the great race. To complete a spectacular year for the teenager, in April 1938 he added the Welsh Grand National to his list of big race victories when guiding Timber Wolf home.

As was the case with many jockeys, the outbreak of World War II brought a temporary halt to his racing career. Hobbs enlisted and served with the Queen's Own Yorkshire Dragoons, reaching the rank of Captain. He was awarded the Military Cross for his role in an assault on a German position near Tunis in 1943. Fortunately he survived the war and, at the age of twenty-five, started a successful training career that lasted until 1985.

No Triple Crown Badge for Blue Peter 6 September 1939

Blue Peter must be regarded as one of the unluckiest horses of the twentieth century. Had the British Government waited just five more days before declaring war on Adolf Hitler's Germany then Blue Peter would almost certainly have been added to the list of Triple Crown winners.

Trained by Jack Jarvis, of Hackler's Pride fame, Blue Peter ran twice as a juvenile. He didn't trouble the Judge on his debut at Kempton, but improved to fill the runner-up position in the Middle Park Stakes later in the season. As a three-year-old he was unbeaten from four races: The Blue Riband Trial Stakes, the 2,000 Guineas, The Derby, and the Eclipse Stakes.

In response to Germany's invasion of Poland on 1st September 1939, Britain declared war two days later. Twenty-four hours after the declaration, the Doncaster racecourse committee announced the abandonment of the four-day St Leger meeting that was due to start on 5th September ending Blue Peter's chance of completing the celebrated treble.

What must have been even more frustrating for the connections of the unfortunate Blue Peter was that, after a short break, racing continued through the war years. Turkhan won the next running of the St Leger in 1940, and two years later Sun Chariot completed the Triple Crown.

Movie Inspiration for Female Jockeys *26 January 1945*

National Velvet was first screened in America on 26th January 1945. It starred Mickey Rooney and two English actresses who were both destined to become Dame Commanders of the British Empire: Elizabeth Taylor and Angela Lansbury. The film centres on a twelve-year-old girl who wins a horse in a raffle. She names the horse "The Pie". With the help of the racehorse trainer, Mi Taylor (played by Rooney), Velvet Brown partners her horse in the Grand National.

Much to the dismay of British racing enthusiasts, the movie was filmed entirely in the USA, with Santa Monica, California, replacing Liverpool in the racing scenes. After watching *National Velvet* many young girls would have been keen to emulate the film's heroine. However, they were unable to do so, not through lack of talent, but simply due to their gender. In 1945 female jockeys were not permitted to ride under Jockey Club rules, and it was not until the mid-1970s that a woman rode in the Grand National.

Riding Barony Fort, a 200/1 chance, Charlotte Brew made history when lining up alongside forty-one male jockeys to tackle the famous fences in 1977. The race was won by Red Rum, his third success; Barony Fort refused at the 27th of the thirty fences. Five years later, Geraldine Rees became the first female jockey to complete the course. On the ten-year-old Cheers she finished eighth. In 1994 Rosemary Henderson guided Fiddlers Pike into fifth in Minnehoma's National, and in 2012 Katie Walsh became the first female jockey to run into the places when her horse Seabass finished third behind Neptune Collonges. The writing was on the wall and it was clear that sooner, rather than later, a female jockey would take the honours.

In 2021, arguably the best female jumps jockey of any era, crossed the winning line in front of the men in the Grand National. On the 11/1 shot Minella Times, an eight-year-old trained by Henry de Bromhead in Ireland, Rachael Blackmore rode a perfectly timed race. Making good headway through the final stages of the contest, Blackmore had a narrow lead at the home turn, which increased to two lengths at the last. At the post, Minella Times held an advantage of over six lengths. It was an historic victory that set the seal on a wonderful year for the talented jockey.

VE Day Guineas   *8 May 1945*

On the 8th May 1945, racegoers made their way to Newmarket looking forward to the 132nd running of the 1,000 Guineas in jubilant mood. After six years of death and destruction, the Second World War had finally ended, in Europe at least. Although many thousands of troops were still overseas, some not to return for a further eighteen months, it was a time of celebration. The erstwhile gloomy headlines that had become a staple of the national newspapers' front pages were replaced by messages that were more positive. 'VE Day – It's All Over' was emblazoned across the front page of the *Daily Mail*, whilst the *Daily Telegraph* went with 'Germany Capitulates!' The Editor of the *Evening Standard* was clearly looking forward to better days with "Advance Britannia" as the main heading although he did add a note of wariness with 'Brief rejoicing – then Japan' as a sub heading. *The Times* refrained from printing headlines on the front page until 1966, but did find room to add 'End of war in Europe' to the masthead.

Many thousands of spectators, now free from the shackles of war and potential invasion by a hostile foe, packed the stands at Newmarket's July course on VE Day. There were far more than expected, and in the 1,000 Guineas the vast assembly enjoyed a master class in horsemanship by Harry Wragg. As the runners raced over the Bunbury Mile, Exotic had the lead, with Wragg's Sun Stream, the 5/2 favourite, fully five lengths behind. To some it seemed that 'even that great judge of pace was waiting too long.' A matter of strides later their doubts were erased as Wragg set to work on the favourite, threading his way through the field. On the ascent to the winning post, Sun Stream, still on the bit, passed the leaders as if they were rooted to the track and was soon clear by three lengths, winning unchallenged.

The concluding remark in the report in *The Times* that 'she is a filly of great brilliance' was confirmed four weeks later when, back at Newmarket, Lord Derby's filly won the Oaks by the narrowest of margins in a hard fought finish. Unfortunately, this brilliant filly never raced again.

Harry Wragg retired from riding at the end of the following season after recording his fourth Oaks success on Steady Aim for trainer Frank Butters taking his Classic tally to thirteen wins. Wragg had a successful training career, winning five Classics before his retirement in 1982. Strangely, the Classic in which he had enjoyed most success as a jockey, the Oaks, was the only one he didn't win as a trainer.

First Use of Photo-Finish Technology   *22 April 1947*

Photographic equipment was installed at five courses in the spring of 1947. The first race in which it was called upon was the Grand Metropolitan Handicap run at Epsom on 22nd April. At odds of 100/7, Star Song won the race by a length. However, the distance between second and third was much closer, necessitating the use of the camera. After a deal of deliberation it was decided by the Judge that Parhelion had crossed the line in front of the third placed Salubrious.

Prior to the introduction of this new technology, race results depended entirely on the Judge's eyesight. Consequently, many dead heats were declared in races where the Judge could not confidently separate the runners. The photographs made it easier to determine the finishing order, but mistakes were still prevalent until the use of a reflected image was introduced in the 1950s. Even so, in very tight finishes it was, on occasion, difficult to determine accurately which horse had gained the advantage and it was necessary for the Judge to resort to a magnifying glass and a print of the finish.

Nowadays the print has been replaced with a digital image with a superimposed finishing line. This speeds up the process of announcing the result as well as reducing the potential for errors.

Top Miler Contests the Derby   *7 June 1947*

Beneath an advert for "Choice Mixed Nuts – Walnuts, Filberts, Popple and Almonds (in shell)" a reporter for Melbourne's *The Age* newspaper detailed the prospects of the runners in the 1947 Epsom Derby. Apparently all turf writers were unanimous in their view that Tudor Minstrel would win the great Classic. To support that prediction the piece included a quote from a former stable lad: 'They could put a cart behind Tudor Minstrel. He would still win.' The public agreed, and the Gordon Richards-ridden colt was sent off the 4/7 favourite, the shortest price for over forty years.

Given his previous achievements it is not surprising that so many racing correspondents were convinced the favourite would prevail at Epsom. As a juvenile he was unbeaten in four starts finishing the season as the highest rated two-year-old in Britain. The following season, Tudor Minstrel returned to action by winning a minor race at Bath, and then tackled the 2,000 Guineas. Arriving at Newmarket on a showery spring day that was chilled by a strong northerly wind, the crowds that packed the stands were unaware that they were about to witness one of the most impressive performances ever seen on the Heath. Gordon Richards had one of the easiest rides of his career, and at the furlong pole he was already looking around for dangers. There were none and the Champion Jockey could confidently ease Tudor Minstrel down, passing the post still on the bit yet fully eight lengths clear of the hard-driven runner-up. Amazingly the time was just 0.2 seconds outside the record for the race despite the ease of success. *The Times* correspondent concluded: 'He was the easiest winner of a Classic race I have seen and must be one of the great colts of the century'. Immediately after this remarkable success the Bookmakers made him 6/4 for the Epsom Classic.

On the morning of 7th June 1947 heavy rain fell on the Epsom turf, though by noon it had mainly cleared leaving the going described as "good". In the year the race was moved to a Saturday, an enormous crowd filled the Downs with the majority expecting to see Gordon Richards win his first Derby. On the way to the post Tudor Minstrel 'put his head in the air and fought against the bit' according to a race report. This was a warning to his backers of what was to come. In the race he failed to settle and pulled hard throughout, expending vital energy in the process. At Tattenham Corner he held the lead but Richards looked far from confident, and within a furlong the favourite was beaten.

In post-race interviews Richards was adamant that Tudor Minstrel failed to stay, despite a pedigree that suggested middle distances should have been well within his stamina range. Dropped back to a mile for the St James Stakes at Royal Ascot he was back to winning form, cruising home by an easy five lengths. Fred Darling tried once more to get a win over middle distances from Tudor Minstrel, but in the ten-furlong Eclipse Stakes at Sandown the 1/2 favourite finished second.

Tudor Minstrel ended his racing career with a win in the Knight's Royal Stakes at Ascot on 27th September. His final tally was eight wins from ten races; his only two defeats were at distances beyond eight furlongs. *Timeform* rated him 144; only two horses have been given superior figures. Tudor Minstrel was, quite possibly, the ultimate miler.

His trainer, Fred Darling, had missed the whole of 1946 due to ill health and retired at the end of the 1947 season. During his illustrious training career he was champion trainer six times, and horses in his care won nineteen Classics including seven wins in the Derby and five in the 2,000 Guineas.

Gordon Richards' had to wait another six years before recording his first Derby success. In a career that spanned three decades, starting in the

1920s and ending in the 1950s, his one and only Derby victory came on Pinza in 1953, the same year he was knighted by the Queen. Richards won fourteen Classics excelling in the St Leger, a race he won on five occasions most memorably on the temperamental Triple Crown heroine Sun Chariot. He was light of frame and could easily ride at 8st without any undue wasting. This meant that he could ride pretty much any horse that was entered and, as a result, he would normally ride in nine hundred races each year. Occasionally his total exceeded a thousand. More rides produced more winners, and this allowed Richards to dominate the flat jockeys' championship from 1925 to 1953 losing out in just three seasons to Tom Weston, Freddie Fox, and Harry Wragg. No flat race jockey has come near to bettering his record of twenty-six jockeys' championships, nor the 269 wins he recorded in a single season.

A serious injury in 1954 meant that Richards could no longer ride, so he turned his attention to training and enjoyed a certain amount of success. Gordon Richards, one of the century's greatest jockeys, the winner of 4,870 races, died on 10th November 1986.

Record Field Size   *13 March 1948*

The Royal Hunt Cup, Lincoln Handicap, and Stewards Cup races are often referred to as "cavalry charges". In 1948 the Lincolnshire Handicap was more of a cavalry charge than most. On a dull spring day, a record-breaking fifty-eight runners lined up at the tapes to take part in the first major handicap of the season. Starter, Captain Chandos-Pole, had his work cut out controlling such a large field but soon had them organised and a smooth start was executed without any undue fuss. At the other end of the race it was Arthur Budgett who was celebrating as his 33/1 shot, Commissar, passed the post two lengths to the good over the favourite Clarion III. In 58th position was Loucose ridden by fifteen-year-old Ron Sheather who was asked to make a weight of 6st 7lbs, and that was before taking his claim into account. Later in life, Sheather had a successful career as a trainer and was associated with a distinctly better miler, the top class Chief Singer.

As well as the Lincolnshire Handicap's record field, the other races were equally well supported and a total of one hundred and fifty-eight runners featured on the six-race card. Those responsible for choosing the races that made up the Daily Double were not making it easy for punters by opting for the Lincolnshire Handicap and Lincoln Plate. Together these two races posed punters the challenge of selecting two winning horses (Commissar and White Ant) from a pool of ninety-six. It paid the lucky winners £72 5s to a 10s stake, and there were sixty-four winning tickets.

Double Exposure for Nimbus   *4 June 1949*

Nimbus made the record books by becoming the first horse to win a Classic as a result of a photo finish. In the 2,000 Guineas of 1949 Nimbus took revenge on the hot favourite Abernant, who had beaten him by six lengths in the Champagne Stakes the previous autumn, winning by a short-head. Abernant's jockey, Gordon Richards, claimed his mount did not stay, and subsequent races supported this view. However, there was a notable gap of four lengths back to Barnes Park in third. Such a significant distance between second and third suggests that if either of the first two had not raced, the winner would had enjoyed a wide-margin victory and been celebrated as one of the better Guineas winners.

Naturally, Abernant was not amongst the thirty-two runners who lined up on soft ground for the Derby a month later. Nimbus was though, and the 7/1 second favourite raced up with the pace throughout the contest. In the final furlong a three-way tussle developed between the Guineas winner, Swallow Tail ridden by Doug Smith, and the French hope, Amour Drake. Nearing the finish Nimbus, under Charlie Elliott, drifted away from the rail towards Swallow Tail, and Rae Johnstone opted to switch Amour Drake to the inside. The three thoroughbreds flashed across the line together, impossible to separate by the naked eye.

After examining the photo finish print the result of the second Classic to be determined by modern technology was given as the same as the first: Nimbus had won by the slimmest of margins, recording a noteworthy double. Amour Drake was placed second, Swallow Tail third and the favourite, Royal Forest partnered by Gordon Richards, fourth. The result closely reflected the view of the betting public with the first four home listed among the first five in the betting.

Not all of the drama associated with the race was confined to the racecourse. As reported by *The Kalgoorlie Miner*, the owner of Amour Drake who, through ill health, had listened to the radio commentary of the race from his bed in Paris died of a heart attack the following day. Whether the heightened level of excitement engendered by the close finish to the race played a part in his demise was not established. Winning owner Henry Glenister, who had bought Nimbus for his wife, may have not suffered from a heart condition, but he faced his own unique set of problems. Glenister was an employee of the Midland Bank and had embezzled large sums of money from his employer in order to finance his racehorse ownership. Unable to live a life of deception any longer, Glenister committed suicide three years later.

Abernant   *23 August 1949*

After Abernant's defeat in the 2,000 Guineas, Noel Murless switched him to sprinting and it proved a wise decision. At Royal Ascot the Owen Tudor colt put up an explosive display to win the King's Stand stakes by four lengths at a price of 4/6. He was the only short-priced winner on a difficult day for punters and was led into the winner's enclosure 'amidst great cheering', no doubt from those who managed to get out of trouble on the favourite.

His price was even shorter when he took on the three-year-old Star King and two older horses in the July Cup later in June. The Times assessed his chances as 'unlikely to be beaten', and so it proved. Making all, Abernant cruised to a three length success with an astonishing eight lengths back to the third.

At York in August, Abernant faced a small field in the five-furlong Nunthorpe Stakes. Heavy rain had fallen in the county prior to the meeting, but not on the Knavesmire which remained dry for the sprint championship. With the race distance and ground in his favour there was only ever going to be one result. This time Richards opted to ride Abernant off the pace and he didn't join the leaders until the final furlong. His supporters were then treated to a burst of speed possibly unequalled in the closing stages of any race. By the winning line, less than twelve seconds later, he had accelerated to a five-length victory in 'effortless style'. This success guaranteed his position as *Timeform*'s highest rated three-year-old of 1949.

The wins continued in 1950, and at Sandown he gave jockey Gordon Richards his 4000th career winner. At the end of the season, Abernant was again the highest-rated horse, a position he held for three consecutive years. With nothing left to prove, or win, Abernant was then retired to stud. Gordon Richards considered him the fastest sprinter he ever rode which supports the view of racing historian John Randall and pedigree expert Tony Morris who assessed Abernant as the best British sprinter of the twentieth century.

1950-1999

||||||||||||||||||||||||||||||||||||||||

In the second half of the twentieth century, the Jockey Club lost its battle against gender equality and women were finally granted training licences.

Shortly after, female jockeys were permitted to ride in races, but only a few select races.

The importance of jumps racing increased with the Cheltenham Festival gaining a level of support that matched Royal Ascot. France found a new champion in Sea-Bird, Italy celebrated the best horse ever to run at the San Siro, and Nijinsky dominated the British Classics.

All-weather racing was introduced in England, a farmer from Wales won the Gold Cup, and Derby glory returned to Beckhampton.

At the end of the century, punters employed artificial intelligence, in the shape of neural networks, to generate new, and far superior, forecasting methods for horseracing.

But most significantly, the two greatest jockeys of any era dominated their respective disciplines.

Champion Hurdle Trebles   *6 March 1951*

As the leaders approached the last flight in the 1951 Champion Hurdle it was obvious to everyone watching from the stands that a record was about to be broken.

Shortly after the start, National Spirit, winner of the race in 1947 and 1948, surged past the two French horses (Pyrrhus III and Prince Hindou) that had set off in front and quickly established a commanding lead. His quick, efficient jumping meant he increased his advantage at every hurdle, and the field was soon well strung out. Almost detached was the eleven-year-old, hat-trick-seeking Hatton's Grace. This order remained much the same until the horses swept down the hill. Heavy rain the previous day, and on the morning of the race, had made the going extremely testing and it was now beginning to take its toll on the free-running horses.

With the leaders beginning to falter, Tim Molony made his move on Hatton's Grace. Trained by Vincent O'Brien in Ireland, where the ground is always soft at best, Hatton's Grace was accustomed to the tiring surface and was far more at home on "heavy" going than National Spirit and many of the other contenders. He started to close on the others and the complexion of the race rapidly changed.

Hatton's Grace had the blinkered National Spirit in his sights and at the last hurdle was at his quarters. With all of the other runners well beaten, there was no doubt that one of these two great horses would prevail and become the first hurdler to claim a third Champion Hurdle trophy. The race was set up for a hard-fought finish, and to the crowd it appeared likely that every yard of the two-mile trip would be needed to determine the outcome. Then disaster struck without warning. Jumping the last, the horse that had given his rivals a lesson in hurdling throughout the race, for once let his jockey down. Whether it was the stamina-sapping ground that gave rise to this aberration, or merely a misjudgement, will never be known with any certainty. On landing, though, National Spirit lost his footing, stumbled, and fell. The race was handed to Hatton's Grace. The oldest winner of the Champion Hurdle had just recorded his third successive win in racing's most highly prized hurdle contest.

There was to be no fourth win for Hatton's Grace. O'Brien's runner lost his crown the following year to Sir Ken who emulated the former Champion by winning the race three years in a row. This meant that in the eight years from 1947 to 1954 only three new names were added to the trophy.

Persian War, who some say was the best hurdler of the twentieth century, recorded his own treble from 1968 to 1970 and See You Then repeated the feat in 1987 for Steve Smith Eccles and Nicky Henderson. His first success in 1985 was also his trainer's first win in the race, though the master of Seven Barrows has since added a further seven victories including the 2020 success by Epatante. No trainer has won the race more often than Henderson.

In 2000, Istabraq became the fifth horse to win the Champion Hurdle in three consecutive years. It is extremely likely that Aidan O'Brien's runner would have won it for a fourth time in 2001 had it not been for the foot-and-mouth crisis that caused the Festival to be first rescheduled for April, and then abandoned.

The Champion Hurdle is a race that horses can dominate. Since its first run in 1927 there have been ninety races, but only seventy individual winners with fifteen horses winning the race on more than one occasion. Whether this pattern continues throughout the 21st century remains to be seen but it can only be hoped that it does. Fans of high quality racing are attracted by the prospect of watching the best thoroughbreds, and to win the Champion Hurdle for three years in a row takes a horse of the very highest calibre.

Youngest Jockey Wins the Eclipse Stakes   *14 July 1951*

Just after three o'clock on the 14th July 1951 a round-faced fifteen-year-old boy perched atop the French-owned horse, Mystery IX, was being led around the paddock at Sandown racecourse in preparation for the Eclipse Stakes. The previous day the apprentice had won the Commonwealth Stakes on Zucchero and was undoubtedly hoping for a quick double. As he looked around the ring he could see the Champion Jockeys Gordon Richards and Charlie Elliott, and not far away the great Doug Smith was looking particularly confident on the favourite, Mossborough. One notable absentee was Scobie Breasley who was prevented from riding due to ill health. He should have been on Mystery IX. The teenager was in exalted company; the Eclipse Stakes wasn't a run-of-the-mill handicap at a low grade mid-week meeting. Poor races were not named in honour of great horses, and Eclipse was one of the greatest racehorses of all time. With a pedigree stretching back to 1886 when it was first won by Bendigo, the Eclipse had become as highly prized by owners and trainers as any Classic. The race had prestige, history, and a prize worth winning: in 1951 the race offered a purse of £9,440 [£300,000] to the winner.

Soon after leaving the starting gate, it was clear that the three-year-old colt, Llanstephan, would make the contest a true test of endurance. His aim was to set the race up for his stablemate, Sybil's Nephew, who possessed stamina in abundance and had recorded two wide margin victories over Mystery IX earlier in the season. With four furlongs to run, the pace-setter dropped away, but it wasn't the other Jack Jarvis runner that took over, it was Doug Smith on Mossborough. At the furlong marker, Mossborough was odds-on to win, the teenager's dream of Eclipse success was fading fast. Sybil's Nephew was staying on and reached the favourite's quarters, Daneshill was also pushing the front two, but all three were painfully one-paced. On the outside, where the more astute jockeys had realised the firmer ground was to be found, a fourth runner was accelerating and rapidly closing on the leaders. With mere yards to go he stole the lead; Mossborough tried to rally and make a fight of it, but he had nothing left. The teenager had timed his run to perfection and a third successive Eclipse went to a runner from across the English Channel.

After pulling up, Mystery IX made his way back to the winner's enclosure, a route his jockey would get to know well in the coming years. While unsaddling the winner, trainer Percy Carter turned to his young jockey, "well done, Lester" he said through a beaming smile. The boy nodded by way of acknowledgement, turned and headed to the weighing room. In his mind there was no need for undue celebration nor extravagant expressions of emotion; it was just another race and there were plenty more to come for the most talented jockey ever to sit on a racehorse.

A Unique Double   *6 March 1954*

Towards the end of 1953 Lester Piggott, who had just turned eighteen, was 5ft 8in tall and struggling to ride at weights under 8st 5lbs. His thoughts naturally turned to Jumps Racing where the weight range was more forgiving to jockeys of a larger physique. On Boxing Day, Piggott rode his first winner over hurdles at Wincanton, and a career as a National Hunt jockey became a very real possibility.

The day before the 1954 Cheltenham Festival Piggott was successful at Worcester on Carola Pride, a horse trained by his father. On the journey home they stopped at Cheltenham racecourse and his father told him that the following day he would be riding Mull Sack in the Birdlip Hurdle. In order to familiarise the teenager with the Prestbury Park track they walked its entire length that very evening, father telling son where to be at each stage of the race in order to preserve sufficient stamina for the famous uphill finish. Twenty-four hours later they were both celebrating his victory on the 10/1 shot; the pre-race walk had proved invaluable.

Just four days later, on 6th March 1954, Piggott was back in the winner's enclosure after winning the Triumph Hurdle on Prince Charlemagne at Hurst Park (the following year the race was transferred to Cheltenham). Of course, in June 1954, after getting his weight under control, Piggott won his first Derby on Never Say Die completing a unique Triumph Hurdle-Derby double within the space of three months.

Over the next five years, Piggott continued to ride in jumps races from time to time. His last ride over hurdles came on 18th February 1959, the same year he enjoyed Classic success with Petite Etoile. On a horse named Jive he signed off with a success, taking his hurdling career tally to twenty wins.

A Missed Opportunity   *11 September 1954*

The 1954 St Leger would have been Lester Piggott's second Classic success of the season, but the talented teenager was not even allowed to attend the meeting. Fifteen days after becoming the youngest jockey to win the Derby, Piggott was involved in a rough race for the King Edward VII Stakes at Ascot. Turning into the short home straight Piggott, on Never Say Die, went for a gap one off the rail. Simultaneously, Gordon Richards started to bring his horse, Rashleigh, across to the inner rail making the Bill Rickaby-ridden Garter the filling in a thirty-mile-an-hour equine sandwich. A certain amount of scrimmaging then ensued between the three runners with Rashleigh coming out best and ultimately winning the race. Never Say Die finished fourth. Piggott was accused of causing the incident and was suspended for the remainder of the day. He was also informed that he would be reported to the stewards of the Jockey Club, something no jockey wants to hear.

Piggott's interview with the stewards the following day did not go well. Unlike the vast majority of the racing public, the Jockey Club's Duke of Norfolk was not a Lester Piggott fan and he decided to make an example of the young jockey. Piggott was banned from riding for six months, and to make matters worse the stewards insisted the eighteen-year-old had to work for a trainer other than his father. In his autobiography Piggott wrote 'I was not to be allowed to set foot on any racecourse for the next six months... I was furious, but there was nothing I could do about the ban, and my season... disintegrated.'

The teenager's ban meant Never Say Die would need a replacement jockey for the St Leger and Charlie Smirke was offered the ride. Smirke was no stranger to the stewards' room either. In 1928 he was banned for riding for five years for, according to the stewards, failing to make sufficient effort to get Welcome Gift to start when contesting a race at Gatwick racecourse. Whether Smirke had made a satisfactory attempt to get the horse started in unison with the others or not, the penalty was harsh in the extreme. Unable to work in racing, Smirke had to support himself with a variety of jobs at a time in the nation's history when getting a job was no easy feat.

After military service during the Second World War, Smirke returned to riding and enjoyed Classic success in the 2,000 Guineas, Derby, and St Leger. He also had a cameo role in a classic of a different genre, the 1951 film *The Galloping Major*.

On 11th September 1954 Smirke was on Never Say Die, the favourite for the St Leger. Although last away he was soon in contention on the inside rail at the back of the leading pack in what appeared to be a fast-run race. Prior to rounding the bend into the home straight there was at least twenty lengths between the leader and the tail-ender. Smirke was content to keep Never Say Die out of the front rank, but on the inside.

With half a mile to travel the field began to bunch up; Never Say Die was still moving smoothly under minimal encouragement from his jockey. Just before the three-furlong marker, Never Say Die, with impressive ease, began to weave through horses. He was soon on the heels of the front-running By Thunder who had been well clear at one stage. By Thunder drifted off the rails and Smirke wasn't going to pass up such an ideal opportunity. He eased his mount through the widening gap. At the furlong pole, Never Say Die was clear and going away. Smirke looked over his shoulder and could see that his ever-growing lead was at least fourteen lengths; he eased the colt down and won pulling up by twelve lengths, the widest margin of victory in the fifth Classic. The Victor Sassoon-owned, Noel Murless-trained, Elopement was a remote second with Marcel Boussac's Estremandier in third.

Charlie Smirke continued riding well into his fifties and rode his last Derby winner in 1958 when he was fifty-one years old. Fortunately for Piggott there would be plenty more Classic opportunities but missing out on such an easy winner of the St Leger was very difficult for him to accept.

The Outstanding Racehorse of the Year   *29 April 1955*

As a juvenile, Meld sustained a serious injury that kept her off the track until the autumn. She followed home her highly regarded stablemate, Corporal, on her debut in a stakes race at Newmarket at the end of September, and then put four lengths between herself and the field in a six-furlong maiden race four weeks later. The style of this success prompted the racing correspondent of *The Times* to comment that 'Lady Zia Wernher's Meld is an attractive filly with reach and size. She was much too good... and being by Alycidon, should stay next season.'

Cecil Boyd-Rochfort's training approach for fillies was not to overwork them, so Meld skipped the springtime trials. At Newmarket on 29th April 1955 Harry Carr, the Royal jockey, was in the plate, hoping the lightly raced filly would give him his first Classic success. He had little to worry about. Meld was prominent throughout the one-mile trip of the 1,000 Guineas, and then pulled away in the closing stages to win by a comfortable two lengths. An overjoyed Lady Zia Wernher embraced her trainer in the winner's enclosure and thoughts turned to more Classic glory in the summer.

The weather was warm at Epsom for the 177th Oaks, and several of the fillies were sweating as they paraded in front of the crowd. At just over sixteen hands Meld stood out amongst her rivals, but not just because of her stature; she oozed class as all well-bred Classic winners seem to do.

Despite the strong field of thirteen runners, the race was run at a slow pace, so Harry Carr shrewdly had Meld running in second place behind Eddie Hyde's Hypermnestra. As the pack turned Tattenham Corner, the favourite was moving so easily that Carr let her stride on. Ark Royal challenged her and managed to go a neck in front, but Carr gave the idling Meld a slight tap with the whip and she was away, galloping clear of her rivals to win by an impressive six lengths. Meld had outclassed her opponents with her performance inciting a great deal of adulation in the media. *The Times* correspondent assessed her perfectly accurately when claiming 'she is the outstanding racehorse of the season... who would probably beat any filly in the country at any distance from six furlongs to a mile and three-quarters'. This was the accepted view amongst all race analysts at the time, one that would be validated later in the season.

Lightning, Strikes, and Rule Changes   *14 July 1955*

The Royal Ascot meeting of 1955 will be remembered for a trio of non-racing events: a delay, a rule change, and a tragedy.

The Delay: the meeting had to be rescheduled for mid-July due to a national rail strike that lasted from 29th May (three days after the general election) to 14th June. The strike was considered so serious that on 1st June the Queen declared a state of emergency. Ultimately the unions won the battle, and the newly-elected Conservative Government, under the leadership of Sir Anthony Eden, acquiesced to their demands for increases in pay.

The Rule Change: ninety-six years after the construction of the Iron Stand, Ascot officials finally agreed to allow divorcees to enter the Royal Enclosure. However, entrance to the Queen's Lawn was by invitation only and Court rules governing divorce still applied.

The Tragedy: on the 14th July, just after the Gold Vase had been presented, fifteen minutes of heavy rainfall forced racegoers to take cover. Lightning then struck a tea-stall and the electrical current flashed along the railings and into the stands. Many of the people that had congregated around the stall were thrown to the ground by the force of the strike. Whilst some were relatively unharmed, others were left unconscious, and one woman tragically died at the instant the lightning hit. The ambulance services were required to transfer forty-six people to emergency units at local hospitals. According to Arden, Harrison, Listed and Maudsley writing in the *British Medical Journal*, 'twelve patients were rendered unconscious for more than a few moments, and two of these died from head injuries'. Naturally, after news of the fatalities became known, the meeting was abandoned.

Incredibly this was the second time the Royal meeting had been adversely affected by a lightning storm in just twenty-five years, with both storms proving to be fatal. The course authorities must have wondered whether there was something attracting the lightning to the track, or indeed the region as a whole. Hopefully the designers of the newly built stand that opened in 2006 took measures to lessen the impact of any such storms in the future.

St Leger Success, Not a Day Too Soon *7 September 1955*

Meld dropped back in distance to a mile for the Coronation Stakes, but that did not stop her winning for the fourth time in as many runs. Her trainer's sights were then fully set on the St Leger and Triple Crown glory.

Many observers thought that taking on the colts at Doncaster would be her downfall, especially with the likes of Acropolis in the line-up who was considered an ideal type for the St Leger. However, there lurked an even greater threat to Meld's prospects of winning the Triple Crown, an almost invisible threat, one which could stop any horse from winning any race. Over the summer many trainers had reported horses coughing and it was only a matter of time before Boyd-Rochefort's Freemason Lodge Stable at Newmarket was affected. Extreme measures were taken to prevent Meld from contracting the cough, but as the final Classic approached it was apparent that this particular strain was singularly virulent and even the most stringent precautions were likely to fail at some point. Bookmakers even stopped taking bets on the race as runner after runner was withdrawn due to the contagion.

After the previous year's race it was decided to restore the St Leger to its traditional mid-week date. Consequently, in 1955 it was scheduled for Wednesday, rather than Saturday. This decision possibly saved the contest. As the cough's impact spread from stable to stable, more and more horses became infected. Had the race date not been switched, there may not have been any healthy runners left to compete.

On the eve of the race, Cecil Boyd-Rochefort assured Meld's supporters that her temperature was normal and she was clear of any infection. Her main equine rival had not escaped the cough, though, and was scratched from the race.

For the most part, the summer had been warm and dry, and St Leger day was no different. In contrast to the humid conditions, Meld remained cool in the parade ring as she had done at Epsom, and although appearing a little lighter was still in magnificent condition. For once she was not the largest horse in the ring, that accolade went to Nucleus, a huge horse that dwarfed the others and appeared more akin to a steeplechaser in size.

The Starter got them underway and Daemon set a slow pace for the first mile in company with Miss Rigton, Marwari, Beau Prince and Meld. In the straight, Carr took Meld to the front but was pressed immediately by the Lester Piggott-ridden Nucleus. Piggott switched his mount to the rails in search of a better racing line, then to the outside again, before mounting a powerful finish. Nucleus may have been physically superior, but Meld was a top class racehorse and she stayed on in determined fashion to secure a three-quarters-of-a-length victory.

Piggott immediately objected to the winner for taking his ground in the final furlong. The stewards were not swayed, though, and quickly announced that the result would remain unaltered. Had the finish been closer, maybe determined by a photograph, then Piggott would have had a better chance of a successful appeal. The video evidence suggested that the final furlong manoeuvrings did not cost Nucleus as much ground as his jockey would have liked to believe and even with a clearer run he would still not have gained the advantage. Confirmation of the result was greeted with a loud roar of approval from a crowd delighted to have witnessed the historic achievement by the exceptional filly. However, none was fully aware of just how much depended on the timing of the race: the following morning Meld started coughing.

A National to Remember   *24 March 1956*

It was the most famous finish to the most famous horserace in the world, but not for the reasons many would suspect. It did not involve several horses battling to the line separated by mere inches, nor did a vastly superior runner canter to a remarkable wide-margin success. The finish of the 1956 Grand National will always be remembered as the race in which Dick Francis and the Queen Mother's Devon Loch were robbed of certain victory by an incident that haunted the jockey for the remainder of his life.

As the leaders rounded the elbow, nearing the end of the gruelling four-and-a-half mile race, Devon Loch held a two-length lead over main challenger, ESB. Moreover, he was seemingly travelling the better of the two. This advantage increased to around nine lengths as he drew level with the water jump on the inner circuit of the course. The crowd were convinced that a Royal victory was on the cards and a deafening roar of encouragement echoed across the course from the stands. Then, with just fifty yards to run, and without warning, Devon Loch, ears-pricked, seemed to attempt to jump an invisible fence, taking his rider by surprise. He landed awkwardly with his legs spread-eagled. Dick Francis was left in a precarious position and was desperately trying to stay on by clinging to Devon Loch's neck in the faint hope that the pair could recover sufficiently quickly to get home in front of his rivals. Nine lengths is a commanding lead when viewed from the stands, and in most cases it's an insurmountable one, but only when both horses are running. With Devon Loch stationary, the gap to his main pursuer closed with great rapidity. Less than two seconds later Dave Dick on ESB passed the stricken pair to score a momentous victory. A forlorn Dick Francis, still mounted on a now fully recovered Devon Loch, could only sit and watch the winner crossing the line in what was the most emotionally painful episode of his racing career.

In 1941 Dave Dick had won the Lincolnshire Handicap (now known as the Lincoln Handicap) so by winning the Grand National on ESB he became the only jockey to win both legs of the "Spring Double". Dick Francis never did win the great race but he achieved more than most in both horseracing and literature. Born in Wales on 31st October 1920, by the late 1930s Richard Stanley Francis was enjoying a successful career riding and training horses. The Second World War put a temporary end to that association and brought him into contact with aeroplanes. As part of his military service as a member of the RAF, Francis progressed from ground crew to fighter and bomber pilot flying Spitfires, Hurricanes, and Wellingtons.

In 1946, his military service completed, Francis returned to racing and became Champion Jumps Jockey in the 1953/54 season. By the late 1950s he had suffered several serious falls and on the advice of the Queen Mother, an owner he rode for on many occasions, he retired from riding and began a new career as a writer. Focussing on crime fiction Francis became known the world over with his books published in twenty-two different languages. Several were also adapted for film and radio. Many writing awards followed his publishing success including the Golden Dagger Award and the Cartier Diamond Dagger Lifetime Achievement Award. An OBE and CBE were bestowed on him in 1996 and 2000.

Dick Francis died at his home in the Cayman Islands in February 2010; he was eighty-nine years old.

Italy's Greatest Racehorse   *10 October 1956*

As Roger Bannister crossed the finishing line at Oxford's Iffley Road track to record the first sub-four minute mile, a two-year-old colt by 1947 Italian Champion racehorse Tenerani was quietly being prepared for his first racecourse experience. Like Bannister, this horse would also become a record breaker.

Bred by Federico Tesio 'the greatest single figure in the history of Italian racing', Ribot, who was named after the French artist, was foaled at

Newmarket in February 1952. He was sent to trainer Ugo Penco and by the summer of 1954 was ready to race. Ribot made a winning debut at the San Siro racecourse in July, and then followed up with two subsequent victories to end his juvenile season unbeaten.

As a three-year-old, Ribot won four more races between March and September 1955, including a ten-length success over Derain when he was first tried over twelve furlongs. He was clearly the best horse in Italy but could he beat the fleetest middle-distance thoroughbreds the rest of the continent had to offer? To answer this question he had to race outside Italy and in October Ribot made the trip to Paris for the Prix de l'Arc de Triomphe, the most valuable race in Europe.

Despite his impressive form, the partisan crowd clearly favoured the home-trained horses and the Italian interloper was available at a very generous 9/1 on the pari-mutuel at off time. Running up with the pace throughout most of the contest, it wasn't until the home straight that Enrico Camici asked his mount for an effort. Ribot then stretched away from the field and, under a hands and heels ride, came home by a comfortable three lengths. Beating the best horses in Europe so easily was an indication of his undoubted ability, and given the tremendous reception he received as he made his way to the winner's enclosure it was clear the Longchamps racegoers realised that they had witnessed the performance of a truly great racehorse. The media had also finally woken up to the fact that Ribot was by no means just another "Arc" winner and flooded into the unsaddling enclosure with note pads and cameras at the ready. 'Miss Marilyn Monroe's press agents would have envied the attention bestowed on him by the photographers' was the view of Vincent Orchard writing in *The Glasgow Herald*.

Showing no ill effects from his trip to France, Ribot signed off the 1955 season with another impressive performance: a fifteen-length win in the Gran Premio del Jockey Club.

Kept in training as a four-year-old, Ribot started the campaign with three easy wins then faced the best British horses in the King George VI and Queen Elizabeth Stakes at Ascot. A wet morning may have discouraged some racegoers from making the trip to Ascot, but not so the Royal family with the Queen, the Queen Mother, Princess Margaret, and the Princess Royal all in attendance. With the rain-softened ground against him, there was a chance of Ribot losing his unbeaten record and High Veldt, carrying the Royal colours, seemed the most likely candidate to benefit if Ribot failed. Sitting just behind Ribot, he was moving better than the Champion for the best part of the twelve furlongs. However, in the last two furlongs Ribot rapidly put a very long-looking five lengths between himself and the Queen's runner to win his fourteenth race. High Veldt may have been a very good horse, but Ribot was a class apart.

A regulation eight-length win at San Siro racecourse followed before he took on the best of the current crop of middle-distance thoroughbreds in the 1956 Prix de l'Arc de Triomphe. On paper the field looked stronger than the one he trounced twelve months previously. This year, two top-flight American horses, Career Boy and Fisherman, had made the trip across the Atlantic to supplement an already powerful twenty-runner line-up.

From the start Fisherman took the lead, which he maintained until the final bend. Once in the straight, though, Ribot turned the race into a procession. He powered away to win by an easy six lengths (some analysts believe the distance to be nearer eight lengths), the widest winning margin for the race at the time. The best middle-distance horses in Europe and America were left toiling in his wake. And his record-breaking achievements did not stop with the margin of success. The "Arc" was his sixteenth successive victory, meaning Ribot had surpassed Nearco's record for the number of consecutive wins by an Italian racehorse.

His magnificent performance was reported as far afield as the United States. *The Sarasota Journal* concluded its race summary with 'Ribot won 33 million francs after stepping off the distance in 2:36'. Once in the unsaddling enclosure, the "Italian wonder horse" was given 'a reception reserved for the very great champions' according to *The Times* racing correspondent. Ribot's two wins in France assured him of a place in this elite set and some highly respected racing historians consider him the best of the lot. After watching these races it is difficult to argue against such a proposition.

The Queen's First Classic Winner   *7 June 1957*

Although Carrozza beat Rose Royale II in the Princess Elizabeth Stakes, the French runner gained her revenge in the fillies' mile Classic. At Newmarket she prevailed by a length with the Queen's filly back in fourth. Classic form is so highly valued by punters that, at Epsom, Rose Royale II was backed down to 11/10 for the Oaks with Mulberry Harbour (also owned by the Queen) the second favourite at 11/4. Carrozza was relatively unfancied at 100/8.

In the race, Rose Royale II was slowly away and both of the Queen's fillies took up positions in the leading pack. After rounding Tattenham Corner,

Lester Piggott slipped Carrozza through a gap against the running rail taking her to the front with three furlongs left to race. Mulberry Harbour, in the Queen's first colours, dropped away tamely and although the favourite moved smoothly into contention, the main threat came from Silken Glider. The Irish-trained filly made up several lengths in the closing stages and appeared to join Carrozza on the line, with a fading Rose Royale II back in third. A photo finish was called and, according to some observers, the result was announced in hardly any time at all. Queen Elizabeth II had her first Classic winner, due in no small part to the strength and brilliance of Lester Piggott. The following day the *Daily Mail* reported that, on returning to her box, the Queen was presented with a print of the photo finish to add to her scrapbook.

Carrozza's win gave Lester Piggott a Classic double; forty-eight hours earlier he had won the Derby on Crepello. It was also a Classic double for trainer Noel Murless who, at the time, was based at Warren Place Stables in Newmarket and was about to embark on a period of domination. Murless won the trainers' championship that season, then again in 1959, 1960 and 1961 with Lester Piggott playing no small part in his ascendency to a position of pre-eminence.

Even the Greatest Get It Wrong Occasionally 5 June 1959

As a two-year-old Petite Etoile could not be considered the outstanding filly of her age group. In fact, she was not even the best filly at Warren Place. Her two wins from four runs in 1958 showed that the daughter of Petition had potential, but Murless and his stable jockey Lester Piggott preferred stablemate Collyria. The Official Handicapper agreed, and at the end of the season Petite Etoile was rated well below the best juveniles such as the exceptionally fast Jack Colling-trained Champion Juvenile Filly Rosalba, winner of the 1958 Cornwallis Stakes.

In 1959 the Prince Aly Khan-owned grey made her seasonal reappearance in the Free Handicap at Newmarket. Piggott opted to ride Short Sentence, so George Moore (who was retained by the Prince to ride his horses in France) took over on Petite Etoile who, under top weight, had no difficulty sprinting away from the field to win by three lengths. Despite this impressive performance, and after discussing the relative merits of the fillies with trainer Noel Murless, Piggott chose to ride Collyria in the 1,000 Guineas a few weeks later. The decision was heavily swayed by the impressive work Collyria had been putting in on the gallops. This time Doug Smith got the ride on Petite Etoile and recorded his second win in the fillies' Classic when the 8/1 shot proved too strong for her thirteen opponents winning by a length from the 9/4 favourite Rosalba. Finally Piggott and Murless realised they had a top class filly on their hands, and at Epsom Lester was not going to pass her over again.

Before the Oaks Petite Etoile's detractors were concerned that she would not have sufficient stamina for the twelve-furlong trip. The explosive speed she had shown in her first two races of the year, and her pedigree, supported that view. However, Epsom's mile-and-a-half track is not as demanding as many, and Piggott was confident she would get home. The market was not so sure: the Guineas winner was sent off the 11/2 third favourite behind the unbeaten Cantelo and Mirnaya. For all of his confidence, Piggott adopted tactics that would give Petite Etoile the best chance of staying the trip. The pair were last to leave the gate and Piggott settled the filly off the pace against the inside running rail, ensuring she took the shortest route around the horseshoe-shaped track.

The 1959 Oaks was not a race for the long shots. At Tattenham Corner the four horses out in front were in the first five in the betting: Cantelo and Rose of Medina led, with Mirnaya and Petite Etoile settled in behind. In the straight, Rose of Medina weakened and Cantelo shot clear followed by Petite Etoile with a motionless Lester Piggott exuding confidence. With two furlongs to go, the favourite was still under a hard drive, whilst Petite Etoile was merely cruising on her inside. It was then that Piggott decided to make his move; switching Petite Etoile off the rails for the first time in the race, she quickly joined Cantelo, and in 'six strides had gone into a long lead.' Piggott looked over his shoulder but could see no dangers and he allowed Petite Etoile to canter to the winning post, three lengths clear of the runner-up with a further five lengths back to the third. This impressive display was supported by a race time that was quicker than Parthia's Derby run forty-eight hours earlier. *The Times* headline writer opted for 'Oaks field spreadeagled by Petite Etoile', and the racing correspondent was as equally impressed, concluding that 'Petite Etoile [was] one of the easiest winners of the Oaks ever seen.'

Wins in the Sussex Stakes, Yorkshire Oaks, and Champion Stakes followed with Petite Etoile ending her three-year-old season unbeaten from six races. Kept in training as a four-year-old, Petite Etoile put up a devastating display in the Coronation Stakes beating the previous year's Derby winner in impressive fashion. In his autobiography Piggott wrote 'she absolutely hacked up, sauntering home in a half speed canter'. A poor effort on soft ground in the King George VI and Queen Elizabeth Stakes followed after which she was rested for the remainder of the season.

In her final season, Petite Etoile repeated her success in the Coronation Cup but it was clear that her previous majesty had lost some of its lustre. Her last race was a defeat in the Queen Elizabeth II Stakes in the autumn. Overall, Petite Etoile had won fourteen of her nineteen races. In any list of the best fillies of the twentieth century there's no doubt that Petite Etoile would be near the top. That's not just the opinion of the racing commentators and ratings analysts, but also of the jockey who knew her best of all but for some time did not appreciate quite how good she was.

A Betting Shop On Every Street   *1 May 1961*

It was all change for the gamblers of Britain on May Day in 1961. The *Betting and Gaming Act 1960* allowed, for the first time, bets to be taken in suitably licensed betting offices. Previously, punters who fancied a wager on horseracing had to either attend the race meeting or possess a credit account in order to stay within the law. For the vast majority of working people these restrictions effectively prohibited them from betting. To satisfy their gambling desires, they had to make use of the services of illegal Bookmakers and place their bets with "Bookmakers' Runners".

This illegal trade in betting was big business in the 1950s and had to be curbed. As one new shop owner commented, 'I used to have four men on the street, they cost me £400 per year in fines, but they took 2,000 bets per day.' Rather than taking a hard-line approach to betting, the Government opted to relax the laws. It was a sensible move, and had the desired effect of reducing illegal betting. Moreover, the law change also increased employment; under the new Act, "Bookmakers' Runners" were now gainfully employed in the new betting offices.

The Church was concerned, with some justification, about this development, fearing that a betting shop would appear on every street and swathes of the public would become addicted to gambling. To appease the opposition, strict regulations accompanied the Act with respect to shop design and opening times. No betting shop could open before 7am and all advertising was prohibited. Shops were required also to be 'cheerless and sombre as possible', but that did not stop punters flocking to their doors. By Christmas 1961 there were 10,000 betting offices in Britain which, according to the Gambling Commission, is roughly the same number as today.

Whilst the volume of bets has increased, the advent of online betting, and the move by Bookmakers to encourage punters to bet on casino style games rather than horseracing, will probably result in the number of shops reducing significantly over the next forty years. It is distinctly possible that by the centenary of their opening, betting offices will have succumbed to the same fate as video rental shops and no longer be a feature on the high street. While that would be welcome by some, there would no doubt be a few hardened punters who would mourn their demise.

A Flying Start Over Hurdles   *28 December 1963*

As America was still trying to come to terms with the assassination of their popular President, John Kennedy's distant relations in County Wexford would no doubt have noticed Flyingbolt's winning debut over hurdles.

Earlier in the year Tom Dreaper's four-year-old had made a less than auspicious start to his racing career when well beaten in a flat race at Leopardstown. However, just a few months later he won a National Hunt Flat Race over two miles at Navan and then put his flat racing hoodoo behind him by taking the Cabinteely Plate. It was jumps racing where he was to excel, though, and by the end of the 1963/64 National Hunt season he had won all four of his hurdle races including the Gloucestershire Hurdle at the Cheltenham Festival. This final victory of the season consolidated him as the top novice hurdler in the British Isles.

Following a summer break, Flyingbolt won the Sandymount novices' chase at Leopardstown. Four further straight wins, which included a success in the championship race at Cheltenham, confirmed the view that he was the best two-mile chaser in training.

A warm-up race over hurdles in the autumn of 1965 brought his winning run (eleven races) to an end, but back over fences next time out he was able to give weight and a five-length beating to his rivals. Three more wins followed before he recorded his most significant win to date: in the two-mile Champion Chase at Cheltenham he cantered home by fifteen lengths. The following day he showed his versatility to run third in the Champion Hurdle, and the following month he demonstrated an unexpected level of stamina when winning the Irish Grand National over 3 miles 2 furlongs whilst carrying 12st 7lbs.

Illness, in the shape of brucellosis, then intervened and whilst Flyingbolt did make a comeback he never regained his former brilliance.

163

To put his ability into a numerical perspective, Flyingbolt was rated just 1lb behind stablemate Arkle, and given his greater versatility it could be argued that he was the better horse. Barry Brogan, Flyingbolt's jockey for his last win, would certainly agree with that sentiment based on the thoughts he expressed in his autobiography.

Arkle   *7 March 1964*

Ask a hundred racing fans for their assessment of the best jumps horse of all time, and at least ninety will opt for Arkle. Although it is over fifty years since his last race, Arkle was so dominant that the impact he made on the sport still endures to this day.

Foaled at Ballymacoll Stud in County Meath, Ireland, Arkle won three consecutive Gold Cups, the King George VI chase, an Irish Grand National when carrying 12st, two Hennessy Gold Cups, and the Leopardstown Chase from 1964 to 1966, amongst other races.

Bought for a mere 1,150gns [£28,000] by Anne, Duchess of Westminster, Arkle was sent to Tom Dreaper who gave the gelding plenty of time to mature. In appearance he was not particularly special, however he did possess an unusually deep chest which required custom-made girths. His two National Hunt Flat Races revealed little to suggest Arkle was a superstar in the making, though he did win four of his six runs over hurdles. It was when he was switched to chasing that his extraordinary ability became apparent.

As a six-year-old, Arkle won the Broadway Chase on the opening day of the Festival meeting at Cheltenham (from 2021 known as the Brown Advisory Novices' Chase) establishing himself as the best novice chaser in the British Isles. Two days later Fulke Walwyn's Mill House won the Gold Cup. Touted as a Gold Cup winner before he ever raced, Mill House's impressive twelve-length success earned his owner a bumper payday after it was revealed that he had taken 200/1 about his horse over a year earlier. Thoughts and hopes of a match between Arkle and Mill House were already on the minds of the racegoers as they left the track. Eight months later their wish was granted.

At Newbury in the Hennessy Gold Cup, Mill House had to concede 5lbs to Arkle who, in turn, had to give the others at least 13lbs. Three fences from home the two great chasers were side by side and whilst they both cleared the obstacle, Arkle knuckled over and almost stopped. His chance of success was gone and Mill House swept to an impressive win. Opinion in the crowd was divided. Some agreed with Pat Taaffe that, without the stumble three fences out, Arkle would have won. The jockey was also overheard saying 'he'll never beat us again' referring to Mill House. Others would not hear of defeat for the Gold Cup hero who Walwyn referred to as 'the best I have ever seen.'

The debate was settled at Cheltenham on a cold, snowy 7th March the following spring. In the 1964 Gold Cup the vast ground-devouring stride of the imposing Mill House took him into a clear lead, and by the second circuit some Arkle supporters feared that it might be an insurmountable one. But Taaffe was not concerned; he closed the gap to what he considered a comfortable distance and then was content to bide his time. Three fences from home Mill House led by three lengths; Taaffe pulled Arkle wide to allow him a clear route to the post. Arkle began to close on the leader and they jumped the second last fence together. At the last Arkle was a length clear, and at the finishing line the margin was five lengths. Arkle's Championship reign had begun.

By the end of his incredible career the Irish-bred horse named after a Scottish mountain was never out of the first three in his twenty-six chases, winning twenty-two of them. Apart from his loss to Mill House in the Hennessy his other defeats were by the design of the Handicapper when he could not give 32lbs, 35lbs, and 21lbs to Flying Wild, Stalbridge Colonist, and Dormant respectively. Though unquestionably amongst the best chasers of all time, one unresolved question does remain: would Arkle have beaten stablemate Flyingbolt?

Starting Stalls Finally Introduced   *8 July 1965*

On 8th July 1965, the day the Great Train robber Ronnie Biggs escaped from Wandsworth Prison, the Chesterfield Stakes at Newmarket marked a new era for flat racing. Rather than lining up at a starting gate, the runners were pushed and cajoled into starting stalls for the very first time on a British racecourse.

The Jockey Club was only around twenty years behind the times with this innovation. Initially invented in the 1930s, starting stalls had been adopted by most other countries for many years and featured in the Kentucky Derby as early as 1941. Clearly a mere twenty years was far too hasty for some racecourse stewards, and it was not until 1967 that starting stalls were used for the Epsom Derby. In the Newmarket race on that historic day in 1965, Lester Piggott took advantage of this overdue modernisation and was first away from the stalls on Track Spare. In typical Piggott fashion he kept the lead throughout and recorded yet another win.

Sea-Bird's Arc   *3 October 1965*

A racehorse can impress in three main ways: a wide-margin win such as Man o' War's success in the Belmont Stakes; an effortless win like Nijinsky's victory in the King George VI and Queen Elizabeth Stakes; and a victory over an established champion still in his/her prime, Arkle's beating of Mill House readily springs to mind as an example. Sea-Bird's win in the Prix de l'Arc de Triomphe comprised elements of all three.

As a two-year-old, the son of Dan Cupid was slowly away in each of his three starts. Whilst this did not prevent him from winning at Chantilly and Maisons-Laffitte, on his third and final outing of the year he had to settle for the runner-up position behind stablemate Grey Dawn in the Grand Critérium. Sea-Bird was a useful two-year-old, but clearly not good enough to give a substantial lead to one of the best juveniles in France. Whatever Sea-Bird achieved as a two-year-old was essentially a bonus; he was always going to be much better the following season.

Stepped up to middle distances in 1965, Sea-Bird readily despatched all comers in the Prix Greffulhe and Prix Lupin by three lengths and six lengths respectively. Next on his schedule was the Derby, a race that would present the French horse with the sternest of opposition and surely test his ability to the full. It didn't.

On that sunny Epsom day, in front of an enthusiastic crowd, Sea-Bird simply sauntered to success from the Lester Piggott-ridden Meadow Court. In the view of *The Glasgow Herald*, 'It was not just a win, it was a slaughter of the innocents'. Piggott was equally impressed 'I rode this Derby in my customary way, and made my move... about the same time as Pat Glennon on Sea-Bird, but it was no contest.' To put the strength of the opposition into some context, on his next start, Meadow Court gave Piggott his first Irish Classic success by winning the Irish Derby. Later in the summer the same combination triumphed in the King George VI and Queen Elizabeth Stakes. Sea-Bird had beaten the best British three-year-olds in emphatic fashion.

Back in France, Sea-Bird followed his Derby win with an easy success in the Grand Prix de Saint-Cloud taking his run to four wins from four races as a three-year-old.

The main target of the season for trainer Etienne Pollet was the "Arc". Given his dominance over the summer, Sea-Bird could have been expected to start at long odds-on for France's premier race. However, he was sent off at 11/10. This was not the consequence of some aberration on the part of the pari-mutuel machine, it was simply due to the strength of the opposition. Sea-Bird faced the unbeaten French Derby winner Reliance, the similarly unbeaten Russian champion racehorse Anilin, and America's finest three-year-old, Tom Rolfe. In the parade ring the favourite was an imposing sight. Powerfully built, the 'beautiful walker' was only matched in appearance by Reliance. Both racehorses were sweating which was possibly a reaction to the huge, excitable, fashionably attired Paris crowd circling the enclosure desperate to get a glimpse of the talented thoroughbreds.

In the race, Glennon settled Sea-Bird mid division whilst the Italian challenger, Marco Visconti, set the pace. The champions from the East and West, Anilin and Tom Rolfe, were both well to the fore along with Reliance. Glennon looked unflustered as Sea-Bird tracked them from the middle of the pack. At the home turn Tom Rolfe made progress on the outside while Anilin continued his battle with Marco Visconti against the rails. Reliance moved up to fourth. Possibly unseen from the stands, Sea-Bird had weaved his way through the pack. As the runners straightened up for home he appeared two off the rails, bearing down on the leader with Glennon totally motionless. The great horse then cruised clear, and despite drifting to the centre of the course, Glennon was able to pat him on the neck and ease him down more than fifty yards from the winning line. Though not strictly accurate, *The Times* asserted that 'it was all over in two sweeping strides.' Arguably it took a little more than two strides but it was still an immensely impressive victory.

Sea-Bird won one of the strongest renewals of the "Arc" by four lengths with his jockey needing to make no effort. This one performance had all the ingredients of a superlative victory, one that can only be achieved by an exceptional horse. *Timeform* evidently agreed and Sea-Bird was allotted a rating of 145, the highest figure given to any horse at the time.

Gender Equality for Trainers   *3 August 1966*

In the summer of 1966, so soon after England's successful World Cup campaign had concluded, thousands continued to revel in the historic joy of this victory. Images of Bobby Moore perched proudly on the shoulders of his beaming teammates, the gleaming Jules Rimet Trophy held aloft, were burned into the consciousness of the nation. Daily routines began again with smiles freshly fixed on every fan's face.

In the world of fashion, mini-dresses were no longer the preserve of the fashionista who frequented Carnaby Street. Jean Shrimpton's scandalous appearance at the 1965 Australian Derby, without gloves or hat and in a white dress cut above the knee, provoked a less than welcoming reaction from the more conservative members of the track's elite. The model's day at the races, though, induced a boom in the sales of mini-dresses that quickly became the most wanted item of clothing amongst the younger female followers of fashion. With respect to music, the *Beatles* were dominating the charts and Eric Clapton, Ginger Baker, and Jack Bruce had formed *Cream*, the first recognised supergroup. The times were a-changing, to paraphrase another musician, and they were changing for the better. Britain had finally shrugged off the post-war austerity years and the whole country seemed to be in a brighter, more carefree, celebratory mode. Well, almost the whole nation: members of the Jockey Club were not in such jubilant spirits. After many years of fighting, they had just lost a battle they so dearly wanted to win. Prospects were grim; they had to come to terms with governing a sport that allowed women to train racehorses.

Whilst women had trained horses for many years, this was in contravention of the rules and could only be undertaken on an unofficial basis. In these cases the licence to train was held by a male employee. Norah Wilmot and Florence Nagle were two such trainers. Nagle was more active in pursuing the Jockey Club with the aim of gaining equality for women. However, it took her over twenty years and a long legal fight, opposed at every possible stage by the sport's ruling body, before she finally emerged victorious. The first licences were granted to Wilmot and Nagel in the summer of 1966, and on the 3rd August Wilmot saddled her horse, Pat, to win the 4:30pm at Brighton, the five-furlong South Coast Stakes for three-year-olds. Interestingly, this significant rule change did not make headline news. In the *Evening Times*, for instance, the issuing of training licences to women for the first time warranted only ten lines of text in a single column, and four of those lines referred to Robert Greenhill and Henry Stickley (the Head Lads who had "officially" trained the horses) relinquishing their permits.

In 1977, more than a decade after women were finally allowed to train horses, for some members of the Jockey Club the unthinkable happened: the Club finally permitted the election of women. The Countess of Halifax, Helen Johnson Houghton, and Priscilla Hastings were the first three women to join this exclusive Club, breaking through another barrier on the road to full gender equality in the sport. Interestingly, Johnson Houghton was "unofficially" the first woman to train a Classic winner. She was responsible for Gilles De Retz when he won the 1956 2,000 Guineas at 50/1, although

Charles Jerdein, her assistant trainer, held the training licence. Twenty-seven years later, Criquette Head became the first woman officially to train the winner of an English Classic.

But it's not just in flat racing where women have had an impact. In 1984 Jenny Pitman added Burrough Hill Lad's success in the Gold Cup to her win in the 1983 Grand National with Corbiere. Though notable achievements, both have been overshadowed by Rachael Blackmore's success in 2021. Her win in the Champion Hurdle on Honeysuckle, a victory that helped her become leading jockey at the Cheltenham Festival, was another first for lady jockeys. And yet better was to come. At Aintree a few weeks later Blackmore recorded a momentous win in the Grand National, a result that will probably have more impact on the future of the race than any other in its long history.

Six of the Best for Doug Smith   *1 October 1966*

Doug Smith won his first Cesarewitch on Canatrice in 1939; twenty-seven years later he was hoping to set a new record with a sixth win in the race named in honour of Tsar Alexander II. Founded in 1839, the same year as the Cambridgeshire Handicap, the two races formed the autumn double. Even though correctly forecasting the two winners required a huge slice of luck on the part of the punter, the races still attracted a great deal of betting. Persian Lancer, Doug Smith's mount for the 1966 contest, had already used up a good deal of his luck just to get to the starting post. He had finished third in the race in 1961, but then broke down and had to spend eighteen months convalescing during which time he reportedly became stuck under a bus.

Notwithstanding this period of concern and frustration for his connections, by 1966 Persian Lancer was back to full health and was well-handicapped for the marathon race. Despite Smith putting up 2lbs overweight, the public were confident of success for Lord Belper's runner and backed him down to 100/7 – some of the luckier punters managed to get 33/1 about the eight-year-old.

At just after 3:20pm on the 1st October Smith settled Persian Lancer well off the pace that was set by Miss Dawn. Riding a waiting race was not merely the preferred style of the jockey, it was a necessity on a horse that didn't like to be in front for too long. No one knew the Cesarewitch course better than Smith, and if anyone could produce the horse at the right time it was the forty-eight year old former Champion Jockey. By the time the leaders reached the *bushes*, many of the runners were well beaten. In contrast,

Persian Lancer was still moving sweetly on the bit. Smith was in no rush though, and it was not until the pair was deep inside the final furlong that he made his move. The timing was perfect, in no small part due to Smith's undoubted skill, and within a matter of strides the race was over. Persian Lancer had repaid the patience of his owner, as well as his trainer, Ryan Price. By recording an unequalled sixth success in the race, Doug Smith had yet again shown every racing fan that he was the master of the Cesarewitch.

Nijinsky   *12 July 1969*

The 1960s had been kind to Lester Piggott. At the dawn of 1969 he could look back over the decade with immense satisfaction having recorded six Jockeys' Championships, eight Classic wins, and three Ascot Gold Cups. He was now partnered with Vincent O'Brien, one of the greatest trainers of the twentieth century, and though he was unaware at the time, by the end of the year he would be riding one of the best thoroughbreds ever to grace the turf.

The previous summer, the American multimillionaire Charles Engelhard, genial in character, rotund in appearance, asked O'Brien to look at a yearling colt by Ribot at the famous National Farm Stud near Toronto, Canada (in 1969 it was renamed as Windfields Farm). Much to Engelhard's disappointment, O'Brien was far from enthusiastic about the colt, his expert eye spotting a potential defect in a foreleg. However, a Northern Dancer yearling with a heart-shaped star and three white socks had impressed the great trainer. O'Brien convinced the former WWII bomber pilot that he should part with $84,000 to buy him. Trusting his trainer implicitly, Engelhard agreed to the purchase, a Canadian record at the time, and the colt was sent to Ballydoyle, County Tipperary.

Just six months later Engelhard must have been doubting his judgement when O'Brien wrote to inform him that he had concerns about the colt's temperament: 'he is inclined to resent getting on with his work' he reported in understated fashion. This is not something any owner wants to be told, especially when such a vast sum of money is at stake and expectations are so high. There was one consolation for Engelhard: the horse could not be in better hands. Ballydoyle attracted the best and most dedicated staff, and through their efforts, skill and patience, the colt steadily improved. By mid-summer 1969 he was impressing anyone fortunate to witness his work.

The first target for the colt, now named Nijinsky, was the Erne Stakes at The Curragh on 12th July 1969. Reports of his impressive homework had found their way to the track and at the post he was the 4/11 favourite. The race was a mere formality for Nijinsky who won with ease, though only by half-a-length. As one of the stable staff recalled, 'after that first race all Ireland was talking of him.' Following three more wins in Irish two-year-old races he was sent to England to contest the Dewhurst Stakes where Lester Piggott would ride him for the first time in public. As was the case in the vast majority of his races, Piggott did not lack for confidence. Settling Nijinsky at the back of the six runners, nearest the far running rail, he was content to bide his time. At the furlong pole he eased the colt through a gap that appeared near the outside of the group and, under minimal encouragement from his jockey, Nijinsky swept clear of his toiling rivals. He was seemingly gliding over the turf while his rivals were ploughing through it. As Brough Scott commented, 'it was Lester Piggott in the irons, and as they toyed with their opposition it was clear that two super talents were blending into something quite exceptional.'

The following year football fans may have been looking forward to a summer of World Cup action with England defending the trophy in Mexico, but for followers of horseracing the big draw was a certain three-year-old colt named after a Russian ballet dancer.

Vincent O'Brien chose the Gladness Stakes for Nijinsky's return to action on 4th April. The colt had apparently put on weight over the winter and O'Brien admitted that he would be fitter on Guineas day. The result of the trial was no foregone conclusion either, with Nijinsky facing a strong field, which included Prince Tenderfoot, True Rocket, and the four-year-old Deep Run who would become well-known to jumps racing fans as a stallion. As Champion National Hunt sire, Deep Run was much sought-after. His progeny included Waterloo Boy who sprang a surprise in the Arkle chase, the 1993 Queen Mother Champion Chase winner Deep Sensation, and the talented hurdler Mole Board who won five of his first six jumps races, then later in his career, added the Grade 2 Long Walk Hurdle Trophy to his list of honours.

After leaving the stalls, True Rocket set the pace with Prince Tenderfoot; Liam Ward who rode Nijinsky in all of his Irish races, and won more races on him than Piggott, didn't let the front pair get too far away, keeping Nijinsky on their heels. With a furlong to go, Ward allowed the favourite to stride on. With the minimum of fuss, the three-year-old was soon clear, winning by a comfortable four lengths. In the post race interview Ward told reporters, 'to my way of thinking the Guineas is at his mercy'. Michael Phillips was equally impressed. Writing in *The Times* he noted that Nijinsky's price for the Newmarket Classic was 6/4 and added 'even that I find generous because, in my present mood, Nijinsky will be a confident selection on the big day.' Hopefully Phillips took the price because at Newmarket on Classic day Nijinsky was down to 4/7.

Under his agreement with O'Brien, Lester Piggott took over from Ward in the Classic. In front of a huge crowd, the Champion Jockey tracked the front runners until the *bushes*. Nijinsky then only needed to be shaken up to go away from the field and win under a hands and heels ride by two-and-a-half lengths from Yellow God and the French-trained Roi Soleil. A few days after his Guineas success, Piggott received a note from Romola Nijinsky, widow of the ballet dancer. It read:

I was tremendously impressed with your magnificent winning of the Two Thousand Guineas race this afternoon on the beautiful horse, Nijinsky, and I send you my congratulations. I ask of you now only one thing – please win the Derby for us!

As his price of 11/8 suggested, the opposition in the Derby was stronger than those he faced in the Guineas, with good horses from France threatening to end Nijinsky's unbeaten run. Some commentators had raised doubts over his stamina. Nijinsky's sire, Northern Dancer, failed to stay the twelve furlongs of the Belmont Stakes and several experts thought the Guineas winner might suffer a similar fate. Piggott had no such concerns over his stamina, but did worry a little about the track. Epsom is not a course that suits all runners, and in the past even the best horses had struggled with its contours.

Not long after the stalls opened, Nijinsky dispelled Piggott's concerns with his smooth, elegant action easily coping with the underfoot undulations. In the mind of the master jockey, the Derby quickly became a 'one-horse race'. At the furlong marker Nijinsky had two horses in front of him, and one upsides. Piggott pulled his whip through and gave his mount a tap and the response was electric. Within a handful of strides Nijinsky surged to the front, then drew clear to win easily. No one in the crowd was left unimpressed with the display, the commanding nature of which was reflected in the race time. Despite not being asked for maximum effort, the colt completed the race in less than a second outside the record set by Mahmoud in 1936. Nijinsky was led back to the winner's enclosure by his owner, Charles Engelhard, supposedly the inspiration for James Bond's nemesis Ernst Blofeld (Ian

Fleming was a good friend of Engelhard). The American philanthropist and war hero was congratulated by the Queen Mother after the presentation; he was in ecstatic mood, his twenty-year ambition to own the winner of the Derby had just been fulfilled.

An easy win in the Irish Derby followed, then at Ascot Nijinsky challenged the best older horses in the King George VI and Queen Elizabeth Stakes. It was a small field, just six runners, but packed with talent including a Derby winner and horses which had won the very best races in France and America. Piggott opted for a waiting race and held Nijinsky back allowing all but one of his rivals to battle it out in front. As they turned into the straight Piggott pulled Nijinsky to the outside and just let him cruise into the lead. Whips were cracking and arms and legs pushing in desperation as the others tried to stay with the champion, but Nijinsky was merely cantering past them. To trackside observers the degree of superiority was unfathomable. As Peter O'Sullevan said in commentary 'he's trotted up' and he had, with a motionless Lester Piggott just enjoying the ride. Piggott claimed that 'he was never better than he was that day'; nobody who had watched the race would disagree.

Throughout August the Ballydoyle team was nursing Nijinsky through a bout of ringworm, and his participation in the St Leger was in serious doubt. O'Brien was not keen to run him at Doncaster, but Engelhard desperately wanted to see his star challenge for the Triple Crown, and O'Brien was not going to refuse the wish of a man who did not have time on his side.

On Leger day, Piggott was in confident mood and blissfully unaware of the events that may have prevented him from riding in the final Classic. In the race before the St Leger, Piggott had the ride on Leander, another Engelhard horse. As the stalls opened Leander stumbled and Piggott hit the ground. Immediately several previously unseen men appeared from behind a cluster of trees. They didn't ask if he was alright, or even inquire as to what had happened. The first question posed was: 'Where have you been shot?' Apparently Piggott's life was in danger. An escapee from the Rampton Secure Hospital had made a threatening telephone call to the racecourse and the police were taking it seriously. Unknown to Piggott he had been shadowed all day by plain-clothes police officers.

During the pre-race preparations, Nijinsky was calmer than usual and to Piggott 'it was clear that some of the gleam had gone out of his eye'. Although he won his third Classic without coming off the bridle, there was a suggestion that he may not be the dominant force he once was.

Taken to France for the Prix de l'Arc de Triomphe two weeks after he completed the Triple Crown, confidence was understandably high among the betting public. Piggott held the colt up as he had done in previous races, and then made his run in the home straight. Although he reached the leaders he didn't go by them as he had at Ascot and Epsom, and Sassafras, ridden by Yves Saint-Martin, was able to get his head back in front on the line. The unbeaten run was over. O'Brien thought Piggott had given Nijinsky too much to do, but it was more likely that the great horse had suffered more from the ringworm than had been appreciated and was simply not at his best.

Nijinsky's final race was in the Champions Stakes at Newmarket. Unusually he was on his toes in the paddock and awash with sweat; this was not the Nijinsky that had thrilled the crowds back in the summer. Ultimately, he was beaten into second place by Lorenzaccio. Interviewed some years later, Piggott was adamant that 'over the summer he was unbeatable, in the autumn he was not the same horse.' Following this defeat, Nijinsky was retired to stud where he sired many Classic winners including Golden Fleece, the unbeaten Lammtarra, and Shadeed.

Vaslav Nijinsky thrilled theatre audiences across Europe with his grace and athleticism. His equine namesake combined those same qualities with power and speed; the result was pure brilliance. The Founders of thoroughbred horseracing, and many who sought to promote it, considered the sport as a mechanism to accelerate the evolutionary process and rapidly improve the breed. Had they been able to witness Nijinsky's performance in the King George VI and Queen Elizabeth Stakes at Ascot in the summer of 1970 there is little doubt they would have been both astonished and satisfied by how well their plans had progressed.

A Guineas to Relish   *1 May 1971*

In the late spring of 1971, the red half of North London was preparing for one of the most important week's of their club's eighty-five year history. On Monday 3rd May, Arsenal would make the short trip to neighbours Tottenham at White Hart Lane and attempt to secure the league title. Then, five days later, they would face Liverpool at Wembley in the final of the FA Cup. Two wins would give them a "double" that had only been achieved once before in English football. At Newmarket on 1st May 1971 an equally prestigious sporting event was taking place. For the first time racing fans would get to see the three best two-year-olds of 1970 compete against each other. That's nothing new, the best juveniles normally take each other on in the Guineas, but what made the 1971 race special was the quality of the runners involved. Any of the three brilliant youngsters would have been Champion juvenile in other years, fate just happened to bring them together in a single season. Whilst that may not have been ideal for the connections of the trio, for racing enthusiasts it made for compelling viewing.

Favourite for the 2,000 Guineas was Mill Reef. In early 1970 it was apparent to trainer Ian Balding that Mill Reef was a special horse. On the gallops he appeared to be vastly superior to his stablemates, so it was no shock to the stable staff when he won on his debut over five furlongs at Salisbury. His starting price may have been a surprise though: Mill Reef was sent off at a generous 8/1 despite receiving 7lbs from the 2/9 favourite. The colt continued to improve throughout the year and he carried Paul Mellon's black and gold colours to success in the Coventry Stakes at Royal Ascot, the Dewhurst Stakes, and most impressively in the Gimcrack Stakes by ten lengths on a rain-soaked Knavesmire. His only defeat came in the Prix Robert Papin in France where the Lester Piggott-ridden My Swallow beat him in a photo finish.

My Swallow was owned by Sir David Robinson and trained at his private stables by Paul Davey. The big, powerful Le Levanstell juvenile had already won two races in England by the time Mill Reef lined up at Royal Ascot for the Coventry Stakes. He then targeted races in France where he gained the victory over the Kingsclere runner. For good measure, he also added the Prix du Bois, Prix de Morny, Prix de la Salamandre, and the Grand Critérium to end the season with seven straight wins. This glorious season elevated My Swallow to the top of the free handicap in Britain and France.

Third favourite for the Guineas, at 11/2, was Brigadier Gerard. The son of Queen's Hussar made his racing debut later than Mill Reef and My Swallow, Major Dick Hern opting to wait until Newbury's late June meeting before introducing the colt to racing. In a field of five, the relatively unbacked 100/7 shot strode away to record an easy five-length success. It could have been ten lengths had Joe Mercer so desired. This impressive victory meant he started at odds-on for his next race, another easy win at Salisbury in early July. The day before Piggott guided My Swallow to success in the Prix de Morny, Brigadier Gerard was back at Newbury for the Washington Singer Stakes, a race in which his trainer often tested his better juveniles. At odds of 4/9 the result was never in doubt and Dick Hern chalked up another win in the race. Despite these impressive successes and the fact that he stood out amongst his rivals in the paddock, Brigadier Gerard was the 9/2 third favourite in the five-runner Middle Park Stakes at Newmarket. With odds-on favourite Mummy's Pet failing to stay the six-furlong trip, Brigadier Gerard had a much easier task than expected. He took full advantage, and extended his unbeaten run by a comfortable three lengths.

At the start of the 1971 season, My Swallow won a minor event at Kempton, and Mill Reef won the Greenham Stakes at Newbury, in their preparation for the 2,000 Guineas. Brigadier Gerard, in contrast, was relaxing at home in West Ilsley the small Berkshire village that is transformed in the early mornings when a seemingly countless number of thoroughbreds make their way via the winding roads from their stables to the gallops.

Given the dominance of these three runners, most trainers decided to avoid the Classic, and at post time only six horses filled the stalls. Despite the small field, it was still one of the best 2,000 Guineas in living memory. My Swallow set the pace with Mill Reef not far away. With three furlongs to race the "big three" were in a line and any could have won. Joe Mercer chose the nearside route, Mill Reef was between horses and My Swallow closest to the centre of the track. With two furlongs to run, all three were moving sweetly, then Mercer decided to let his colt stretch. The pair quickly secured the lead and the whips were drawn on the other two. Brigadier Gerard accelerated and went clear with his jockey merely waving his whip, not needing to make contact. In the final half-furlong the lead increased and it was clear that Brigadier Gerard was well in command. The other two battled on but they were outclassed, and Mercer was able to ease the three-year-old home to win in exhilarating fashion by three lengths. Mill Reef outstayed My Swallow to take second place with the tail-swisher Minsky back in fourth. There was no doubt about the result, no hard luck stories, no excuses: the best miler in the land had won, and won decisively.

My Swallow raced twice more as a three-year-old but did not add to his tally of victories. Mill Reef enjoyed better fortune. After the Guineas he won the Derby, the Eclipse Stakes, the King George VI and Queen Elizabeth Stakes, and the Prix de l'Arc de Triomphe. The following season he won the Prix Ganay by ten lengths then scrambled home in the Coronation Cup. Unfortunately, his career was then brought to an untimely halt. Mill Reef suffered a serious training injury and had to be retired to stud.

Brigadier Gerard picked off the top mile races of the year then stepped up to ten furlongs in the Champion Stakes in the autumn. For the first time in his career he was made to struggle, and at the line had only a short head to spare over the four-year-old Rarity. By the summer of 1972, Brigadier Gerard was unbeaten from fifteen races and had won at a range of distances from five furlongs to a mile-and-a-half. Then, in the Benson & Hedges Gold Cup, his winning run came to an end with a defeat to the Derby winner Roberto. He was soon back to his best though, with repeat successes in the Queen Elizabeth II Stakes and the Champion Stakes. In total Brigadier Gerard won seventeen of his eighteen races, mostly at the very highest level. He was certainly the best horse the Hislop family owned, and several commentators considered him the best horse ever to have raced in England.

First Win by a Female Jockey   *6 May 1972*

Meriel Tufnell became the first female jockey to win a race under Jockey Club rules when she partnered Scorched Earth to success at Kempton on 6th May 1972. Until then women had not been permitted to compete under rules but, following sustained pressure from various factions of the industry, the Jockey Club finally relented and scheduled a series of twelve ladies' races. Tufnell won three of these contests and was awarded the first Lady Jockeys' Championship.

Although not sanctioned by the Jockey Club, women did compete in matches in the early 1800s. One such example took place on 25th August 1804 at York. It was announced as follows:

> *A match for 500 gs., and 100 gs. Bye, four miles, between Colonel Thornton's Vingarillo, and Mr. Flint's br. H. Thornville, by Volunteer. Mrs. Thornton to ride her own weight against Mr. Flint's.*

A detailed account of the event was provided by the *York Herald* in which it was claimed that over 100,000 spectators assembled on the Knavesmire to witness the race, more than ten times the number that were present when the great Eclipse raced. Between them, these racegoers wagered in excess of £200,000 [£20 million] on the day.

The horses and riders paraded at 4pm and, a short while after, the race was underway. Alicia Thornton, the 'daughter of a respectable watchmaker of Norwich', in '"leopard colour", blue sleeves and cap', clearly had a plan and was soon building a lead over her opponent. To a significant number in the crowd a notable upset was looking more and more likely as the race progressed. With three of the four miles completed, Mrs Thornton still held the lead. Then, without warning, Vingarillo's stride shortened and her opponent quickly joined her. A few strides later, Thornville was well clear. Despite her best efforts, Mrs Thornton could make no headway against her stronger challenger and 'drew up, in a sportsmanlike style. Mr Flint riding in all white was able to coast home; all his opponent could do was accept his success.' The *York Herald* concluded its analysis of the contest in a style which would possibly enrage modern-day feminists, 'Never, surely, did a woman ride in better style. It was difficult to say whether her horsemanship, her dress, or her beauty was most admired – the *tout ensemble* was unique.'

The following year Mrs Thornton made a return to racing. At York's August meeting she was scheduled to ride in a match for 'four hogsheads of claret as well as the stakes' against Mr Bromford. For reasons unknown, on the day of the contest, Bromford declined to race and paid the forfeit. Mrs Thornton simply cantered over the course to collect her prize. Later in the afternoon, she took on the best male jockey of the era, Frank Buckle, a protégé of Samuel Chifney 'for a considerable sum of money' over a distance of two miles. On this occasion Mrs Thornton rode her husband's horse, Louisa, putting up a weight of 9st 6lbs. Buckle was on Allegro who had to shoulder 13st 6lbs.

At a little after 3:30pm the flag fell and Mrs Thornton again set the pace; Buckle was content to sit in behind until the closing stages, a style of race-riding that was often adopted by Chifney. Approaching the *distance*, Buckle made his move and poached a slight lead; but Mrs Thornton was not to be outdone. By 'collecting her horse with great power and skill' she gained a half-neck advantage at the line. Returning to the unsaddling area, Mrs Thornton was met with cheers and applause from the huge crowd that fully appreciated the significance of her success. Much to the frustration of women riders, racing's authorities did not.

Queen Elizabeth's Classic Double   *10 September 1977*

By the end of 1976 Dunfermline had raced three times without success. But as is so often the case with horses bred to stay middle distances and beyond, she would be seen to better effect as a three-year-old. At Newmarket the following April it was clear that Dunfermline had improved over the winter, and in the ten-furlong Pretty Polly stakes the daughter of Royal Palace was far too good for Olwyn and On The Fringe, winning by four lengths.

Dunfermline's next target was the Oaks which, for Lester Piggott at least, did not go to plan. Cantering past the stands on the way to the start, the saddle on Piggott's mount Durtal slipped. As the pair approached the entrance to the paddock the saddle then slid completely beneath the filly causing Piggott to fall. To make matters worse, Piggott's foot remained trapped in the stirrup, a scenario that gives all jockeys nightmares. Durtal bolted, and Piggott was dragged at speed across the Epsom turf. The horse seemed to head directly for a wood and concrete fence. In all probability she was just simply trying to get free from her jockey who, in turn, was desperately hoping that she would succeed before causing any more damage. This was not to be though, and Durtal crashed into the fence with sufficient force to splinter the wood. Luckily for Piggott the impact smashed the stirrup iron, freeing him, and possibly saving his life. Durtal was not so fortunate and impaled herself on the splintered shafts of wood.

The Oaks went ahead minus the favourite, and despite meeting trouble in running on several occasions Dunfermline, under Willie Carson, powered home to win by just under a length from Freeze The Secret giving the Queen and trainer Dick Hern their first win in the race.

The Queen's Silver Jubilee year was to be very successful for the monarch. In September Dunfermline added the St Leger to Her Majesty's list of winners. Under an inspired ride from Carson, the filly managed to wear down Alleged in the final furlong to win by a length-and-a-half, with a long gap back to the third. This was a top class performance from Dunfermline as an analysis of Alleged's subsequent races demonstrates. A few weeks later the colt gained his revenge by winning the "Prix de l'Arc de Triomphe" then, the following year, he retained his "Arc" crown by winning the most prestigious race in France for the second time.

A Tough Introduction   *7 April 1979*

Unquestionably, Steve Cauthen was expecting racing to be different on this side of the Atlantic. Whether he was quite prepared for what he was about to encounter at Salisbury racecourse on 7th April 1979 is extremely unlikely.

Incessant, heavy rain had turned the lush, green turf into something resembling the ancient marshlands of the south west that had provided a stronghold for King Alfred 1,100 years earlier. Cauthen certainly wasn't in Kansas, or even sunny California, anymore. From the moment one of the official's cars became bogged down in the mud, unable to move in either direction, the afternoon was in danger of descending into farce. A broken public address system did little to enhance communication with the record crowd excitedly awaiting the "Kentucky Kid's" first ride on a British racecourse. Nor did it engender any degree of confidence in the equipment used at the track.

Whilst the appearance of an unattended interloper on the track lifted the spirits of the racegoers, it must have rung even more alarm bells in the American's thoughts. The small pony, strolling nonchalantly along the home straight, appeared oblivious to the crowd and completely unconcerned that his appearance on the course at a different time could have caused a serious incident involving several much larger ungulates. As the miniature horse passed the winning post a congratulatory cheer, akin to the ovation that greets the Derby winner, echoed across the course. Could England really be the home of the most prestigious horseraces in the world? By this point Cauthen must have had some serious doubts.

Whatever opinion he formed about racing in rural England, he did not let it influence his riding and he remained his usual calm self. In the very first race on the card, Cauthen's first-ever ride in Britain, the eighteen-year-old showed that he was already a master of his craft. His innate appreciation of pace, and precise judgement of where to position his horse at each stage of a race, was seen to brilliant effect. On Marquee Universal he gradually wore down the front-running Twickenham and then forged ahead in the closing stages of the Grand Food Stakes. The youngest jockey to win the American Triple Crown had won his first race on the other side of the Atlantic and like so many American jockeys before him, he would have a profound impact on the sport in Britain.

A Racing Fairytale   *4 April 1981*

A two-mile novices' hurdle race at Ascot on 10th January 1975 was chosen as Aldaniti's introduction to racing. It was a shrewd choice by Josh Gifford because the five-year-old won it with plenty to spare. The remainder of his career did not go quite so smoothly. Long periods of lameness interrupted his training and Gifford had to use all of his expertise to get him ready for action after so much time was spent recuperating from various operations.

By the end of the 1977/78 season Gifford's tireless efforts had resulted in Aldaniti running into the places in both the Scottish Grand National and the Cheltenham Gold Cup, but injury was to intervene again. And this time it wasn't just Aldaniti who needed medical attention. His jockey, Bob Champion, who had ridden the chaser in all of his races, was diagnosed with cancer and had to undergo a long period of treatment. Remarkably, both horse and rider made full recoveries and in the spring of 1981 they faced another significant challenge together. This time it was one of their choosing: the thirty fences of the Aintree Grand National.

With just 10st 13lbs on his back, Aldaniti deserved to be amongst the favourites for the race, though his training setbacks were a note of caution to punters. At off time, Spartan Missile, with John Thorne hoping to become the oldest jockey to win the great race, had been backed into favouritism at 8/1; Aldaniti was next best on the books at 10/1.

It was a fine, sunny day in Liverpool when the forty runners went to post for the 135th Grand National. The ground, described as "good", would not be a serious impediment to front-runners, so it was not too surprising to see Champion take Aldaniti up to the leading trio at the eleventh fence. Six fences later he went clear of the group, but was cautiously tracked by Royal Mail and Rubstic. Favourite backers were somewhat concerned because Spartan Missile was well off the pace and seemingly with little chance of success.

Three fences from home, Rubstic weakened, and Aldaniti appeared to have only Royal Mail to beat. A glance over his shoulder must have worried Champion because Philip Blacker had Royal Mail travelling easily in his slipstream. On the run to two out, Aldaniti maintained his lead over Royal Mail, the pair well clear of the third. Almost unnoticed, Spartan Missile had moved into fifth place, but still had at least a dozen lengths to find. Royal Mail hit the next fence hard, a mistake that cost him a couple of lengths. Spartan Missile was still improving though, and was now in fourth.

With one fence left to jump, the fairytale win looked a distinct possibility for Champion and Aldaniti, if only they could keep going. The stamina-sapping marathon was beginning to take its toll, and the two leaders were visibly slowing with every stride. Whilst Aldaniti jumped the last fence two lengths clear of Royal Mail in second, John Thorne had stealthily moved the favourite into third. From a hopeless position with five fences to jump, Spartan Missile was suddenly in contention and looking dangerous. At the elbow he raced smoothly past the exhausted Royal Mail and was clearly gaining on Aldaniti. His jockey was getting every ounce of effort from the tough nine-year-old, and the pair was gradually closing the gap on the long-time leader. To quote from Peter O'Sullevan's commentary: 'John Thorne is putting in a storming finish'.

Thoughts of Crisp's defeat in 1973 must have flashed through Bob Champion's mind. From being in a position every jumps jockey dreams about, Bob Champion was now in danger losing an epic finish. It may have made exciting viewing for the millions watching at home, but for Champion a gentle canter to the line would have been the preferred ending to the contest. In typical determined fashion, Champion asked Aldaniti for one last effort and, as the favourite drew even closer, he responded. Like his jockey, Aldaniti also did not want to lose, and from somewhere he found an extra reserve of stamina. In the last one hundred yards they pulled away again as Spartan Missile's valiant run petered out. Champion and Aldaniti secured the victory by four lengths.

The Official Handicapper will tell you that the extra 6lbs Spartan Missile carried compared to Aldaniti made the difference. That's true, it would have had an effect, but there was far more to the race than pounds and ounces and handicap marks. For those of a certain age, what unfolded that day became the stuff of equestrian folklore. This was consummate drama that transcended the sport and seized the hearts of a nation. As horse and rider approached the starting line, two hapless victims of life-endangering illness, no one could have foreseen the timeless glory that beckoned them both. Not even their most misty-eyed admirers dared to believe. But the indomitable duo had other ideas and two legends were created that day. It was a perfect day at the races and one that would never be forgotten or surpassed.

Record Breaking Grand National   *3 April 1982*

The 1981 Grand National may have been the highlight of Bob Champion's racing career, but the following year's race was definitely one of his unluckiest. Back on board Aldaniti, Champion failed to get over the first fence. At least he did have nine other jockeys on the Aintree turf with him for company. This early catalogue of disasters was a sign of what was to come, and by end of the 1982 contest only eight horses from the thirty-nine that went to post remained on their feet.

As a successful hunter chaser, Grittar went into many notebooks as a potential Grand National winner after his success in the Aintree Foxhunters' Chase. His useful-looking form propelled him to the head of the betting market and in the main event he started as the 7/1 clear favourite. Much to his credit, Grittar's owner-trainer Frank Gillman insisted that his runner's amateur jockey, Dick Saunders, retained the ride despite many so-called racing experts imploring him to reconsider his decision and replace Saunders with an established professional.

In the race it was clear that Saunders was not going to let this golden chance of success slip by without making the most of it. He could have opted for the easier path around the outside of the track. This would keep him well out of trouble and away from the bulk of the fallers. Such an approach would all but guarantee a clear round. He also calculated that this safer, less-attacking plan would markedly increase the distance he had to travel and, therefore, reduce his chance of winning. Instead, he backed himself as a jockey, and Grittar as a reliable jumper, and took the more challenging route against the inside running rail. It may have been shorter from flag to post, but it meant he had to negotiate the ditches where the drops on the landing sides were at their greatest. The inside route is not a sound recommendation for jockeys and horses of a nervous disposition, but for Saunders it made perfect sense.

Grittar completed the first circuit without issue, and at Becher's Brook the second time around he took the lead, still travelling very easily. The plan was working, the risk had been worth taking, and the pair was in pole position with a mile to go. Grittar maintained the advantage until the last when, being pressed by Hard Outlook, he made his first serious mistake and ploughed through the fence scattering a considerable portion of the spruce. It could so easily have been his demise and a disappointing end to the race for favourite backers. The tough, experienced chaser had made jumping mistakes in the past, though, and knew how to stay on his feet. With Saunders sitting tight, Grittar kept his footing, regained his momentum, and quickly picked up speed again. From there to the finishing line he comprehensively out-stayed his only serious rival, winning by fifteen lengths. Hard Outlook crossed the line in second, and Loving Words, after remounting, was a fast finishing, though remote, third. It was a polished display from both horse and jockey and those who had doubted Saunders' ability to handle the course were left feeling suitably embarrassed.

Two records were set in the 1982 Grand National: Dick Saunders was forty-eight years old when he recorded this success, the oldest jockey to do so, and by finishing in eighth place, Mrs Geraldine Rees became the first lady rider to complete the course.

Abduction of a Champion   *8 February 1983*

Shergar was not a precocious two-year-old. He needed time and Michael Stoute did not rush him. It wasn't until mid September that he made his debut. Over a mile at Newbury the Great Nephew colt with the white blaze and four white socks recorded a comfortable two-and-a-half length win under Lester Piggott prompting Michael Seely to write in *The Times* 'It is becoming more and more obvious that the Newmarket trainer has an exceptionally powerful team of young horses'. It was a performance full of promise, so a defeat by Beldale Flutter in the Futurity Stakes on his only other start in 1980 was somewhat perplexing and those of a superstitious nature were quick to quote the ancient adage: "If thou hast a fole with four white feet, keep him not a day".

It was only as a three-year-old that Shergar's full potential would be realised. He returned to action at Sandown in April a much stronger colt. His eight opponents in the ten-furlong contest had little chance, and with Walter Swinburn in the plate he strolled home to win by a huge margin. The Bookmakers were certainly impressed and his Derby price was reduced from 25-1 to single figures. Shergar followed up at Chester in May, winning by twelve lengths, and was now a short price for the Derby.

In the Epsom Classic the result was much the same as at Sandown and Chester. Despite being eased by "The Choirboy" in the last furlong, Shergar recorded the largest winning distance in the history of the race. At the winning line he was ten lengths clear of the runner-up, Glint Of Gold. Old sayings referring to horses with four white socks were appropriately denounced as nonsense. Wins in the Irish Derby, with Piggott replacing a suspended Swinburn, and in the King George VI and Queen Elizabeth Diamond Stakes left no one in doubt that he was the best three-year-old for some considerable time. In Piggott's view '[he] was a great horse, one of the greatest we have seen'.

After such a successful racing career Shergar was extremely valuable, and was in great demand as a sire. Despite offers from abroad, the Aga Khan placed him at the Ballymany Stud in Ireland and in his first season Shergar produced thirty-six foals. In many minds, Shergar was set to become an influential sire, one that might even shape the future of the breed; no one would have guessed that he only had a few short months to live.

On 8th February 1983 a contingent of masked, armed men broke into the home of Ballymany's head groom Jim Fitzgerald. At gunpoint they forced him to load the Derby winner into a horsebox which disappeared at speed into the night. Fitzgerald was also abducted and driven around the Irish countryside for most of the night before being released in the early hours of the morning near the village of Kilcock, about twenty miles from the stud.

The kidnappers made contact by telephone the same day and demanded a ransom. They also insisted that negotiations would be held only with the racing personalities Derek Thompson, John Oaksey, and Peter Campling of *The Sun* newspaper. Negotiations were ongoing over the next few days with proof requested that the horse was indeed in the kidnappers' possession. Photographs were provided but this did not satisfy the negotiating team. In a telephone call they explained that they needed definitive proof that first, the horse was Shergar and second, that he was still alive. The reply to this was as simple as it was alarming: 'If you're not satisfied, that's it'. Shergar was never seen again.

Years later it was established that the kidnappers were members of the terrorist organisation, the IRA. Their assumption was that by kidnapping such a valuable sire, a considerable ransom would be raised providing much needed funds to allow them to continue, and possibly expand, their terror campaign in Britain. Fortunately, no money changed hands so the kidnappers did not profit. But that's scant compensation for the loss of such a potentially influential sire. The whole episode was just another display of unnecessary brutality, and the only outcome was to deny the racing public the chance of watching the possibly brilliant offspring of this racing great competing in the most prestigious races in Europe throughout the remainder of the decade. Whether the abductors' plans had worked or not, nothing positive could have been achieved from the act.

The First Five Home   *17 March 1983*

It's fair to say that, in terms of results, Paul Nicholls has had a better than average start to the twenty-first century. In fact the list of major races that the horses in his care have won seems unending. There are the three Gold Cups, nine wins in the King George VI Chase at Kempton, three wins in the Queen Mother Champion Chase, four wins in the Stayers' Hurdle (now the World Hurdle), a Champion Hurdle, a Grand National and virtually every race at the Cheltenham Festival, some many times. But arguably his crowning achievement was in the 2008 Gold Cup when he saddled the first three home: Denman, Kauto Star and Neptune Collonges.

For most trainers simply having a horse in the race would be a lifetime's achievement, and winning it would only ever happen in their dreams. To saddle the first three home would not even be on their radar. Yet Nicholls' remarkable performance in 2008 cannot match that achieved by Michael

Dickinson twenty-five years earlier. In 1982 Dickinson recorded his first win, and first one-two, in the race when Silver Buck got the better of stablemate Bregawn. The following year he achieved the near impossible and beat odds of 150/1 offered by Bookmakers to train the first five home in the Gold Cup.

Naturally doubts have been cast over the quality of the 1983 race, but it should be noted that three non-Dickinson trained horses were priced shorter than Ashley House, Dickinson's outsider. With Combs Ditch, Fifty Dollars More and Brown Chamberlain in the race it was far from certain that one of his quintet would even win the contest. Had it been a foregone conclusion then odds of 150/1 would never have been offered. It was, without any doubt, a momentous achievement.

The tendency for a small number of trainers to dominate jumps racing has been criticised on many occasions. However, it is just part of the natural evolution of the sport; the best trainers will always attract the best horses. So in the future there must be a chance, albeit slim, that Dickinson's remarkable achievement will be equalled, and possibly even bettered.

A Jockey's Near Death Experience   *25 February 1984*

The safety of chasing has improved over the years since those first few races run across ploughed fields, stiff fences, and wide brooks in the early 1800s. But it remains to this day a dangerous sport in which jockeys risk their lives every time they leave the starting gate. Racegoers at Doncaster in late February 1984 witnessed just how treacherous jumping obstacles at thirty miles per hour can be.

As a jockey, Hywel Davies had experienced many bad falls in his distinguished career breaking a range of bones including his collarbone six times, pelvis, arms, and ribs. Whilst such a catalogue of injuries would make many riders reconsider their chosen sport, for Davies it was just part of the game. There was a point where he must have wished he had opted for a safer route through life, though. Whilst riding for David Barons in a handicap chase at Doncaster on 25th February 1984 Davies had a fall that was altogether more serious, and for many jockeys it would have been life-changing. His horse, Solid Rock, had made good headway to be up with the pace in the closing stages, but at the last fence suffered a crashing fall. Davies was concussed and in his words, as reported in the *Liverpool Echo*, 'on the way to the hospital I died for a bit. They had to revive me seven times.' That would have been enough for most riders, but not for Davies. Just over twelve months later the Welshman was guiding Captain Tim Forster's Last Suspect to victory in the Grand National.

Of course, it is not just jumps racing that is fraught with danger, flat racing falls can be just as horrific, and on rare occasions even worse than Davies' life-threatening incident. Manny Mercer was a leading jockey in the 1950s regularly recording over 100 winners in a season. The brother of Joe Mercer was a stylish, accomplished jockey and to many observers would have been champion jockey had it not been for the dreadful events of 26th September 1959. While catering to the post, Mercer's mount Priddy Fair slipped and Mercer fell, striking the rails (at this time rails were constructed of concrete and steel) before hitting the ground. In a blind panic, the colt lashed out kicking Mercer twice in the head. Anyone who witnessed the horrifying scene knew at once the outcome would not be anything but tragic. The thirty-one-year-old was immediately transferred to an ambulance but never regained consciousness. His death was announced via the public address system and the meeting cancelled; racegoers quietly left the track in shock, hats removed as a mark of respect for 'one of Britain's most brilliant jockeys'.

More recently the talented Lorna Brooke lost her life after a fall at Taunton racecourse on 8th April 2021. Riding Orchestrated for her mother, Brooke fell at the third fence in a handicap chase. She was taken to Southmead Hospital in Bristol and although initially assessed as "critical but stable", various complications resulted in her death some days later. This tragic episode was a reminder that no matter what changes are made, nor how well the protective equipment is improved, horseracing will always be one of the most dangerous of sports.

Unlucky Seventeen   *22 March 1984*

Provideo made his debut in flat racing's traditional curtain raiser, the Brocklesby Stakes, at Doncaster on 22nd March 1984. According to the official formbook, Provideo was a neat juvenile with scope for improvement. In the race he disputed the lead until half way when he took over, then ran on well in the final furlong to win by four lengths. The two-year-old was off the mark at the first time of asking and six days later he doubled his tally when taking the Toytop Stakes at Catterick by a comfortable seven lengths.

Back-to-back defeats followed at Lingfield and Thirsk. On both occasions the less than straightforward Godswalk colt filled the runner-up position. However disappointing these losses were, they led to a change which ultimately paid dividends over the course of the season. The race at Thirsk convinced trainer Bill O'Gorman that his colt would benefit from blinkers and he was soon proved correct in his assessment. At Ripon on 28th April Provideo, fitted with the new headgear, romped to a six-length victory over Alan Bailey's Halcyon Cove. Following this success, a run of ten wins from just twelve races took Provideo's score to thirteen, equalling the twentieth century record set by Nagwa and Spindrifter.

At York's Ebor meeting he was defeated in his record-breaking attempt by Vaigly Oh in the Prince of Wales's Stakes, Steve Cauthen getting the verdict in a photograph. However, Tony Ives, who rode Provideo to all his juvenile wins, soon had the colt back in the winner's enclosure. At Ripon on Bank Holiday Monday, Provideo proved too strong for the George Duffield-ridden Lobbit in the Champion Trophy Sakes and in so doing set a new record. The Bard's remarkable record of sixteen juvenile victories was now in the sights of Team Provideo. However, the last ten weeks of the season were not about to go to plan.

A third to Northern Chimes at Kempton followed his Ripon win, then ill health intervened and Provideo was prevented from returning to the racecourse until the end of October. With just a fortnight of the season remaining, Provideo was taken to Doncaster where he 'held on gamely' to win a five-furlong contest by a head from Pacific Gold. The star two-year-old had fifteen wins to his name and needed just one more to equal The Bard's record set in 1883. With opportunities running out fast, and the threat of inclement autumn weather further reducing the number of potential races, Provideo made the trip to Redcar for the Dinsdale Spa Stakes. He faced five opponents and had to concede upwards of three pounds, but the tough front-running juvenile loved racing and, more importantly, he loved winning. Provideo was first away from the stalls at Redcar and dominated the race throughout, turning it into a procession and winning by an impressive seven lengths.

Provideo had equalled The Bard's achievement in an era when racing was far more competitive. One more win would set a new record. O'Gorman sent Provideo to America searching for the single success that would give him the record outright. It was a poor decision as O'Gorman freely admitted. Provideo contested the Buckpasser Stakes over a mile, a distance that was far beyond his best. The outcome was a defeat and the only time in twenty-four races that he failed to make the frame. With no other races left to contest, Provideo had to settle for a share of the record.

In 1990 Timeless Times matched Provideo's record of sixteen wins as a juvenile. Also trained by Bill O'Gorman, Timeless Times was sent to the USA in an attempt to break the record but, like Provideo, he failed in his bid for the elusive seventeenth victory. Some records are clearly more difficult to beat than others, and this one which was set over 150 years ago is proving to be particularly challenging.

Bookmakers' Palpable Error Rule   31 March 1984

Anyone entering a Tote Bookmakers shop on the morning of the 1984 Grand National would have been greeted with large posters advertising a new speciality bet for the race. To win the bet all that was required was to identify correctly four horses that completed the course in the big race. It was that easy, and many were tempted to have a go.

The inspiration for the bet was straightforward to see. In 1983, ten horses managed to complete the course from a starting line-up of forty-one, and the year before produced just eight finishers from thirty-nine runners. Based on those races, it might be fairly assumed that around nine of the forty horses contesting the 1984 race should make it home. That would make the odds of any four horses completing over 350/1. So perhaps it was not that easy after all. However, no race is entirely a lottery, so allowing for an element of skill on the part of the punter the chance of success would naturally increase. An equally important factor was the ground. In 1984 the going was officially classified as "good" which would, based on historical evidence, increase the number of finishers, possibly to somewhere around the twenty mark. Consequently, the 33/1 offered against the exotic bet made a great deal of appeal to many punters.

As it turned out, for those who risked their cash, finding four horses to complete the race was much easier than expected since twenty-three of the forty runners crossed the finishing line. Getting paid out, though, was not as simple.

On Monday morning hundreds of punters made their way to the Tote's shops, thoughts of new cars and Caribbean cruises widening their already beaming smiles. Winning betting slips were passed across the counter and gratefully accepted by the odds settler. Then, without any warning or preamble to soften the blow, they were given the bad news. The price of 33/1 was offered in error; the correct price was 16/1. In an instant, smiles had been replaced by frowns, delight had become bewilderment, and expected profits had been halved. There would be no new cars, no exotic holidays, nothing even approaching the mildest form of extravagance. With the winning slip now stapled to the counterfoil and money counted out, any challenge by the punter was utterly pointless and was met with 'it's in the *Sporting Life*, check it for yourself'.

This was an excellent example of the "palpable error" rule in action and punters had no option but to accept the payout at the lower odds. The rule is a safeguard for Bookmakers and can be applied if they have incorrectly quoted a price. In this case it was difficult to see how the price could be claimed to be incorrect when it was displayed prominently on hundreds of posters throughout the country, but it was. Moreover, when was it decided that a mistake had been made? Before the race started? Or after it had been run when it was apparent that, with twenty-three horses completing the course, this particular exotic bet was going to be very costly to the company? These questions, though asked, were never answered.

Remarkably, even in the current digital age of betting, the palpable error rule is still invoked even for bets placed on websites over which the Bookmakers' software governs each and every click. Unfortunately, under the regulations relating to betting which apply at the present time, the palpable error rule is not available to punters.

Oh So Sharp's Triple Crown Bid   *2 May 1985*

Oh So Sharp, the most exciting juvenile of 1984, started her three-year-old campaign in the Nell Gwyn Stakes at Newmarket. The Kris filly was partnered by Steve Cauthen, Henry Cecil's new stable jockey, and on his first public appearance on the stable star the American wasn't in the mood to take any chances. Oh So Sharp hit the front fully two furlongs from home and Cauthen drove her out to the line to win by a comfortable length from Bella Colora. It was an impressive display by an impressive filly, but many tougher tests lay ahead.

Two weeks later on 2nd May 1985 Oh So Sharp made the short trip from Warren Place to the Rowley Mile where she started the 2/1 favourite for the 172nd running of the 1,000 Guineas. Three fillies that had finished behind Oh So Sharp in the Nell Gwyn Stakes decided to try their luck again and with just over a furlong to go it looked as if one of these might succeed: Oh So Sharp was two lengths behind Bella Colora and Al Bahathri, and seemingly beaten. Cauthen though had other ideas and in a power-packed finish forced a three-way photograph. The wait for the result seemed to take far longer than usual, but when it was finally announced the distances between the winner, runner-up and third placed horse were given as two short heads. In what was the closest finish to the race in living memory, Oh So Sharp had prevailed from Al Bahathri and the Lester Piggott-ridden Bella Colora. Steve Cauthen had his first win in the great race, Oh So Sharp's owner, Sheikh Mohammed, had his first Classic success and the 1,000 Guineas had a new record time.

Following the 1,000 Guineas win, Oh So Sharp was taken to Epsom for the Oaks. She faced eleven opponents on ground that was very different from Newmarket. The sun-dried surface in April had seemed to suit her, but at Epsom it was much softer, which was far from ideal. Most commentators considered Triptych to be her main danger, and for the Irish-bred filly deep ground posed no problems at all.

On the downhill approach to Tattenham Corner, Cauthen was niggling along a fourth-placed Oh So Sharp. In contrast, Triptych moved smoothly on the quarters of the leader. At the top of the straight Oh So Sharp jumped the path as the horses drifted away from the rails into the centre of the course. For some reason, whether it was the more level racing surface, or a subtle change of pace, Oh So Sharp seemed now to be travelling much better. At the two-furlong pole she joined Triptych at the head of the field. Then, under a drive from Cauthen, she powered clear, impressing everyone in the stands including commentator Graham Goode who claimed: 'the race looks over in a matter of strides'. He was correct, it was. Oh So Sharp lengthened away in majestic style to win by six lengths from the Irish runner.

At Ascot in July her winning run came to an end. A combination of very hard ground and being hampered on the turn into the straight was too much for her to overcome and she went down by a neck to Petoski. At York the following month she came up against Lester Piggott at his very best. Riding Commanche Run, the previous year's St Leger winner, Piggott conjured up one of his magical rides setting the perfect tempo throughout and keeping just enough in reserve to fend off a late challenge by the filly to win by just under a length.

The Fillies' Triple Crown was still the target though, and at Doncaster in September the punters made her the 8/11 favourite to match Meld's 1955 achievement. Piggott was riding Henry Cecil's second-string runner Lanfranco and, encouraged by his success on Commanche Run, he adopted similar forcing tactics. Piggott faced two problems though: Cauthen was awake to his manoeuvrings, and Lanfranco was nowhere near as good as Commanche Run. With three furlongs to race, Lanfranco was still in front, and Piggott took the opportunity to look over his shoulder to see how far Oh So Sharp was behind him. It must have been utterly dispiriting for him to see her loom up on his outside, moving sweetly. Cauthen put Oh So Sharp into top gear and she pulled clear, despite edging towards the middle of the track. Phardante came between the two horses to snatch second place on the line but couldn't get to the favourite. Oh So Sharp had completed the Triple Crown, Henry Cecil had become the first trainer to win over one million pounds in a single season, and Steve Cauthen had won his fourth Classic of the year on an exceptional filly. No wonder in an interview with Tim Richards for *The Owner Breeder* magazine, Cauthen remarked 'I rode Indian Skimmer, Time Charter and Triptych, three outstanding fillies, but Oh So Sharp was the best.'

The Big Freeze   *6 February 1986*

In the early months of 1986 movie fans were enjoying recent releases such as Sidney Lumet's *Power* and Woody Allen's *Hannah and Her Sisters*. Horseracing fans, on the other hand, had little to smile about. All racing on the final three days of 1985 had been abandoned, and January was not proving to be much better with thirty-two meetings lost to the weather. Worse was to come though. When the snow and ice descended on 6th February it initially seemed like just another cold winter's day with no racing to enjoy. However, what we did not know then was that there would be no racing at all for the next four weeks.

Racing finally returned at Catterick on 5th March but by then the sport's authorities were already counting the financial cost of the cold spell in the millions and decided that action needed to be taken to avoid similar situations in future. One solution was all-weather racing. Three years later the continuity of racing, even through the coldest of weather, was assured when the artificial tracks at Lingfield and Southwell came into operation.

Britain's first all-weather race was run on Lingfield's equitrack surface on 30th October 1989, 168 years after the first artificial dirt track appeared in New York. The race was won by Niklas Angel and was ridden by Richard Quinn. This claiming contest formed part of a bumper twelve-race card to kick-start this new form of racing. A second meeting on fibresand at Southwell followed a few days later. Since those first races, all-weather racing's popularity has been steadily growing, along with the number of fixtures.

Interestingly, that first Lingfield meeting featured eight non-handicaps and four handicap races. The second meeting, at Southwell, was also heavily biased against handicaps. Unfortunately, this well-balanced pattern has not survived. In 2021 a standard eight-race all-weather meeting would have probably six or seven handicaps, which does nothing to improve the overall quality of British racing.

Dawn Run   *13 March 1986*

Triskaidekaphobia may curtail the activities of a notable proportion of the population, but not so the connections of Dawn Run. In fact, by the end of her career, "thirteen" had become quite a lucky number. After winning the Irish Champion Hurdle in mid-February, at Cheltenham on 13th March 1984 Dawn Run won the second leg of the European Champion Hurdle treble. Later in the year she made history by becoming the first horse to win all three Championship races when taking the French equivalent. It's fair to say that for owner Charmian Hill and trainer Paddy Mullins, 1983/1984 was a pretty good season.

As good as the early months of 1984 were, the following season was definitely one to forget. Dawn Run had been switched to chasing, and after her first race in November she sustained an injury that would keep her off the track for many months. Finally returning to racing in mid-December 1985, the Champion Hurdle winner 'put up a totally exhilarating performance' to win her comeback chase at Punchestown prompting Bookmakers to clip her odds for the 1986 Gold Cup to 5/1 even though this was only her second start over fences.

Later in the month Dawn Run made it twelve wins from her last thirteen starts when getting the better of Buck House in a three-runner race at Leopardstown. Keen to gain more chasing experience, the eight-year-old made her way to Cheltenham the following month to contest the Holsten Distributors Chase. Another easy win was expected and at the off she was priced at 4/9. However, nothing's certain in racing, and at the sixteenth fence she unseated Tony Mullins. Though he was able to remount, Dawn Run could only finish a distant fourth. It was far from ideal preparation for the main target of the year.

Her failure to complete the course did not dissuade her connections, and on 13th March 1986 Dawn Run was back at Cheltenham lining up alongside the likes of Wayward Lad, Forgive 'n Forget, Run and Skip, Combs

Ditch, and Fred Winter's Observe to race for the Gold Cup. Lack of chasing experience was considered by many racing experts as her major weakness, but with Jonjo O'Neill in the saddle the huge Irish contingent in the stands had faith in her abilities. Their confidence was reflected in the prices on offer and the mare started the contest as the market leader.

In the race, Dawn Run matched strides with Run and Skip some three or four lengths clear of the main group throughout the first circuit, both seemingly determined to make the contest a thorough test of stamina. At the water jump on the second circuit, Dawn Run dropped her hind legs allowing Run and Skip to take the advantage. The two main dangers, Wayward Lad and Forgive 'n Forget, were content to sit third and fourth, awaiting their chance. At the final ditch, six fences from home, Dawn Run skipped over it economically and was back in front, but only just, from a tenacious Run and Skip who was still moving easily. The favourite clattered through the next at the top of the hill giving Run and Skip a length lead. A slow jump at the fourth last fence allowed Run and Skip to increase his lead, and for Wayward Lad to draw upsides. With two fences to go, Dawn Run was under the whip; it appeared that her race was over.

Forgive 'n Forget and Wayward Lad took over at the last and it looked like the fight would be between the two geldings. Wayward Lad surged clear but drifted to the rails, undoubtedly exhausted; Forgive 'n Forget edged towards the stands' side. O'Neill was forced to switch Dawn Run off the rails to give her any sort of chance of mounting a challenge. As they raced up the hill to the line, Forgive 'n Forget faded, Wayward Lad could give no more, but from somewhere Dawn Run found extra and began to close. Had the race been twenty yards shorter then Wayward Lad would have won; as it was, in the shadow of the post, Dawn Run passed her rival to win by a very hard-fought length. The Champion Hurdle Gold Cup double had been completed for the first time, and Jonjo O'Neill and Dawn Run had become the toast of all Ireland.

Gunning for Success   *16 June 1988*

While the Harwood-Starkey combination was irresistible to some punters, for form students who were unswayed by particular trainer-jockey pairings, the combination's Ile de Chypre was still the stand out selection for the 1988 King George V Handicap. The Ile de Bourbon colt had raced just twice at the back end of the 1987 season, showing promise on both occasions. On his only start of 1988 the three-year-old came up against the strongly fancied, and heavily supported, Knight Line Dancer at Newmarket and did well to finish in the runner-up position. This run not only confirmed his wellbeing following the winter's break but demonstrated that he would be well suited by twelve furlongs. Just as importantly it gained him a handicap mark: Ile de Chypre was now qualified for his early season target at Ascot's Royal meeting

Before the race he attracted plenty of money both on and off the course. Those who watch market movements would have spotted his price shortening on the day from a generous 6/1 to 4/1 second favourite.

Ile de Chypre's supporters would have been smiling throughout the race - well almost. The colt hit the gates and took the field along at a pace that had many of his rivals struggling. Deep inside the final furlong his lead was over three lengths, with a further significant gap back to the third. Guy Harwood must have had a wonderful feeling of satisfaction as he watched the relatively inexperienced Ile de Chypre striding towards the finishing line with the race at his mercy. Then, without warning, the leader swerved violently away from the crowd on the far side of the track, unshipping jockey Greville Starkey. Understandably there was an audible gasp of disbelief from the spectators packed into the stands, followed by a period of utter bewilderment.

So, what had happened? At the time no one knew for sure, and various theories were put forward. It was generally accepted that the horse was a little unreliable. However, this dubious temperament did not stop Ile de Chypre winning two races by ten lengths and three lengths at Newbury later in the season, nor a Group 2 contest at The Curragh, and the Group 1 International Stakes in 1989. Something else must have caused him to react in such a fashion, but quite what it was remained a mystery.

Over twelve months later the issue of Ile de Chypre's Ascot run resurfaced, but not at Portman Square in front of an assembled collection of Jockey Club members. Instead, it became the focus of a trial at Southwark Crown Court. James Laming, a London-based car dealer, was accused of conspiracy to supply cocaine as part of a Peruvian drugs ring. Laming's defence, as reported in *The Herald*, was that banknotes in his possession, on which trace amounts of cocaine were found, were payment for stopping Ile de Chypre winning at Ascot. He strongly denied any knowledge of drug dealing and instead admitted to taking part in an illegal betting operation. He alleged that, in partnership with Mr Renee Black, he modified a set of binoculars so that they would emit a high frequency sound that only animals could hear. He further claimed that when fired the sound would, to the horse, feel 'like he has got a hornet or wasp in his ear.' The defence suggested that being able to stop any horse in any race would allow Mr Black to launder more easily the proceeds from his drugs operation without Laming's knowledge of the source of the money. As part of the trial, the "ray gun" as it became known, was tested on ponies and it did cause an amount of distress to some. However, a test in a field is very different than from a distance of over twenty-five yards in front of many thousands of racegoers all cheering their fancy home.

After assessing the evidence, Laming's claim that he was merely a race fixer fell on deaf ears and the jury convicted him of conspiracy to supply drugs. Whether the "ray gun" was the cause of Ile de Chypre's defeat will never be known with absolute certainty. However, if the horse you have backed is leading in the final furlong and the person in the stands next to you suddenly raises an inordinately large pair of binoculars, a certain amount of inadvertent blocking on your part would probably be advisable.

A Gold Cup Double   *10 December 1988*

To racegoers of a certain generation, the first major race of the Jumps season will still be known as the Mackeson Gold Cup. Founded in 1960 and won for the first time by Fortria for Tom Dreaper, the "Mackeson" held a special place in the Calendar until 1995. Since then the race has had a variety of names, none of which have ever replaced its initial sobriquet in the minds of many race fans. Over the years this two-and-a-half mile chase has been won by some top class horses such as Peter Cazalet's Dunkirk, the Grand National winner Gay Trip, Fred Winter's duo Fifty Dollars More and Half Free, David Nicholson's Very Promising, Josh Gifford's Bradbury Star and, of course, Pegwell Bay.

Pegwell Bay was trained by Captain Tim Forster at his stables in Letcombe Bassett, a mere stone's throw from the ancient watercress beds that populate Letcombe Brook and have provided soothing post-gallop therapy for horses ever since they first galloped through this remote, yet beautiful part of Southern England. Old Manor Stables is an historic yard, which in the past housed such racing greats as Golden Miller when he was in the care of trainer Owen Anthony.

As a young horse, Pegwell Bay was extremely nervous and unsure of people. Even loading him into a horsebox was a task beyond the abilities of many experienced racing staff. However, under the expert guidance of

Henrietta Knight, who broke-in many of Forster's and Fred Winter's horses, he gradually became more accustomed to working with humans and less prone to displays of nervousness. It was soon apparent that Pegwell Bay had a great deal of potential.

Forster was a renowned pessimist, something that was apparent to anyone who spent time in his company. He freely admitted to this somewhat negative attitude towards life and horses, reasoning that if anything ever did happen to go in his favour his devout pessimism would mean that it was doubly joyous. According to David Ashforth in his excellent profile for the *Racing Post*, before the 1980 Grand National the advice Forster gave to Charlie Fenwick, rider of his representative Ben Nevis, was to 'keep remounting'. In the race Ben Nevis skipped over the fences and won by twenty lengths.

Despite his negative take on the world, the Captain was also a very kind and generous man with a well-honed sense of humour. He could also tell a good tale as the following anecdote demonstrates. One summer a brother of one of the stable jockeys was employed at the yard before returning to University. He wasn't allowed near any of the horses and spent his time cutting the lawns and tidying the flower borders. Some months later he won a point-to-point race in Devon on an ex-stable runner now owned by his jockey brother. The day after the victory Forster was in bullish mood about the success. Anyone who was prepared to listen was told about the media lauding other stables for bringing through young jockeys but "after working here for a few weeks, even the gardener is good enough to ride a winner. They never report that" he grumbled, with his tongue firmly in his cheek. Of course, many jockeys had developed their skills at Old Manor Stables under Forster's guidance including Richard Dunwoody, Luke Harvey, and Chris Maude, and his expertise was well known and appreciated throughout the industry.

In the autumn of 1988 even the greatest doom and gloom merchant in racing must have had some positive thoughts about Pegwell Bay. The seven-year-old gelding was an improving chaser, the only type of racehorse that mattered to Forster. Of his ten races under National Hunt rules, he had won six, including a warm-up race for the Mackeson. Furthermore, Pegwell Bay was working well at home and looked perfectly primed for his early season target.

On a dry, sunny October day, thirteen runners went to post for the 29th running of the Mackeson Gold Cup. The ground was described as "good to firm" which was ideal for Pegwell Bay whose six previous wins came on ground that was "good" or firmer, surfaces on which he was thus far unbeaten. When it was announced that Brendan Powell would miss the ride due to injury, the first call Forster received was from Peter Scudamore. In what turned out to be a momentous year for the Champion Jumps Jockey (he was the first to record in excess of 200 winners in a single season), Scudamore wasn't going to miss the chance of securing such an exceptional spare ride.

In the race, Gee Armytage set the pace on Gee-A, but it was clearly not fast enough for Pegwell Bay who had pulled himself to the front rank by the sixth fence. Over the eighth fence, Scudamore took Pegwell Bay clear. By the next, second favourite Giolla Padraig had closed the gap, and no doubt Forster would have been thinking that defeat was not far away. Scudamore harboured no such thoughts, he had simply given Pegwell Bay a breather. Jumping the second last fence the pair went clear again, a bad mistake putting Giolla Padraig out of contention. Another impeccable jump took him three lengths clear at the last from which point he extended his lead to record a decisive victory.

As he did after the majority of his races, Pegwell Bay spent most of the following few days lying down. Normally, horses prefer to stand, and in many cases a horse laying down would set alarm bells ringing amongst the stable staff, but it was just one of Pegwell Bay's quirks. Those who cared for him simply ascribed this unusual behaviour to the fact that, when racing, Pegwell Bay gave everything he could.

A month later on 10th December 1988, Forster and his Gold Cup winner were back at Cheltenham, but this time Pegwell Bay was partnered with Brendan Powell. Fortunately, the ground was ideal, unlike his handicap mark which had risen 10lbs for his Mackeson win. The opposition was stronger though, with Martin Pipe's often free-running ten-year-old, Beau Ranger, sitting at the head of the market.

As expected Beau Ranger, who had won the race in 1984, set off in front; Powell had Pegwell Bay nicely settled in the following pack. At the fifth fence Powell let Pegwell Bay stride on, and he took the lead, much to the surprise of many in the stands. Rounding the bend at the end of the first circuit, Beau Ranger slipped along the rails to join Forster's runner at the head of affairs. They were both moving well but Pegwell Bay's quick, efficient jumping soon had him back in front. At the top of the hill the runners were beginning to get strung out with the first three, Pegwell Bay, Beau Ranger and Comeragh King pulling away from the remaining group. At the second last fence there was little between the leading trio and the winner would be the one with most determination. Beau Ranger and Pegwell Bay landed in unison over the last; there was just the hill to go and both jockeys realised they would be tested to the full. Beau Ranger had the running rail to help him, but Pegwell Bay didn't like to be beaten and he was soon at full stretch trying to gain the advantage. By the line his battling efforts had taken him into the lead and he secured length-and-a-half victory. One of the toughest horses in training and one of the sport's greatest trainers had completed a unique Gold Cup double.

In 1997 Senor El Betrutti became the second horse to win both Cups in the same season, and in 2006 Exotic Dancer repeated the feat. Pegwell Bay's stablemate, Dublin Flyer, also won both races within a twelve month period but not in the same racing season. As good as these subsequent achievements were, to many racing fans they didn't quite match Pegwell Bay's victories in the autumn of 1988. This was partly because he was first to record this special double, but there were other reasons. Pegwell Bay was not overly big and he was not the best chaser of all time, but his courage, determination, and will to win were unparalleled. He was the type of horse that racegoers take to their hearts; the type of horse that gets spectators to the track on a cold winter's day. Pegwell Bay was the epitome of Jumps Racing.

Desert Orchid   *4 February 1989*

In the late 1980s, when it came to races featuring Desert Orchid there were days when the result was never really in doubt. And not at a point where he had an unassailable lead on the run-in, nor even as he jumped clear of a tiring rival at the last fence. There were days when it was clear he would win while the runners were walking around the parade ring. That may appear to be an outlandish statement, a fanciful boast benefitting from hindsight; but anyone who was lucky enough to see Desert Orchid in the flesh would probably agree with it. The 4th February 1989 was one of those days.

Four runners were declared for the Gainsborough Chase, to the racing purists the highlight of the Sandown card. Pegwell Bay, Kildimo and Charter Party ambled around the pre-parade ring, Pegwell Bay was his usual calm self taking little interest in the surroundings. Then, from the far end of the ring the fourth runner appeared: a huge grey thoroughbred. The closer he came the larger he looked and not in a tall, leggy, unfurnished way. He was solid muscle from head to hoof. The other three were all in top shape, but the impression Desert Orchid gave when walking alongside them was, in the human terms, comparable to Arnold Schwarzenegger standing next to Ghandi as one paddock side observer memorably remarked. Of course, his light grey colouring may have accentuated his physique causing some form of optical illusion, but to those scattered around the ring, physically he was in a different league to his rivals that day. He didn't just have the edge in conformation. As he paraded before the growing crowd of racegoers, Janice Coyle by his side, he exuded an air of superiority. Desert Orchid believed he was the best, and he knew that the race would soon prove it beyond any doubt.

Desert Orchid did not always dominate though. The 1984/85 season is not particularly memorable for his followers. After a sparkling winter as a novice hurdler which produced six wins from eight starts and culminated in a run in the Champion Hurdle for which he was second favourite to the odds-on Dawn Run, the following season generated just one win from another eight races. The front-running grey started with three placed efforts behind some good horses, notably See You Then and Browne's Gazette, then ended the campaign with two pulled ups and a fall.

Two hurdles from home on his return race in the autumn of 1985 it looked as if the 4/9 favourite was back to his best. Having led from the off he was well clear of the field, but a crashing fall brought his race to an unexpected and disappointing end. The race was won by Wing And A Prayer ridden by Simon Sherwood the jockey who, in later years, would have a successful association with the grey. David Elsworth then made the shrewd decision to switch Desert Orchid to fences. Given his somewhat erratic jumping this was considered to be a courageous decision by some; others argued that the bigger obstacles would mean that "Dessie" would need to slow down and focus more on his jumping, an approach that could pay dividends.

At Devon and Exeter racecourse on 1st November 1985, Desert Orchid jumped well, made all and won a novices' chase unchallenged by twenty-five lengths, confirming the fact that Elsworth knew the horse better than anyone. Three more wins followed in quick succession before he unseated Colin Brown in a three-runner race won by Pearlyman. After three placed efforts, an unlucky defeat at Ascot ended an interesting season that promised more than it actually delivered.

On his return to racing in the autumn of 1986, Desert Orchid won a handicap chase over two-and-a-half miles, beating the other joint favourite, Very Promising, by seven lengths. He was receiving 25lbs, though, which gives an idea of how the Official Handicapper rated his previous chasing performances. To be able to contest the best weight-for-age races with a realistic chance of success he would need to improve somewhere around twenty pounds. After a disappointing effort, he won the Frogmore handicap chase over two miles by a comfortable twelve lengths. Elsworth then made another surprising decision. Until that point Desert Orchid had been campaigned over distances between sixteen and twenty furlongs. Elsworth's next target for his improving chaser was the King George VI chase at Kempton, over three miles.

To most racing fans, the King George VI is the key chase of the year when it comes to identifying the best chasers. Kempton is a fairer track than Cheltenham, and the three-mile distance requires speed and accurate jumping, as well as stamina. The Gold Cup is more of a "stayers race" especially when the ground is soft. The 1986 running of the "King George" certainly attracted a strong field. Alongside Desert Orchid was stablemate Combs Ditch partnered by Colin Brown, Forgive 'n Forget, Wayward Lad, Western Sunset, and Beau Ranger to name just a few. Simon Sherwood was on the grey and, confounding most experts' forecasts, he did not sit in behind the leaders an attempt to conserve the seven-year-old's stamina. Desert Orchid made all, quickened two fences from home and won by a comfortable fifteen lengths. By any measure it was an impressive display which surely left the Handicapper wondering why he had previously allotted the runner such a low handicap mark. Three more wins followed during the season. Desert Orchid's only two defeats were against the great Pearlyman in the Queen Mother Champion Chase over two miles, and a heavy defeat in the Whitbred Gold Cup where he attempted to give upwards of 13lbs to the field in a race over a stamina-testing three miles five furlongs.

In the 1987/88 campaign, Desert Orchid ran nine times making the frame on each occasion and winning four races including the Chivas Regal Cup at Aintree and the Whitbred Gold Cup Handicap Chase by two-and-a-half lengths from Kildimo who, incredibly, was trying to concede a 1lb. Desert Orchid's run in the "King George" ended in defeat to the French-trained Nupsala.

The following season, Desert Orchid regained his "King George" title, and then beat his three rivals at Sandown on 4th February as easily as his body language suggested he would. This race was, in essence, a "prep" race for the main target of the spring, the Cheltenham Gold Cup.

Prolonged rain had made the ground soft by the time the Festival began in March making the race an even greater test of stamina than usual. This didn't change Sherwood's race plans though. Adopting the same forcing tactics as he had in the past, Desert Orchid set off in front, and maintained the lead for the whole of the first circuit. As the runners turned away from the stands he was joined by Ten Plus who forged ahead with ten fences left to jump. Sherwood kept his mount to the inside rail, but Ten Plus was moving well and at the final ditch had gained a three-length advantage. With four fences to go Ten Plus extended his lead to four lengths and it looked like Fulke Walwyn might claim his fifth win in the race. Yahoo, a lover of soft ground, stealthily moved into third. The race was warming up nicely.

At the tricky third last fence the race was over for Ten Plus as he over-jumped and knuckled on landing. Desert Orchid was back in front, but Yahoo was moving ominously well against the inside running rail. At the second last the yellow colours of Yahoo were visible in front and the stamina-sapping surface was clearly taking its toll on Desert Orchid who was tiring with each stride. He looked like a beaten horse, and favourite backers wondered if the grey had anything left. Sherwood asked for an extra effort, and at the last fence the two leaders landed together. He was back in the race but started to give ground away by drifting towards the centre of the track in the same way so many horses had in the past when encountering the uphill climb. Halfway along the run-in the result was far from certain, but Yahoo would have been clear favourite to win.

Then, from somewhere, the grey seemed to find more; the accompanying words of commentator Peter O'Sullevan giving so many racing fans hope: 'he's beginning to get up, Desert Orchid is beginning to get up'. With fifty yards to race, the grey was in front again, and the tough Yahoo was finally beaten. At the line there was just over a length between the two. It was Dessie's eighth straight win, and arguably the highlight of his career.

The Cheltenham Gold Cup victory may have been his most memorable, but it was not his last. Desert Orchid ran a further sixteen times, his long career coming to an end on Boxing Day 1991. Those sixteen races produced seven more victories including an Irish Grand National success under top weight, and another two wins in the King George VI chase taking his tally to four, which was a record until the brilliant Kauto Star won the race five times between 2006 and 2011.

A race between Arkle, Flyingbolt, Golden Miller, and Desert Orchid would have been a wonderful spectacle. Arkle would probably have started favourite, but he would have needed to be at his very best to stay on terms with the other three. Predicting the winner would not have been a straightforward task. Each Champion would have had his supporters, and many would have sided with the grey who, at times, looked to have a race in safe-keeping even before it had even started.

From Farmyard to Winner's Enclosure *15 March 1990*

At his farm in rural Carmarthenshire, Sirrell Griffiths owned a herd of cattle and three racehorses that shared their stables with a few bantams and some Rhode Island Reds. On the morning of the 1990 Gold Cup he milked his cows, loaded one of the horses into a trailer, then drove the 125 miles to Cheltenham. A little before 3:30pm, Griffiths watched his runner, partnered by Graham McCourt, canter to the start. It was only by chance that he was there at all; that day Griffiths should have been back on the farm doing whatever cattle farmers do between morning and evening milking. The intended Festival target for his representative was the Mildmay of Flete Challenge Cup run on the second day of the meeting. An unexpected delay at the local market meant he was too late to declare his runner for that two-and-a-half mile contest, and had to settle for a Gold Cup entry instead. So here he was, on day three, nervously watching his horse milling around at the start alongside the best stayers in Britain and Ireland.

The 1990 Gold Cup had brought together the very cream of British jumping bloodstock. Taking on the 1989 winner, Desert Orchid, was Yahoo, the horse that had pressed him so hard in the finish twelve months earlier; the Welsh National winner, Bonanza Boy; recent winners Cavvies Clown, Nick The Brief and Ten Of Spades; the highly-regarded Toby Tobias and dual cup winner Pegwell Bay. It was a quality line-up through and through and those experts, the Bookmakers, had given his horse next to no chance of winning. But Griffiths had faith, he knew his runner had been working well and fully deserved his place in such lofty company. He knew Norton's Coin had a chance, in his mind, a good chance.

When the tapes went up, Cavvies Clown seemed reluctant to race and gave the others at least a twenty-length advantage; Desert Orchid and Kildimo made the running. McCourt was content to sit mid-division on Norton's Coin. There was little change in the position of the runners throughout the first circuit. As they reached the top of the hill for the second time, Ten Of Spades was matching strides with Desert Orchid at the front of affairs; Norton's Coin, who was still moving smoothly, had progressed into fourth. Two fences from home, Desert Orchid led on the nearside, Toby

Tobias ran against the rail and, much to the amazement of the racegoers watching from the stands, Norton's Coin had moved into third. A good jump at the last was critical for all three. With the crowd's cheering ringing in their ears they all cleared the last but, surprisingly, the favourite began to weaken and Toby Tobias took the lead followed by a "staying on" Norton's Coin. The rising ground was now making the chase to the line even more strenuous, which appeared to favour the outsider. With fifty yards to go his gathering momentum took him upsides Toby Tobias, then propelled him into the lead. By the time he crossed the finishing line he held a three-quarters-of-a-length advantage. At 100/1 Norton's Coin was the longest priced winner of the race – a good result for most Bookmakers except, of course, for the offices in Wales, especially Carmarthenshire.

Beckhampton's Classic History   *6 June 1990*

Beckhampton has been the source of Classic winners stretching back to the early 1800s. Located near to the mythical Avebury Stone circle and Silbury Hill in one of the most ancient parts of England, Beckhampton even has a reference in the *Domesday Book*. Judging by the names of its patrons, back in late eleventh century there was a definite Nordic influence in the region.

Initially a coaching inn located near to the tollgate on the Devizes road, it was converted into racing stables in the late 1820s by owner William Treen. Beckhampton Stables' first Classic winner was a filly named Deception who won the Oaks in 1839. Some years later Treen was replaced by Harry Woolcott who was responsible for five Classic winners including Formosa who won the Fillies' Triple Crown as well as dead-heating in the 2,000 Guineas. Sam Darling, the next trainer to run the famous establishment, added a further seven Classics to the roll of honour including Galtee More who became the first Beckhampton trained winner of the Derby, set a record time in the 1897 2,000 Guineas, and went on to complete the Triple Crown by winning the St Leger.

Fred Darling, Sam's second son and a strict disciplinarian who insisted that his staff were all well groomed and smartly attired even when working in the yard, recorded his first Classic success at Beckhampton when Hurry On won the 1916 St Leger. Classic victories would then come thick and fast, with two 1,000 Guineas wins, five successes in the 2,000 Guineas, two more Oaks victories, and an amazing seven wins in the Derby. In 1926 Fred Darling had a second St Leger winner when Coronach took the oldest Classic, then added a third when Sun Chariot completed the Fillies' Triple Crown in 1942 for His Majesty King George VI. Noel Murless was the next trainer to enjoy Classic success at Beckhampton by adding a 1,000 Guineas and St Leger to the ever-growing list during his short association with the yard.

Jeremy Tree followed Murless and, as well as claiming victories in the Oaks and 2,000 Guineas, he trained Khalid Abdullah's Rainbow Quest, winner of the 1985 Prix de l'Arc de Triomphe. However, by the time of his retirement at the end of the 1989 season, the stable had not seen a Derby winner since Fred Darling's Owen Tudor won the race in 1941. Neither Tree nor his successor Roger Charlton knew that this dry spell was about to be broken in dramatic fashion just six months later.

Sanglamore was by Sharpen Up the sire of Sharpo the champion sprinter who won the Nunthorpe Stakes on three successive years when in Jeremy Tree's care. He was barely mentioned around the yard in 1989 when other juveniles were preferred. With the exception of Illusory who, in the early part of the year was considered by some to be a potential stable star, it was a very low-key year for Beckhampton's juveniles. Prospects for Classic glory in 1990 looked bleak.

Making his debut at Leicester in the closing days of the turf season, Sanglamore was second under Steve Cauthen to the favourite, Lover's Moon. He clearly benefited from the winter's break because his next run showed a marked improvement. At Nottingham over ten furlongs he stayed on well to get the better of Helen's Guest. Then, just over two weeks later, he was caught close to home by Clive Brittain's seemingly unfancied, but clearly useful, Anvari in the May Stakes at Newmarket. Taken to York for the Group 2 Dante Stakes in mid-May, the three-year-old was far too strong for the other eight runners, and at the line had a length-and-a-half to spare in a comfortable success over Karinga Bay who was to win the Group 3 Gordon Stakes later in the season. Sanglamore was on the upgrade and was primed and ready for his main target of the year, the Prix du Jockey Club.

Like Sanglamore, Quest For Fame had only one run as a juvenile and also took the runner-up position. He was well fancied for the race at Newbury and although he managed to get the better of stable companion Deploy, he found Henry Cecil's Tyburn Tree too strong. It was an encouraging run from both of the Beckhampton inmates. Unlike Tyburn Tree who did not train on as a three-year-old, Quest For Fame made good progress over the winter and got off the mark in good style in a twenty-one runner maiden race at Newbury on his return to racing in the spring of 1990. A second to Belmez, a well-regarded Cecil runner, Quest For Fame was slightly disappointing in the Chester Vase for those who thought he had Classic potential. But he was still improving, and with a month to go before Epsom there was still hope.

On Sunday 3rd June, Sanglamore went to Chantilly hoping to match the success of Henry Cecil's Old Vic twelve months previously. He faced eleven opponents including his old adversary Anvari, the French favourite Epervier Bleu, and the lightly raced, but impressive and heavily backed Theatrical Charmer. As the stalls opened, Pat Eddery restrained Sanglamore and settled him at the back of the field. He seemed determined to conserve Sanglamore's stamina for the final stages of the contest that was likely to be run at a strong pace on the "good to soft" ground. With well under a mile to go, Eddery still had Sanglamore in last position. The favourite went for a run on the outside and that was Eddery's cue to get his runner into the race. At the two-furlong maker, Sanglamore still had ten lengths to find, but Eddery was getting into the drive position. He rapidly made ground into fourth; then quickened impressively to pass the favourite deep inside the final furlong and record a half-length win. Sanglamore had won *a* Derby for Beckhampton, and three days later all eyes would be on his stablemate Quest For Fame in *the* Derby.

Razeen, Steve Cauthen's choice of Henry Cecil's runners, was favourite for Epsom's big race on 6th June 1990; Quest For Fame was generally around the 7/1 mark, fourth favourite. Eddery, seeking a quick Derby double, positioned Quest For Fame much closer to the pace than he had Sanglamore, and rounded Tattenham Corner on the heels of the leaders. Hitting the front two furlongs from home at first seemed too early, but Eddery was well aware of the colt's stamina and knew exactly what he was doing. Quest For Fame gradually increased his lead and crossed the winning line three lengths to the good.

After such a long wait, Beckhampton Stables had sent out two Derby winners in less than a week, giving Roger Charlton the start to his training career at the historic stables of which he could have only dreamed.

Phoenix Park to Buckingham Palace   *1 September 1990*

The racegoers who stayed for the last race at Phoenix Park on 1st September 1990 were unaware that they were about to witness the first ride in public by a jockey who would become recognised as the best jumps jockey of any era. Riding Nordic Touch for Jim Bolger, Tony McCoy put up 1lb overweight on the 4/1 favourite, but it made no difference to the result. Even with just 6st 11lbs on his back the three-year-old couldn't make the frame.

Given his height, McCoy had little chance of maintaining such a low weight and it soon became apparent that his future would be in National Hunt races. In 1994 he moved to England and rode as a conditional jockey for National Hunt trainer Toby Balding. It was at this point his undoubted natural ability became apparent. McCoy won the conditional jockeys' championship in 1994/95, then became Champion Jockey in 1995/96, a title he held for an uninterrupted run of twenty years. During this time McCoy won every race worth winning and demonstrated time and time again that he was better than any of his contemporaries in every aspect of jumps racing.

By the time he retired at the end of the 2014/15 season, McCoy had ridden over 4,000 winners, including 289 in a single season, had been appointed a Member of the Order of the British Empire, and an Officer of the Order of the British Empire. If that wasn't enough, he also won the BBC Sports Personality of the year award, the first jockey to do so. In 2016 he received the ultimate accolade from the Queen and Tony McCoy became Sir Anthony Peter McCoy.

He's Back   *15 October 1990*

Almost forty years after riding his first winner when aged twelve, Lester Piggott retired from race riding. A spell as a successful trainer followed as well as a short period at Her Majesty's Pleasure for evading tax, a transgression for which individuals are punished harshly but multinational corporations are seemingly excused without censure. Then, in 1990 he shocked the racing world again. Piggott was back riding horses and, more importantly, riding as well as he ever had. His return at Leicester on 15th October attracted a huge crowd of racegoers to the Midlands venue all keen to watch the Master at work. The press were not thin on the ground either with camera crews and journalists taking up every possible vantage point in an effort to interview the fifty-four-year-old. His time away from the limelight had clearly had little impact on Piggott and his dry sense of humour was at its sharpest. When asked by a journalist if his riding technique had changed, Piggott merely replied 'No, still one leg on each side.' Unfortunately the day did not produce any winners. However, at Chepstow the following day he recorded a double and another winner followed at Newmarket's Dewhurst meeting. At the Curragh the following week Piggott deputised for the injured John

Reid and, riding for Vincent O'Brien, he picked up another four winners in a single afternoon. Unfortunately, he didn't have a ride in the nursery in which a future great, sixteen-year-old Tony McCoy (claiming 10lbs), guided the two-year-old Nordic Wind into the runner-up position.

Four days later Piggott was in America, a jockey's licence in his hand (cost: $300), and the thought of winning the Breeders' Cup Mile foremost in his mind. The stands were packed at Belmont Park that autumn day with many of the racegoers wondering if the "old Brit still had it in him". They were about to find out in no uncertain terms. In one of the most exciting races of the century, Piggott took Royal Academy, who lost his action when hitting a false patch of ground on turning into the straight, from last to first to win the celebrated race in a photograph. It was vintage Piggott, and those who questioned whether he should be allowed to ride in public "at his age" were left to wonder why they ever doubted him. More success followed over the next four years and by the end of his career Piggott had won every race worth winning including an incredible thirty English Classics.

Back in 1983 his Derby win on Teenoso took his tally in the Epsom race to nine victories, more than any other jockey has ever achieved. Even the great Fred Archer only won the race on five occasions and although Frank Buckle managed fourteen wins in the two Epsom Classics, nine of them were in the Oaks. After adding seven French Classics, sixteen Irish Classics, eleven Gold Cups, including three in a row on Sagaro, and a total of just under 4,500 winners to Piggott's record-breaking number of Classic victories, it becomes not just the profile of a great flat racing jockey, but the profile of the greatest flat racing jockey that ever sat on a thoroughbred.

Racing on a Sunday Afternoon   *26 July 1992*

The first Sunday race meeting staged in Britain under Jockey Club rules was held at Doncaster on 26th July 1992. It was a strange affair. The course was not permitted to charge for admittance for those wanting to watch the racing, and there was no on-course betting. To get around these restrictions, course admission was charged, ostensibly, for the privilege of hearing the band of the Irish Guards, and any bets had to be placed the previous day when betting shops were open.

The move to allow racing on Sunday, even in this very restricted form, was fiercely opposed by various factions. One argument in favour of racing seven days a week was that it would bring Britain into line with most other countries. Sunday racing had been a regular fixture in Ireland for seven years and was an accepted part of the sporting week in France.

It was not for another three years, and an amendment to the Sunday Trading Bill, that bets could finally be placed on Sundays. Newmarket was the venue for the first Sunday meeting that allowed on-course betting and the feature race was the 1,000 Guineas. It was won by Richard Hills on Harayir, his first Classic win.

While Sunday racing is now part of the fixture list, it has, with a very few exceptions, become synonymous with low-grade racing. In France many of the most prestigious races are run on Sundays, the "Arc" being an example. The same applies in Ireland. Taking the 2019 flat racing season as an example, there were thirty-four meetings held on Sundays in Great Britain. These meetings featured 245 races of which just one was a Group 1. Group race classifications actually accounted for just three races, whereas handicaps made up 170 of all contests run. In Ireland, twenty-five Sunday meetings produced 165 races of which six were Group 1 standard, with a further fourteen spread between the other two Group classifications. Less than half of the races held in Ireland were handicaps, compared to two-thirds in Britain.

The reason for this bias towards the lower grade races is that Bookmakers prefer them. Their highly competitive structure suits the layers by allowing them to generate maximum profit from minimal input. Essentially handicaps 'are the closest a live sporting contest can get to a casino game'. More handicaps means greater profits for Bookmakers, which in turn means increased revenue for racing. Whilst the additional income is undeniably good for the sport, the replacement of quality weight-for-age races with an endless stream of low-grade handicaps is not. Nor does it appeal to those interested in racing as a sport rather than purely a medium for betting. Those hoping to explain why, in the 21st century, Irish racing is producing higher quality racehorses than British racing may find a comparison between the two race programmes a good place to start.

The Welsh Grand National   31 December 1994

To most racing enthusiasts, the Welsh Grand National has become as much a part of Christmas as mince pies. But that has not always been the case; in its early days the race was run at Easter. The evolution of the Welsh Grand National stretches back to 1895 when it was first staged at Ely racecourse in

Cardiff, and it was not until 1949 that the contest was moved to Chepstow. It then took a further thirty years before the race was given its Christmas position in the calendar. Throughout all that time, and the various changes, there was one constant: the race was always run in Wales. At least it was until 1994 when, for the only time in its history, the Welsh Grand National was run in England.

The winter of 1994/95 was one of the wettest in living memory, and by race day the Chepstow turf was completely waterlogged. A switch of track was agreed, and Newbury was the chosen venue not least because it staged a regular meeting between Christmas and New Year. Like Wales, Berkshire had received more than its fair share of rain in the pre-Christmas period and, much to the disappointment of racegoers, the first day of the Newbury meeting had to be abandoned due to water-logging. Prospects for the National looked bleak, but fortunately a dry night meant that, in the space of twenty-four hours, underfoot conditions improved just enough to make the track raceable. The National was back on, which was good news for cricket-loving Kim Bailey, trainer of Master Oats.

Bailey took charge of the somewhat fragile gelding in the autumn of 1991 and placed him well to win the Plough Maiden chase at Southwell near the end of the season. Following a break of 545 days, Master Oats tackled a handicap chase at Uttoxeter, and off an official handicap mark of 107 proved too strong for his six opponents. More wins on "soft" and "heavy" ground followed, and by the start of the 1994/95 season his handicap mark had risen to 148.

A delayed preparation meant he didn't return to racing until early December when he gave weight and a beating to the 1992 Gold Cup winner Cool Ground. Party Politics finished closest to the improving eight-year-old, but even he was a well-beaten runner-up. Bailey now set his sights on the Welsh Grand National, which would be only the second time Master Oats had contested a race beyond three-and-a-half miles, the other time being the 1994 Aintree National where he fell at the thirteenth fence when still going well.

Thankfully, the 31st December 1994 was a dry, albeit windy day. By race time the Members' Stand was packed with tweed jackets and cigar smoke. The favourites had won the first four races (one was a joint favourite) and supporters of Master Oats were hoping that the trend would continue. The ground was certainly in his favour, and Norman Williamson looked confident as he settled Master Oats at the rear of the field in the early stages of the contest. After jumping the thirteenth of the twenty-one fences

Williamson moved Master Oats into contention just behind the leader, Dakyns Boy; and four fences from home he hit the front. Williamson looked over his shoulder, he could see that most of his rivals were toiling. Earth Summit was the only possible danger but he was under pressure whereas Master Oats was cruising without any significant encouragement from his jockey. At the last fence he was well clear and could be eased on the run-in to record a twenty-length success. In commentary Peter O'Sullevan remarked that he would be 'well fancied for the Grand National', but before that he had an even more important race to contest.

Ten weeks later Master Oats was at Cheltenham taking on the best chasers in the country in the Gold Cup. The wet winter had continued well into February, so there was plenty of give in the ground at the Prestbury track - ideal for Master Oats. Williamson opted to ride a waiting race, as he had done at Newbury and, apart from clipping a couple of fences, the race went to plan with the 100/30 favourite outclassing the field and winning by a comfortable fifteen lengths.

Master Oats was at the top of his game in the winter of 1994/95 which resulted in Raceform assigning him a rating of 186, at least twelve pounds higher than all other chasers in the country. His Newbury run was astounding, and his Gold Cup performance was one of the most impressive in the history of the race. In fact, only three horses have won the race by a greater margin: Easter Hero, Arkle and Alverton; not a bad trio to be associated with.

Hitting former England fast bowler Gladstone Small for six may have been the highlight of Kim Bailey's cricketing career, but the 1995 Cheltenham Festival was definitely the pinnacle of his training career. Forty-eight hours before the Gold Cup, Bailey's Alderbook won the Champion Hurdle setting up a noteworthy double that was completed in emphatic fashion by Master Oats – the only horse to win the Welsh Grand National without leaving England.

21st Century

The new millennium started with a revolution in betting and in the sport in general. Exchanges offered punters a new way to bet and their impact was immediate and profound. There was a shift in focus away from a sport designed to determine a hierarchy based on ability, to one aimed at maximising revenue. Consequently, the BHA's obsession with handicap races continued unabated with weight-adjusted contests soon accounting for the majority of horseraces run in Great Britain.

Despite this negative structural change to racing, there were many horses that demonstrated what racing should really be about.

Fans of jumps racing who didn't get to see Arkle were able to enjoy the spectacular sight of a horse matching his remarkable achievement of winning three Gold Cups; and on the hurdling front, Big Bucks dominated staying events like no other horse ever has.

For flat racing connoisseurs, there were several top class horses that raised the pulse rate and one in particular that could challenge the very best that competed in the Classics over the last two-hundred years.

A New Way to Bet   *9 June 2000*

When the *BetFair* betting exchange started trading in June 2000 it marked the most significant change to the betting industry since betting shops were legalised in 1961. The exchange offered punters an alternative to betting on the Tote or with Bookmakers. Crucially, it provided a means for punters to lay horses, in other words back them to lose. Naturally, this was open to abuse and made it far easier for connections of horses to profit from defeat or even failure to run. For ante post races, for instance, an owner could lay his/her horse, safe in the knowledge that it was never an intended runner. This way a profit could be guaranteed.

Of course, exploiting loopholes such as this had happened many times in the past. In 1845, *The Sportsman's Magazine* published a letter in which the correspondent strenuously urged all readers to lay a horse named Zanoni in the Chester Cup adding 'at the eleventh hour... get a friend to object to the horse's pedigree, and to call for proof of his age.' Such a move would allow layers to collect if Zanoni lost but, according to this master of betting strategy, 'if he wins, refuse to pay on the plea of the objection, and he must be a clever fellow to get the better of us in a court of justice.' Zanoni was Maccabeus, also known as Running Rein, the horse disqualified in the 1844 Derby. Whilst the letter was not meant to be serious advice, it did highlight an area which needed addressing by the Jockey Club, and similarly in the years following the introduction of the exchanges, rules needed to be amended to accommodate this new style of betting.

One of the main benefits the exchanges offered punters was the ability to bet purely by computer. Systems could be established on home computers, and programs written which automatically placed bets without the need for human intervention.

The 1998 book *Forecasting Methods For Horseracing* illustrated the potential of neural networks (a branch of artificial intelligence) for horseracing prediction. Although networks were able to formulate forecasting models that were superior to human experts, at the end of the twentieth century their creation was a slow process due primarily to lack of computing capacity. Rather than relying on a set of rules designed by a human researcher, neural networks learn by examining previous examples, the more examples the better. Many real-world tasks are extremely complex, and it often took a network a great deal of time to establish the necessary relationships between the data that were required to form a usable model. Fortunately, this issue was soon overcome as computers rapidly increased in speed and capacity. In a short space of time, artificial intelligence-based systems were developed that could beat the very best humans in games such as Chess and Go, to accurately detect the presence of cancer from mammograms, and even drive cars. They are also used by many punters who generate a healthy living by trading on the exchanges. The impact which artificial intelligence will have on the way we live is only just starting to become apparent; this new technology could alter our lifestyles to the same degree that the expansion of the railway network did in the nineteenth century.

Twenty years on from their inception, the betting exchanges are still growing, mainly due to their ability of offer markets with a lower over-round and Bookmakers' keenness to close down accounts held by successful punters. Despite this upheaval in the betting market, the golden rule of profitable betting has not changed. Punters should always consider all available prices when placing a bet, including those offered by Bookmakers and exchanges, and attempt to secure the best one available. Following this rule undoubtedly increases the chance of securing a long-term profit.

Galileo   *28 October 2000*

It is often the case that the better juveniles start their careers later in the season, but the end of October is extremely late by any measure. Aidan O'Brien finally allowed Galileo to grace the turf on 28th October 2000. His long-awaited debut took place over a mile of Leopardstown's famous track in the shadow of the Dublin Mountains. It was, without any doubt, worth the wait.

Lining up in a field of sixteen, Mick Kinane soon had the Sadler's Wells colt tracking the leaders, Sky View and Taraza. Inside the two-furlong marker, Galileo hit the front and smoothly drew clear. Without being asked a serious question he ran out the easy fourteen-length winner. His detractors would say that, impressive as he was, wide-margin victories on "heavy" ground are always misleading, adding that his opponents did not pose a significant threat. Both claims have some merit, although runner-up Taraza won two of her next three starts. A better guide to the value of this stunning success is in comparison with other performances on the day. In the next race on the card, Dermot Weld's 109-rated four-year-old won in good style carrying 1lb more than Galileo in a time of 1 minute 49.6 seconds. Galileo completed the mile in 1 minute 48.2s seconds and could probably have shaved at least half-a-second off that time had Kinane so desired. On those figures alone

Galileo's win was one of the most remarkable of the year and it prompted one racing analyst to write 'it is easy to over-estimate these youngsters after just one run, but Galileo really does look something very special', and very special he turned out to be.

In the early months of 2001 there was speculation that Galileo may run in the 2,000 Guineas. When questioned, Aidan O'Brien would emphasise often how much speed his colt possessed. But it was not to be. As soon as he was declared for a ten furlong Listed contest at Leopardstown it was clear that he would be kept to middle distances through his three-year-old campaign.

After an easy win on his return from the winter break, Galileo was upped in class to a Group 3 race where he readily despatched his four opponents. With his two "prep" races out of the way, Galileo was ready for the Derby where he would face the 2,000 Guineas winner, Golan.

At Epsom he was always up with the pace and Mick Kinane allowed him to hit the front at the two-furlong pole. Galileo immediately lengthened his stride and pulled well clear; Golan came out of the pack and stayed on well, but Galileo was far too good and won by a long looking three-and-a-half lengths without feeling the whip. This impressive victory confirmed the promise of his juvenile run the previous October and ensured that he would be ranked amongst the best Derby winners.

Kinane rode a similar race to take the Irish Derby even more easily, but on his next start, in the twelve-furlong King George VI and Queen Elizabeth Diamond Stakes at Ascot, the 1/2 favourite had to fight for the first time in his racing career. As usual, Kinane timed his run to hit the front at the two-furlong marker, but this time a horse came with him, the five-year-old Fantastic Light. In a tussle, Galileo finally out-stayed his rival in the last two hundred yards prompting some observers to suggest that Fantastic Light might have his measure over a mile-and-a-quarter. Five weeks later their theory would be put to the test as the two great horses met in the Irish Champion Stakes.

On a sunny autumn day, the crowd packed the stands at Leopardstown to see the rematch. As the stalls opened, Galileo's stablemate, Ice Dancer, raced into a lead setting a furious pace. Clearly Aidan O'Brien felt compelled to ensure the race was a true test of stamina; he could not risk a slowly run contest that would produce a sprint finish. Rounding the final bend the "big two" made their moves: Fantastic Light up the inside and Galileo from the outside of the pack. They joined each other clear of the field, and battled along the straight. At times it looked like Galileo would maintain his unbeaten record, a fraction of a second later Fantastic Light looked the stronger. They flashed past the finishing post together, but not quite in unison; Fantastic Light had prevailed by a neck. Galileo had tasted defeat for the first time.

Taken to Belmont Park, New York, for the Breeders' Cup Classic, Galileo ran well below par as many European horses do at the meeting. He was immediately retired to stud.

As good as he was in the mid-summer races, Galileo was to make an even greater impact on horseracing as a sire with his offspring quickly amassing a vast number of significant victories. Galileo was leading sire in Great Britain and Ireland in 2008 and again from 2010 to 2019. Just as importantly, he has sired numerous Group race winners including Frankel, considered by many to be the greatest ten-furlong horse ever to set hoof on a course in Great Britain.

The World's Best Juvenile   27 October 2001

Aidan O'Brien's Johannesburg made his racing debut on 30th May 2001 just seven months after Galileo, and ten days before his stablemate won the Derby. On paper, the colt by Hennessey had a straightforward task at Fairyhouse, which was confirmed by his starting price and the race itself. At odds of 1/3 he easily beat his seven rivals. The Bookmakers were not giving much away though with an over-round of 133% for an eight-runner race.

A solid win in the five-furlong Norfolk Stakes at Royal Ascot followed. Stepped up to an extended six furlongs for the Anglesey Stakes at The Curragh, he was much more impressive. Quickening clear in the closing stages he won by a comfortable four lengths, showing that he was just as good on ground that had some ease in it. This success prompted his trainer Aidan O'Brien to remark that Johannesburg was a 'very good colt... [with] speed and stamina.'

After some debate, the Group 1 Phoenix Stakes at Leopardstown was chosen for his next run. In the race, Mick Kinane tracked the leaders then let Johannesburg stride on at the furlong pole. The colt's impressive acceleration settled the affair in a matter of seconds and he pulled clear to win by five lengths. Stablemate Wiseman's Ferry who was four lengths behind the favourite at The Curragh, was around seven lengths behind in fourth, possibly giving a guide to Johannesburg's degree of improvement.

At Deauville in August he made it five wins from five races and recorded a second Group 1 win. Then, in the Middle Park Stakes at Newmarket, he added a third win in the top tier with an imperious display. O'Brien then set his sights much further afield.

Many good horses run well in Europe then perform poorly in America at the end of the season. Timing is clearly one issue that contributes to these many failures, but also the stresses associated with travelling, a different time zone, and a different environment, all conspire to reduce their chances of running to their full capabilities. Therefore, there's always a concern when an unbeaten runner makes the trip across the Atlantic. Even so, the Breeders' Cup Juvenile on 27th October 2001 at Belmont Park was the target for Michael Tabor's champion two-year-old. To have a chance of winning, Johannesburg needed to adapt to a new surface, stay the extended mile, two furlongs more than any distance he had so far tackled, and get the better of Bob Baffert's unbeaten colt Officer, who was rated a 4/6 shot in the race. It was asking a lot, and the majority of punters did not think he was up to the challenge; hence his starting price of just over 7/1.

Kinane settled Johannesburg on the heels of the leading group in the early stages, keen to preserve his stamina. Officer set the pace. As they started to round the oval, O'Brien's runner was fifth, on the inside running rail, and moving smoothly. Straightening up for home there was a wall of three horses in front of Kinane and one on his outside. He had plenty of horse, but nowhere to go. Would this become one of those "if only he got a run" races? Officer was still in the mix at the head of affairs and there were plenty of runners behind Johannesburg with good finishing speed. It was a wide-open race and success could depend on a single decisive move.

From nowhere there came a fortunate break for O'Brien's star. The runner on Kinane's outside began to weaken, so the jockey quickly pulled Johannesburg wide of the leading group and asked for an effort. The response was immediate. Johannesburg swooped past his toiling rivals making the finest juveniles in America appear altogether pedestrian. Repent finished fast on the outside but it was too late. The best juvenile in the world had won his fourth Group 1 race in four different countries.

Unlike Galileo who continued to improve and enjoyed a successful three-year-old campaign, Johannesburg failed to train on. This was not too surprising, as one commentator wrote at the end of 2001 'physically Johannesburg looks well developed and there must be a doubt whether he will progress as much as his contemporaries over the winter.' After three modest efforts in 2002 Johannesburg, one of the most brilliant juveniles ever to race in Britain, was retired to stud.

Best Mate Matches Arkle   *18 March 2004*

When Best Mate won the Gold Cup in 2002 his record was eight wins from thirteen runs under National Hunt rules. In each of the five races he failed to win, he finished second, including the King George VI Chase at Kempton eleven weeks before his Cheltenham success.

The following season he added three more races to his tally and three more wins. The first came at Huntingdon in the Grade 2 Peterborough Chase where he outclassed a small field. In the "King George" at Kempton he gained compensation for his defeat the previous year, and then gave the Gold Cup field a lesson in jumping when retaining the trophy. In so doing he became the first horse to win back-to-back Gold Cups since L'Escargot in 1971 which illustrates the magnitude of the achievement.

His warm up race at Huntingdon did not go as planned at the start of his 2003/04 campaign. An uncharacteristic mistake four fences from home put paid to his chances and the Champion had to settle for the runner-up spot. Henrietta Knight then opted to take her stable star to Leopardstown rather than allowing him to defend his Kempton crown, a move which produced a quick Grade 1 double for the stable. Edredon Bleu won at Kempton and Best Mate proved to be nine lengths too good for his seven opponents in the Ericsson Chase that featured Gold Cup fancy Beef Or Salmon.

On 18th March 2004 Best Mate, still only a nine-year-old, joined a trio of great Champions comprising Golden Miller, Cottage Rake and Arkle, by winning his third consecutive Gold Cup. It was a remarkable achievement by a horse that some believed never received the recognition he deserved. His detractors, and surprisingly there were some, seemed always to be ready with a barbed comment, whether relating to the style of success, the number of times he raced each season, or some other minor related issue. After the 2004 Gold Cup, critics claimed that the margin of success should have been greater, and it is true that Beef Or Salmon was much closer than he was when the pair met in Ireland.

However, Best Mate was again fluent at his fences and showed steely determination when faced with stiff competition in the closing stages of the contest. Whether the winning distance is a short-head or impressive twenty lengths, the owner still gets to lift the trophy.

In the Lexus Chase the following December, the improving Beef Or Salmon gained his revenge on exceptionally soft going but, despite this defeat, Best Mate was still on course to gain a fourth Gold Cup success in

March. Only Golden Miller would have remained ahead of Knight's chaser with respect to the number of Gold Cup victories had he succeeded which seemed very likely until just a few days before the Festival. As his trainer was putting the final touches to the Champion's preparations for the race, his season was brought to an abrupt halt. In fact it was probably an indication that Best Mate's career was all but over. After completing a routine piece of work on the gallops, Best Mate broke a blood vessel. For many horses this is something that occurs from time to time and they make a full recovery. As former biology teacher Henrietta Knight said at the time 'Whenever they break a blood vessel it is serious, but it is not career-threatening'. While Knight was correct in her assertion, for Best Mate this seemingly innocuous incident was indicative of something more serious. As a precautionary measure he was forced to miss the chance of winning his fourth Gold Cup, for which he was the clear favourite. Best Mate did not reappear on a racecourse until the following November.

On 1st November 2005 at Exeter, the scene of his first victory over fences back in 2000, Best Mate was attempting to concede weight to his rivals when Paul Carberry pulled him up before the second last fence. It was the only race in which Best Mate failed to finish in the first two, and it was to be his last race. Seconds after his jockey had dismounted Best Mate collapsed.

Although the race had ended, few in the stands knew that Monkerhostin had won. All binoculars were focussed down the track; all eyes were on the stricken champion. An uneasy low murmur filtered through the crowd that seemed to be making one last telepathic effort to "will" Best Mate back to his feet. It was not to be. A single voice, audible to more than its owner had probably intended, uttered in a simple monotonic fashion eight words which expressed what everyone was thinking and no one wanted to accept: 'I think I just heard Henrietta's heart break.'

Best Mate's devoted trainer was the first person to reach him, 'I was actually on the track where he came down... I knew immediately he had died,' she told reporters.

His death made headlines in the national press and television news reports. Best Mate was one of those rare horses that do more than just win races, they become part of the national consciousness and appeal to the racing and non-racing public alike.

As his owner Jim Lewis explained, his popularity throughout the country 'helped us raise thousands of pounds for charity and he made a lot of difference to many people's lives.' In racing terms Best Mate won fourteen of his twenty-two races, including three Gold Cups, but his contribution to horseracing, and society in general, was immeasurable.

A Most Inexperienced Guineas Winner   *3 May 2009*

Ghanaati, a Giant's Causeway filly out of a Mr Prospector mare (Sarayir), was foaled in March 2006. As a two-year-old she ran only twice. Both races were at Kempton on its all-weather surface. Although she was over three lengths behind the winner on her debut when ridden by Michael Hills, she was made a short-priced favourite for her second run, winning by a very easy six lengths when partnered by Michael's older twin brother, Richard. Her next start was in the 1,000 Guineas at Newmarket. Starting at 20-1 she was given little chance of success but proved the punters wrong by winning a shade comfortably in a record time, becoming the only filly to win this great race having never before competed on turf.

Four in a Row for Yeats   *18 June 2009*

Since Master Jackey won at Ascot in 1807 there have been many great winners of the Gold Cup. Isonomy won the race in 1879 and 1880 for trainer John Porter, then four years later St Simon won the contest by an easy twenty lengths. Bayardo's Ascot win confirmed him as one of the greatest horses of the twentieth century and, in the mid-1970s, Sagaro became the first horse to win the race in three consecutive years, his first success starting a period of dominance for Lester Piggott who won the race six times in an eight-year span. In 1995, Double Trigger added the Gold Cup to a long list of "Cup" victories that included three wins in both the Doncaster and Goodwood Cups. Then, of course, we get to Yeats.

Trained by Aidan O'Brien in Ireland, Yeats won his first Gold Cup as a five-year-old in 2006. Remarkably, it was his first run of the season after a break of 242 days. The Goodwood Cup followed before an unexpected defeat at The Curragh and a disappointing run in the Melbourne Cup.

The following season he was back in action in April and put together four straight wins including his second Ascot Gold Cup. Four wins from five runs in 2008 brought him his third consecutive Gold Cup as well as his first win in France when he took the two-mile Prix Royal Oak.

Prospects for a fourth Gold Cup win looked decidedly poor when he returned to action in 2009 with a thirty-two length defeat in the Vintage

Crop Listed Stakes, a race he had won the two previous seasons. This defeat was put down to the soft going and a lack of early season fitness with the *Racing Post* reporting that he 'blew a lot after the race'. At Ascot on the 18th June 2009 it was a very different story. On more suitable going, Yeats led over three furlongs from home and was well in command from that point onwards. By winning the race for a fourth time he has a valid claim to the title of best stayer in history although connections of Stradivarius and Alycidon may hold an alternative view.

Remounting Rule Modified   *2 November 2009*

Allowing jockeys to remount in races had been a contentious issue for many years. In 2009 the BHA, which had taken over the rule-making powers from the Jockey Club, banned the remounting of a horse once the race had started. This issue had been brought into focus when Kauto Star fell two fences from home in the Weatherbys Bank novices' chase at Exeter in early 2005. Kauto Star had been on his way to an impressive victory when taking the tumble. Given his commanding lead, Ruby Walsh quickly remounted and without the use of irons jumped the last. In the meantime Mistral de la Cour had passed them, and was well on his way to the finishing line. Walsh made a valiant effort to get Kauto Star back in front, but at the line the favourite failed by a short head. After the race it was found that Kauto Star had sustained an injury, probably when falling, and as a result he missed the remainder of the season, including the Cheltenham Festival.

Naturally, there were many who disagreed with the new ruling. When all four horses fell in a novices' chase at Towcester in 2011, causing the race to be declared void, the detractors were quick to blame the new ruling. But at least punters had their stakes returned which would have been welcome news to those who had backed Zhukov, a faller at the fourth, providing they had not destroyed their betting tickets by the time Radharc Na Mara unseated his jockey at the last.

This was not the first time the remounting rule had been changed. For much of the nineteenth century the rule regarding remounting was given as follows:

If a rider fall from his horse, and the horse be rode in by a person that is sufficient weight, he shall take his place the same, as if his rider had not fallen, provided he go back to the place where the rider fell.

In other words, anyone of equal or greater weight could complete the race in the event of an injury to a rider. Consequently, it was quite possible that a spectator, with no race-riding experience who was merely enjoying a day out at the races, could return home that evening as a successful jockey.

As for Kauto Star, after a nine-month break he returned to racing action and embarked on a remarkable career. He made the frame in twenty-six of his thirty-one races that included back-to-back wins in the Tingle Creek Stakes, four BetFair chase victories, two Gold Cups, and a record-breaking five wins in the King George VI Stakes at Kempton.

Frankel's Guineas   *30 April 2011*

After experiencing such a remarkable degree of success in the closing three decades of the twentieth century, Sir Henry Cecil's fortunes started to dip at the beginning of the new millennium. The number of Group winners declined rapidly, his stable of horses, once the dominant force in European racing, shrank to a quarter of its previous size, and his personal life, at times, was far from harmonious and not helped by his own failing health. As he watched his two-year-olds working on the Limekilns, there must have been days when he hoped that just one of them would be the new Oh So Sharp, or Indian Skimmer. Maybe a Reference Point or Ardross was striding across the gallops in front of his very eyes, or perhaps an Old Vic or Slip Anchor. In 2010, there was no horse on a par with these equine giants of the past but, quite incredibly, there was one even better.

The big, long-striding colt by Galileo out of a Danehill mare, made a pleasing debut at Newmarket's July course in mid-August 2010. Starting the 7/4 favourite he readily got the better of Nathaniel by half-a-length with a wide margin back to the third. The time looked reasonable for the debut run, but nothing exceptional. It was, though, the only race in which Frankel started at odds against.

Dropped back in trip, and on more suitable going, Frankel gave weight and a thirteen-length beating to his two rivals on his second start. According to some speed experts, his rating was now into three figures, exceptional for a juvenile, and his price for the 2011 Guineas was cut to 16/1. The result was similar on his next run in the Group 2 Royal Lodge Stakes at Ascot. Held up by Tom Queally in the early stages, he led on the bit three furlongs out then surged away to put ten lengths between himself and the field. Frankel was now favourite for the 2,000 Guineas and the Derby.

In the Dewhurst Stakes, a race that brought together three of the best two-year-olds of the season, including the unbeaten Dream Ahead a nine-length winner of the Group 1 Middle Park Stakes a fortnight earlier, the winning margin may have been only two-and-a-quarter lengths but the victory was emphatic. Frankel's race time for the seven furlongs was 1m 25.73s, faster than the three-year-olds managed in the preceding fourteen-runner Group 2 Challenge stakes and over a second quicker than the juvenile fillies in the Rockfel Stakes. His main danger, Dream Ahead, was fully seven lengths adrift at the line.

Brilliant two-year-olds do not always train on, as was the case with Johannesburg. Fortunately, after the winter break, there was nothing in the gallops reports to suggest that Frankel would suffer the same fate. Quite the contrary, in fact. According to the *Racing Post*, he outpaced a Newmarket-to-Cambridge passenger train prior to his Guineas trial. Whether true or not, at Newbury he showed that he was as good, if not better, than he had been the previous autumn, coming home four lengths clear of Excelebration, a horse that would follow him home in a further three contests. By this stage of his career most race analysts considered Frankel to be exceptional, but to some he still needed to prove himself in a Classic. On the 30th April 2011 Frankel would get his chance to dispel any doubts.

Two Thousand Guineas day dawned dry and breezy. As the thirteen runners went to post for the mile Classic, the crowd moved from parade ring to betting ring, then to the stands and rails. Regular attendees took up viewing positions they had done so many times in the past, positions that had allowed them to marvel at performances by Bosra Sham, Salsabil, Miesque, Oh So Sharp and Pebbles, Zafonic, Nashwan, Dancing Brave and El Gran Senor, some of the greatest thoroughbreds ever to race at Newmarket. Was Frankel about to be added to this list of memorable horses?

The favourite was drawn in stall one, his pacemaker in thirteen, a far from ideal situation but it made no difference. As the gates opened Frankel was quickly into his stride and was leading after a furlong, the pacemaker unable to match his speed. After just two furlongs he had powered into a lead of around five lengths. This margin steadily increased as the runners covered the historic Newmarket Mile. At the *bushes* Frankel's advantage was fully fifteen lengths. Many observers thought he had gone too fast and would tire in the closing stages. In their view, no horse could be that much better than his contemporaries. As the pair neared the furlong pole, Tom Queally started pushing on Frankel, but the others were already under the whip and being forcefully driven, in an attempt to close the gap. The leader wasn't stopping though, and at the line he had six lengths in hand over the runner-up; the fourth horse home, Slim Shadey, was beaten seventeen-and-a-half lengths. This astonishing performance increased his handicap rating by twenty pounds and he was beginning to look like a freak, a "one in a million" thoroughbred.

Three more wins followed in 2011, including a five-length defeat of the four-year-old Canford Cliffs in the Sussex Stakes and a four-length win in the Queen Elizabeth II Stakes at Ascot in October. Frankel went into the winter with a perfect nine from nine and comparisons were being made with other unbeaten champions such as Ribot and Ormonde.

Much to the delight of racing fans the world over, Frankel was kept in training as a four-year-old. Four straight successes, with a narrowest winning margin of five lengths, showed that he had lost none of his ability. His stunning win at Royal Ascot was at least on a par with his Guineas success and to some judges was even better. In the autumn he approached the last race of his career unbeaten from thirteen starts.

At Ascot on 20th October 2012 the 2/11 favourite faced just five opponents in the ten-furlong Champion Stakes. The French star, Cirrus Des Aigles who won the race in 2011, was seen as the main danger and at 9/2 was priced accordingly. Frankel had won over ten furlongs in the Juddmonte International Stakes on his previous start, but it was felt that he was better at a mile and the soft going was not in his favour. In fact he had only encountered a similar surface once before, on his very first start back in 2010.

The race could not have started any worse for Frankel fans; for the first time in his career the great horse was slowly away, losing around three lengths as the gates opened. Queally soon had Frankel on the tails of the leaders but making up ground on a testing surface is far from ideal. As the pack rounded the bend and straightened up for home Frankel had over two lengths to find on the new leader Cirrus Des Aigles and a first defeat looked a distinct possibility. Queally didn't panic though, and asked his mount to improve; the French horse was under the whip. At the distance, Frankel was upsides the leader, still under hands and heels.

Then, with the crowd in full voice, Queally got serious with the unbeaten Champion and gave him one sharp crack of the whip. The response was decisive and within a couple of strides he was clear. The margin of victory was under two lengths, but with conditions so much against him, it was one of his most impressive performances.

An amazing career was over, and the debate naturally turned to Frankel's place in the pantheon of great horses. *Timeform* rated him 140, two pounds clear of Dancing Brave, which appears to be a very conservative estimate of his ability. It did represent an improvement on his three-year-old assessment though which put him behind Sea-Bird, Tudor Minstrel, and Brigadier Gerard. Of course, comparing horses from different eras is a virtually impossible task. Eclipse, St Simon, Ormonde, and Bayardo were all brilliant horses, but can any meaningful comparison be made with today's runners a century or more later? Ribot was undoubtedly the best horse in Europe in the 1950s, and Tudor Minstrel excelled at a mile, but could not replicate the form over further. Brigadier Gerard has a claim to be Frankel's equal but, unlike the 2012 Champion, he was beaten. The same comment also applies to Sceptre, Pretty Polly, Alleged and Shergar. Whether or not he was the greatest thoroughbred can never be known for certain, but the person who knew him best definitely put him amongst the greats. Sir Henry Cecil said of Frankel in the *Racing Post*: 'He's the best I've ever had and the best I've ever seen. I'd be very surprised if there's ever been better'.

Most Expensive Stubbs Painting Sold   *5 July 2011*

George Stubbs was born in Liverpool in 1724, the son of a leather currier and cutter. It was assumed that he would join the family business, but the young Stubbs' talents lay elsewhere. Often, when he was supposed to be working for his father, he would disappear to the stables where he could practise and develop his artistic skills. He did not have to wait long before his undeniable talent was recognised. One of his earliest efforts was the model of a horse for which he received a gold medal from the Society for the Encouragement of Arts. From that point, his career path was set.

Though mostly self-taught, Stubbs spent time in southern Europe and northern Africa where he was able to observe more exotic animals in their natural environment. On one such visit he witnessed, at close quarters, a lion kill and devour a horse. These observations coupled with his detailed understanding of anatomy became the basic building blocks of his work.

His immensely detailed paintings have grown in popularity in the centuries since his death. At Christie's on 5th July 2011 his "Gimcrack on Newmarket Heath, with a Trainer, a Stable Lad, and a Jockey" was auctioned. It attracted bids up to £22 million, making it the most expensive Stubbs ever sold.

Estimate Makes History   *20 June 2013*

Estimate, owned by Her Majesty Queen Elizabeth II, made a modest start to her racing career when well beaten on her only run as a juvenile in the autumn of 2011. However, she was a stayer in the making, and over twelve furlongs on her return to racing the following May she was far too good for the eleven maidens she faced at Salisbury. On the back of this form, Estimate was made the 3/1 favourite for the Queen's Vase at the Royal meeting in June. The greater test of stamina clearly suited the Monsun three-year-old, and she powered away from the field in the last two furlongs to win by an impressive five lengths. Twelve months later, on 20th June 2013, she was back at Ascot, this time racing for the most prestigious trophy of the June meeting.

Estimate's "prep" race, the two-mile Group 3 Sagaro Stakes, had given her a third win from six races, and Sir Michael Stoute was sure to get more improvement from her by the time she lined up for the Gold Cup. At Royal Ascot, Estimate was sent off the 7/2 favourite.

Ryan Moore kept her on the heels of the leaders as the runners made their way at a modest gallop through the early stages of the race. At Swinley Bottom, Estimate was only fifth, but moving well. Turning into the straight Moore asked Estimate to quicken and whilst her reaction wasn't on a par with St Simon's over a hundred years earlier, she did begin to stay on. At the two-furlong marker she only had Colour Vision, winner of the race in 2012, in front of her.

With a furlong to go she ranged upsides the leader and appeared to have the advantage, but a greater threat came from the centre of the track where Simenon was quickening from off the pace. Simenon edged nearer and nearer as Estimate gained the upper hand over Colour Vision, and in the last fifty yards it was a battle between the two. Estimate held a crucial lead though, and no matter how determined Simenon was, he could not get past the filly. At the winning line Estimate had a neck to spare. Despite a history stretching back to the early years of the nineteenth century, Estimate was the first horse owned by a reigning monarch to win the Ascot Gold Cup.

A Long Winning Run Finally Ends   *25 January 2014*

On 25th January 2014 Big Bucks was finally beaten. His winning run started on New Year's Day in 2009 when he ran out a comfortable winner over Don't Push It who memorably won the Grand National a year later when partnered by Tony McCoy. From that race onwards, Big Bucks just kept winning, accumulating eighteen straight wins for trainer Paul Nicholls. In 2009 he won the prestigious World Hurdle, Liverpool Hurdle, and Long Distance Hurdle, amongst other races. Big Bucks then won these same three races in 2010, 2011 and 2012 despite injuries curtailing his appearances. When he retired, the undoubted champion staying hurdler of the age had won twenty of his thirty-three hurdle races in addition to three chases.

Enable   10 May 2017

After making an encouraging debut on the all-weather at Newcastle in late November 2016, Enable only managed a third to stable companion Shutter Speed on her return over ten furlongs at Newbury in 2017. Three weeks later, the daughter of Nathaniel lined up for the Cheshire Oaks over a distance just shy of twelve furlongs. Before the race the main danger appeared to be Alluringly, Aidan O'Brien's even-money favourite. However, in the short Chester home straight there was no danger at all to John Gosden's filly. At the furlong pole Enable was three lengths clear of the field, and Frankie Dettori was able to ease her down in the closing stages to win by just under two lengths. This win kick-started a stunning run of success.

In June Khalid Abdullah's three-year-old added the Epsom Oaks to her tally, then a third Oaks when she won at The Curragh in July. Later that month she made short work of the older generation when scoring in the King George VI and Queen Elizabeth Stakes by four-and-a-half lengths. Her five opponents in the Yorkshire Oaks proved no match for the 1/4 favourite, the victory giving her a remarkable four Oaks successes in a single season. By this stage Enable, and her stablemate Cracksman, were the highest rated middle distance horses in Britain, and on 1st October the filly extended her winning run to six when beating the best European horses in the Prix de l'Arc de Triomphe by a comfortable two-and-a-half lengths.

As a four-year-old the success continued. A regulation win in the September Stakes, her first run of the season, was followed by a second "Arc" victory, and then a win in the Breeders' Cup Turf at Churchill Downs.

Enable added three more wins to her ever-growing list in 2019. In the Eclipse Stakes she always had the measure of her rivals, winning a shade comfortably by just under a length. At Ascot in the King George VI and Queen Elizabeth Stakes she was pushed out to win by a neck from Sir Michael Stoute's Crystal Ocean then secured another Oaks victory at York when getting the better of Magical, Aidan O'Brien's filly that had finished runner-up to her on three occasions.

It was disappointing that when attempting a record-breaking third win in the "Arc", Enable could only manage a second to Waldgeist. Nevertheless, by that stage of her career Enable had won eleven of her thirteen races, a pretty decent record for any horse. In the 2019 World's Best Racehorse Rankings, Enable was rated 128, the same as Crystal Ocean and Waldgeist at the top of the table, having been placed fifth in 2017 and only joint eighth in 2018 the year she won in France and America, which does cast some doubt over the accuracy of these figures.

In the coronavirus-ravaged season of 2020, Enable made her debut in the Eclipse stakes and ran second to Ghaiyyath. Two wins followed before she returned to Longchamps seeking that elusive third "Arc" victory. The heavy going was not in her favour, though, and she suffered the heaviest defeat of her long career finishing just over six lengths behind the winner. Just over a week later it was announced that Enable would be retired.

Enable was one of the greatest mares to grace the turf and it will be interesting to see if her progeny can emulate her achievements over the coming seasons.

Reshaping the Sport   *Autumn 2021*

Studying horseracing is a fascinating business. Over the years its enduring popularity has proved a genuine rival to all of this country's most prestigious sporting institutions, including association football. Its mass appeal across decades saw stands packed with avid racegoers, their backgrounds transcending every walk of life and every social class. At its zenith, betting shops buzzed with energy as punters shared information and "whispers" from "those in the know", the promise of which would enrich them all.

In more recent times, truth to say, the sport of kings has had to weather a rather concerning decline as the focus has shifted away from a sport designed to provide a means of determining the best and improving the breed, to a mechanism that merely serves the Bookmakers.

The authorities are as much to blame. Their "stack it high, sell it cheap" policy toys with the dignity of the game and, left unchecked, jeopardises its very future. Today, we are witnessing a huge expansion of the British flat racing calendar, from 3,700 races in 1990 to 6,350 contests in 2019. Moreover, in terms of racing performances, there were 39,000 for punters to digest in

1990, compared to 60,000 in 2019. Unsurprisingly, such a radical increase in volume has only been matched by a sadly proportionate reduction in quality and appeal.

This issue might not have been nearly so serious had the overall programme retained some of its traditional balance. Whereas fewer than half of all flat races run in 1990 were handicaps, the ratio has increased to seven out of every ten races run in 2021. A large proportion of maiden races, claimers, sellers, and stakes contests have been replaced, leaving owners of all but the best thoroughbreds compelled to run their horses in the seemingly endless stream of weight-adjusted races. In turn, these overrated affairs are gradually suffocating the general standard of the nationwide calendar. The consequent disaffection of once loyal followers now too often leaves meetings bereft of the atmosphere that only a paying public can afford.

Is the cause a lost one? Certainly urgent action is required to address an increasingly one-dimensional spectacle. If real racegoers are to once again grace the greatest courses in the land in numbers, change is imperative, before the dignity of the sport is sacrificed at the online altar of casino-style games. Racing has so much more to offer than the dull simplicity of a saddle cloth denoting a winning number and, fortunately enough, there's an abundance of wonderful history to support this claim.

Over the last 500 years horseracing has been associated with remarkable human and equine achievements. Americans may know where they were the day Kennedy was shot, but racing fans not only know where they were the day "Dessie" won the Gold Cup, but also who they were with and what they had for lunch. Heroic tales of the magnificent performances by Eclipse, St Simon and even Ormonde may not be on the lips of every racegoer, but no one who witnessed Bob Champion winning the Grand National on Aldaniti will ever forget it; the faithful at Cheltenham the day Best Mate won his third Gold Cup will have a bedtime tale to tell their grandchildren again and again; and the fortunate ones in times gone by who watched Frankel, Dancing Brave, Oh So Sharp, Nijinsky or Ribot are still bathing blissfully in simply magical memories.

Horseracing is not just about betting, about winning and losing money, it's about the jockeys, the trainers, the owners, the grooms, the races, and perhaps most of all, the four-legged legends that have decorated so many races with their fabulous talent and tenacity. Since racing's Tudor days' inception, these truths have never changed. It's up to the guardians of our beloved sport to ensure that they never will.

Notes and References

In many instances citations are given in the text. However, in order to improve readability, not all quotations have been referenced directly and, instead, are detailed in the following section. Many quotes will have multiple references that could be found in a range of books and journals. I have provided a single reference for each quote in an attempt to limit the number of works included. A comprehensive list of all books, periodicals, and websites used is given in the Bibliography.

20 March 1519 - The First Horserace Run Under Rules
'the grand point is, to prevent a competitor...' *Whyte, J.*

8 October 1665 - The Newmarket Plate
'to be given to him who shall run the best and fastest on horseback' *Rice, J.*
'the noblemen and gentlemen, and the more opulent class of yeoman' *ibid.*
'No man is admitted to ride for the plate or prize...' *Sporting Magazine.*

11 August 1711 - First Race Meeting At Ascot
'horses to gallop at full stretch' *Holland, A.*
'making and fixing the posts and other work' *Cawthorne and Herod.*
'engrossing the Articles for Her Majesty's Plate' *ibid.*
'reigning beauty of the period' *ibid.*
'dressed like a man...' *ibid.*

24 June 1740 - Minimum Prize-Money Levels Introduced
'The decline of demoralising pastimes... ' *Sports, Pastimes, & Customs of London, Ancient & Modern.*
'did nothing towards the advancement of the Turf' *Rice, J.*
'no very amiable character' *ibid.*
'an end to the objectionable race meetings' Cawthorne and Herod.

Mid October 1762 - Owners Select Their Colours
'for the better convenience of distinguishing each horse... ' *Baily's Sports and Pastimes, vol 90.*

1 April 1764 - Eclipse By A Distance
'ridden all day and occasionally all night' *Holland, A.*
'by way of a crooked-syringe' *Rice, J.*
'object of universal comment' *ibid.*
'His shoulders had great size...' *ibid.*
'gall of a pike or partridge, or the juice of celandine' *Sporting Magazine, vol 7.*
'set fire to the wide end and as it burns..' *ibid.*
'any of the black legged fraternity' *Whyte, J.*
'possessed extraordinary speed and power' *Rice, J.*
'unequalled in those days as a racehorse...' *Baily's Sports and Pastimes, vol 18.*

24 September 1776 - The First St Leger Stakes
'there are no people so strongly imbued with a love...' *Rice, J.*
'quarrels, murders and bloodsheds' *ibid.*
'makinge the waye at the horse-race.' *ibid.*

14 May 1779 - First Running Of The Oaks Stakes
'extremely disagreeable saline matter' *Rice, J.*

'did drink four pints' *ibid.*
'plantation of oaks' *ibid.*
'homebrewed [ale] of the most bucolic kind' *ibid.*
'added to the extent and elegance of the building...' *ibid.*

18 June 1784 - A Duel At Ascot
'try their fortune with copper, silver or gold' *Cawthorne and Herod.*
'of character unimpeached...' trial records, *oldbaileyonline*
'a little too fond of attending...' *ibid.*
'rascal and a scoundrel' *Sporting Magazine vol 7.*
'deported himself with the utmost steadiness and composure...' *ibid.*
'rescue his name and honour from the invidious reports... ' *ibid.*
Character witness descriptions of Richard England were taken from *Sporting Magazine* vol 7.
'proper to set you forth...' trial records, *oldbaileyonline*

28 June 1791 - Baronet Wins The Oatlands Stakes
'Rich and poor, high and low, made common cause...' *Cawthorne and Herod.*
'each seating from two to three hundred ladies...' *Rice, J.*
'your Baronets are more productive than mine...' *Cawthorne and Herod.*
'Your single Baronet is worth all mine put together.' *ibid.*

20 October 1791 - Samuel Chifney
'laid it on thick in the right way' *Baily's Sports and Pastimes, vol 69.*
'no gentleman would start against him' *Roche, J.*
'slogging match to a mounted chess game' *Tanner, M., Cranham, G.*
'the finest rider that ever threw his thigh over a racer' *Rice, J.*
'material for a small town' *Sportsman's Magazine of Life in London and the Country, vol 1.*
'was a perfect character in his way...' *ibid.*
'without seeing the parson' *Rice, J.*

21 May 1801 - Eleanor's Classic Double
'amiable temper' *Whyte, J.*
'made preparations for...' *ibid.*

11 June 1807 - Evolution Of The Ascot Gold Cup
'a very large concourse of people...' *Cawthorne and Herod.*
'Her Majesty was received by the Prince of Wales...' *ibid.*

18 April 1809 – Expansion of Betting Opportunities
'cut the reins asunder, and fastening the several parts to his feet' *Ashton, J.*
'127 English miles in nine hours' *Sporting Magazine vol 4.*
'a mouthful of brandy and water' *ibid.*
'considerable sum' *ibid.*
'twenty-one and a half successive hours' *ibid.*
'sixpence [would] roll a hundred yards' *Rice, J.*
'perfect ease and great spirit' *ibid.*

22 May 1828 - Dead Heat In The Derby
'the real disgrace of England…' *Trolloppe, A.*
'in the greatest of horse-races…' *Baily's Sports and Pastimes, vol 18.*

8 March 1830 - First Recognised Steeplechase
'upwards of one hundred yards' *New Sporting Magazine, vol 3.*

7 May 1835 - Nat Flatman
'entirely without showy qualities' *Cawthorne and Herod.*
'savagely attacked by The Libel' *ibid.*

22 May 1844 - Derby Day Fraud
'any booth or public place…' *The Times.*
'comic singers and dancers…' *Rice, J.*
'innumerable… and the vast majority…' *The Times.*
'…between the intervals of the races…' *ibid.*

6 June 1844 - The Emperor's Plate
'stern despot and haughty autocrat' *Cawthorne and Herod.*
'purpose of ascertaining how far the people..' *The Times.*

23 May 1849 – The Flying Dutchman
'magnificent specimen of power' *The New Sporting Magazine vol 18.*

14 September 1853 - West Australian's Triple Crown Bid
'pick of the lot, to look at' *The Times.*

7 November 1861 - The First Melbourne Cup
'three courses for a shilling' *australianfoodtimeline.com.au.*
'private room for ladies' *ibid.*
'beds for one shilling with hot and cold baths' *ibid.*

31 May 1865 - Gladiateur's Derby
'a rough-looking, angular horse, without any quality' *tbheritage.com.*
'thence ensued one of the finest races…' *The Times.*
'innumerable vehicles from the four-in-hand drag…' *Rice, J.*
'triple barrier round the course' *The Times.*
'nothing numerically compared with those…' *ibid.*
'incessant, and from among their occupants a full quorum…' *ibid.*
'busy and crowded city' *Rice, J.*
'propagating vice, or robbing the bystanders.' *ibid.*

'dense, swarming, excited mass of humanity' *The Times.*

9 September 1868 – Formosa's Four Classics
'a rich harvest was made…' *The Durham Chronicle.*
'the best looking mare in the race…' *The Times.*
'she walked away with Fordham a very picture…' *ibid.*
'her coat could not be equalled by any loom of Lyons…' *Baily's Sports and Pastimes, vol 15.*

22 October 1878 - A Cambridgeshire Gamble
'nearly all of them [racegoers] have gone for Macbeth' *The Times.*
'rattling sticks in their hats' *Porter, J.*
'threading his way through the others as if determined to get to the front.' *ibid.*
'felt… quite equal to the others and entitled to the same respect.' *ibid.*
'a beautiful young coquette, with direct, impudent speech…' *Macnair, M.*
'in a canter by two lengths' *The Times.*

29 October 1881 - Danny Maher
'bright, warm-hearted character, and delightful personality' *The Advertiser (Adelaide).*

12 June 1884 - St Simon's Ascot Gold Cup
'stride over straw' *Welcome, J.*
'beneath his fashionable vapid and foppish exterior…' *ibid.*
'prodigious… the number of coaches and vehicles…' *Cawthorne and Herod.*
'going leisurely enough' *The Times.*
'strode gaily to the front' *ibid.*

14 October 1885 - A Champion Makes His Debut
'the place for which he had been heavily backed' *The Times.*
'consummate ease' *ibid.*

29 May 1895 - Sir Visto's Derby
'tremendous applause, sustained…' *The Times.*

17 September 1897 - Tod Sloan
'all that had to be done was send for Sloan' *Sloan, T.*
'because of the loud clothes… instead of any merit as a rider.' *ibid.*
'doing the neck crouch, the horse's stride seemed to be freer' *ibid.*
'I wait for no jockey.' *ibid.*

31 May 1899 - A Most Expensive Flying Fox
'bright and bold in his eye' *Baily's Sports and Pastimes, vol 73.*
'he made so unfavourable an impression…' *The Times.*

2 May 1900 - A Royal 2,000 Guineas Victory
'by throwing his rider and bolting to the stands.' *The Times.*
'it was pretty clear that the Prince would win' *ibid.*

10 September 1902 - Sceptre's Triple Crown
'multitudes on the broad expanse…' *The Times.*
'going so easily that there did not seem…' *ibid.*
'hurricane of applause' ibid.

27 June 1903 – A Filly to Rival Sceptre
'if anyone…' *tbheritage.com*

28 October 1903 - Hackler's Pride And The Confederates
'they had the Bookmakers by the throat'. *Mathieu, P.*
'done a canter for a month.' *ibid.*
'charming autumn day.' *The Times.*
'could not hold his own in the betting…' *ibid.*
'it cannot be said that the quality… ' *ibid.*
'you won't need that' *Mathieu, P.*
'shot clear away from Burses, Kilgalss, Ballantrae and Simony' *The Times.*

26 September 1905 - Development Of Newbury Racecourse
'level stretch of land…' *Porter, J.*
'conducted in a very friendly atmosphere' *ibid.*

26 May 1909 - A King's Derby
'tumult of jubilation was overwhelming…' *The Times.*

16 June 1910 - Turning Silver Into Gold
'passed the others simply at his leisure' *The Times.*

4 June 1913 - A Memorable Derby
'the most delectable English cricket ground' *Sengupta, A.*
'It is not true that women are banned…' *ibid.*
'turned a complete somersault' *The Times.*
'an irresponsible person without official instructions.' *ibid.*
'at once telegraphed all over the world…' *ibid.*

14 June 1919 - Royal Hunt Cup Record
'trebled the franchise' *nationalarchives.gov.uk*
'something to which the…' *Heffer, S.*
'Arion will catch him, the weight must tell' *The Times.*
'marvel' *ibid.*
'one of the most magnificent performances…' *ibid.*

12 June 1920 - Man o' War's Record Breaking Win
Louis Feustel's paddock comments were recorded by the Daily Racing Form.

12 March 1924 - First Cheltenham Gold Cup
'I cannot believe that the winner at Aintree…' *The Times.*

2 July 1929 - Introduction Of The Tote
'brown bungalow-like' *The Times.*
'figures went wrong on the total board' *ibid.*

18 June 1930 - Stormy Times For Ascot And England
'he pulverized the English bowling…' *The Times.*

20 January 1931 - Dorothy Paget And Golden Miller
'scarcely such form as to warrant such short odds' *The Times.*

8 May 1945 - VE Day Guineas
'even that great judge of pace was waiting too long.' *The Times.*

7 June 1947 - Top Miler Contests The Derby
'put his head in the air and fought against the bit' *The Times.*

23 August 1949 - Abernant
'amidst great cheering' *The Times.*
'effortless style' *ibid.*

10 October 1956 - Italy's Greatest Racehorse
'the greatest single figure in the history of Italian racing' *Randall, J.*

5 June 1959 - Even The Greatest Get It Wrong Occasionally
'six strides had gone into a long lead.' *The Times.*

1 May 1961 - A Betting Shop On Every Street
'I used to have four men…' *The Times.*

12 July 1969 - Nijinsky
'one-horse race' *Piggott, L.*
'Where have you been shot?' *ibid.*
'it was clear that some of the gleam had gone out of his eye'. *ibid.*

6 May 1972 – First Win By A Female Jockey
'collecting her horse with great power and skill' *Whyte, J.*

8 February 1983 - Abduction Of A Champion
'[he] was a great horse, one of the greatest we have seen' *Piggott, L.*

25 February 1984 – A Jockey's Near Death Experience
'one of Britain's most…' *The Age.*

13 March 1986 – Dawn Run
'put up a totally exhilarating performance' *The Times.*

15 October 1990 - He's Back
'No, still one leg on each side.' *Piggott, L.*

26 July 1992 - Racing On A Sunday Afternoon
'are the closest a live sporting contest' *May, P.*

28 October 2000 - Galileo
'it is easy to over-estimate these youngsters…' *May, P.*

27 October 2001 - The World's Best Juvenile
'very good colt… [with] speed and stamina' *Racing Post.*
'physically Johannesburg looks well developed…' *May, P.*

18 March 2004 - Best Mate Matches Arkle
'Whenever they break a blood vessel…' *Racing Post.*
'helped us raise thousands of pounds…' *ibid.*

Bibliography

Books

Aston, J.: *The History of Gambling in England.*
Baerlein, R.: *Shergar and the Aga Khan's Thoroughbred Empire.*
Banks, S: *A Polite Exchange of Bullets: The Duel and the English Gentleman, 1750-1850.*
Brake, L and Denmoor, M.: *Dictionary of Nineteenth-century Journalism in Great Britain and Ireland.*
Cawthorne, G. J. and Herod, R. S.: *Royal Ascot its History and its Associations.*
Cavendish-Bentinck, W.: *Memories of Racing and Hunting.*
Craven: *The Sporting Review.*
Elringont, C. R. (ed.), *A History of the County of Cambridge and the Isle of Ely*: Volume 5.
Farrer, V.: *First Past the Post: The Melbourne Cup of 1861.*
Grant, T.: *Count No. 1 The Old Bailey.*
Griswold, F.G.: *Sport on Land and Water – Recollections of Frank Gray Griswold* – Volume 2.
Heffer, S.: *Staring At God.*
Holland, A: *Classic Horse Races.*
Holland, A: *Stride By Stride, The Illustrated Story of Horseracing.*
Howes, M.: *Emily Wilding Davison: A Suffragette's Family Album.*
Huggins, M.: *Flat Racing and British Society, 1790-1914: A Social and Economic History.*
Macnair, M.: *Lady Lucy Houston DBE: Aviation Champion and Mother of the Spitfire.*
Mathieu, P.: *The Druid's Lodge Confederacy.*
May, P.: *Forecasting Methods For Horseracing.*
May, P.: *The Two-Year-Old Review of 2000.*
May, P.: *The Two-Year-Old Review of 2001.*
Murray, A.: *All the King's Horses: A Celebration of Royal Horses from 1066 to the Present Day.*
Nicoletti, J.: *On the day: Phar Lap's Death Shocks the Racing World*, Australian Geographic.
O'Brien, J and Herbert, I: *Vincent O'Brien: The Official Biography.*
O'Brien, L.: *What's The SP? Oxford Dictionary of National Biography*
Parsons, P.: *Newmarket: or, an essay on the turf.*
Piggott, L.: *Lester: The Autobiography of Lester Piggott.*
Plumptre, G: *Back Page Racing.*
Porter, J.: *John Porter of Kingsclere: An Autobiography.*
Rice, J.: *History of the British Turf, from the earliest times to the present day*, volumes 1 and 2.
Roche, J: *Horse-Racing: Its History and Early Records of the Principal and Other Race Meetings.*
Sloan, T.: *By Himself.*
Sandford, C.: *The Final Over.*
Tanner, M., Cranham, G.: *Great Jockeys of the Flat.*
Thomas, D.: *The Victorian Underworld.*
Trolloppe, A: *He Knew He Was Right.*
Unaccredited Author: *Sports, Pastimes, and Customs of London, Ancient and Modern.*
Walder, D: *The Chanak Affair.*
Welcome, J.: *Fred Archer – A Complete Study*
Whyte, J. C.: *History of the British Turf*, volumes one and two.

Periodicals

Baily's Magazine of Sports and Pastimes – various volumes.
Bell's Life and Sporting Chronicle
British Medical Journal, June 1956: Arden, G. P., Harrison, S. H., Lister, J., and Maudsley, R, H,: *Lightning Strike At Ascot*
Daily Racing Form
Sarasota Journal
The Advitiser (Adelaide)

The Age
The Durham Chronicle
The Edinburgh Gazette
The Gentleman's Magazine, 1801
The Glasgow Herald
The Herald
The Mercury
The New Sporting Magazine – various volumes.
The Sporting Magazine – various volumes.
The Sportsman Magazine, 1828.
The Sportsman's Magazine of Life in London and the Country, Volume 1.
The Sydney Morning Herald
The Times
Towyn-on-Sea and Merioneth County Times
York Herald

Web Articles

Ashforth, D.: *Paget did as she pleased,* www.thefreelibrary.com
Balic, A., *Sandwiches, Savouries and Strawberry Fizz: Dining at Speed on the Flying Scotsman*
Down, A.: *Gold Cup Hero Who Was More of a Flete-ing Fancy,* www.racingpost.com
May, P.: *Rise of the Handicaps,* www.attheraces.com
Pinfold, J, Lake, T and Gay, D: www.sites.google.com/site/jockeypedia9/home
Proceedings of the Old Bailey: www.oldbaileyonline.org
Randall, J.: *A Century of Racing: Geniuses, Giants and Grandees,* www.thefreelibrary.com
Randall, J.: *Armistice centenary: racing's involvement in the Great War,* www.racingpost.com.
Salleh, A.: *Phar Lap Killed by Arsenic,* Expert Confirms, ABC Science Online, www.abc.net.au
Sengupta, A.: *Suffragettes burned down the pavilion on Nevill Ground, Tunbrdige Wells,* www.cricketcountry.com
Sayers, S: Sievier, *Robert Standish (1860-1939),* www.adb.anu.edu.au
Thorpe, V.: *Truth Behind the Death of Suffragette Emily Davison is Finally Revealed,* www.theguardian.com
www.allertonoak.net
www.ascot.co.uk
www.australianfoodtimeline.com.au
www.bbc.co.uk/news/
www.britannica.com/biography/emily-davison
www.broughscott.com
www.bwm.org.au
www.eclipsemagazine.co.uk/remembrance-sunday-at-the-races/
www.greyhounddderby.com
www.jockeysite.com
www.nam.ac.uk
www.nationalarchives.gov.uk
www.racingpost.com
www.tbheritage.com
www.thoroughbreddailynews.com
www.undyingmemory.net/newmarket/
https://wansteadmeteo.com/2015/06/26/premier-league-of-heatwaves-1850-2015/

Acknowledgements

Naturally, a book focussing on the history of horseracing will draw on many varied sources from newspapers to books and websites. The remarkable **greyhoundderby** website was an invaluable source of results for the Classics. Details for every Classic run in Great Britain are listed on the 70,000-page site including jockey, trainer, owner, and starting prices where available. *History of the British Turf*, volumes one and two provided a greater depth of information for a shorter time period. The rules of racing, as well as the requirements to become a member of the Jockey Club rooms, were taken from these texts. Furthermore, the details of the races in which Mrs Thornton competed are given in the second volume of these books. *Horse-Racing: its History* added further to the information already gleaned along with the two volumes of *History of the British Turf*, from the earliest times to the present day by James Rice.

A great deal of horse-specific information was found on the **tbheritage** website. For a vast number of sires the site details in-depth analyses and anecdotes; it's a remarkable work and the contributors have created an essential database for anyone interested in thoroughbred racing. George Plumtre's *Back Page Racing* is an excellent read and it informed the structure of the sections covering the twentieth century. Other quotes are attributed to John Randall's excellent *A Century of Racing: Geniuses, Giants and Grandees*. The early descriptions of Ascot relied on two primary sources, the Ascot racecourse website and the book: *Royal Ascot its History and its Associations*.

In 1914 many jockeys left racing in order to enlist in the armed services. The **jockeypedia** website provides many details but the work of John Pinfold, Tony Lake and Derek Gay deserves a special mention. They have trawled through thousands of documents to generate as comprehensive a list of jockeys lost in the Great War as possible. The section headed The Ultimate Sacrifice, refers to their work as well as drawing from the **undyingmemory** website, the **eclipsemagazine** website and John Randall's Armistice centenary: racing's involvement in the Great War.

Biographies were especially useful and informative. John Welcome's *Fred Archer – A Complete Study* provided many of the quotes given in the section relating to the great jockey as well as the description of the Duke of Portland in the St Simon essay, whilst John Porter's autobiography was the source for much of the information relating to Isonomy and the development of Newbury racecourse. Tod Sloan's ghost written *By Himself* is a fascinating insight into the life of the talented jockey. Lester Piggott's autobiography is a must-read for any fan of horseracing. The unreferenced quotes in the sections relating to the horses he rode are all taken from this book, as well as the note from Romola Nijinsky. Paul Mathieu wrote the definitive guide *The Druid's Lodge Confederacy* and many quotes in the Hackler's Pride section are taken from this exceptional book. The primary source of data relating to the history of Beckhampton was Roger Charlton's website.

Various sources were used for the Socio-economic data. *Flat Racing and British Society, 1790-1914: A Social and Economic History*, was particularly interesting, but the main source was the national archives website which is accessible online. There exists a whole tranche of information relating to Emily Davison. The quotes used in the section relating to Aboyeur's Derby are attributed to the **Britannica** website, and the online articles: Suffragettes burned down the pavilion on Nevill Ground, Tunbridge Wells and Truth Behind the Death of Suffragette Emily Davison is Finally Revealed.

Richard Baerlein's *Shergar* and the Aga Khan's *Thoroughbred Empire* was consulted for the information relating to the abducted Derby winner, and three main sources were used in the chapters that covered Australian racing: First Past the Post: The Melbourne Cup of 1861; On the day: Phar Lap's Death Shocks the Racing World; and Phar Lap Killed by Arsenic, Expert Confirms.

For in-running details of many races, where possible, I have reviewed videos and generated my own summaries. It is amazing how many races are now available to watch online, so if you're still not sure whether Ribot was as brilliant as commentators say, have a look at his races on the internet. Naturally, the **www. racingpost.com** website is a treasure trove of information, and not just race results. There are articles by the best writers in the racing, possibly any sport, such as Brough Scott, David Ashforth, Steve Dennis, and the incomparable Alastair Down. Ashforth's brilliant piece on Dorothy Paget provides background information for the Golden Miller item, and Down's hugely entertaining article about Sirrell Griffiths is quoted in the rendering of the 1990 Gold Cup.

For court case and trial information the **oldbaileyonline** website was extremely helpful. It holds information on all the trials held at the Old Bailey from 1674 to 1913 and is definitely worth exploring. All other unattributed quotes are taken from various newspapers, especially *The Times* whose archive provides access to the daily editions from 1785 to 1985 and is a wonderful resource for anyone wishing to explore the past.

On a personal note, I would like to thank all those who have helped me with this project. Brough Scott, Dave Rossiter, John Slusar, Kim Bailey, the poet Andy Fincham, and John Randall all replied to queries at crucial stages in the writing of this book. Henrietta Knight for the Foreword, and also the members of my family who contributed so much (I hope one person in particular notices the reference to Rosalba, a horse that won him enough cash to buy a new car), and especially Sara for everything she does all the time, Rhianna, Dan and Mr "Duke" Lynton; Mike for always finding the correct phrase, and the members of the Plough Angling Club for distracting me with fishing matches, phone calls about fishing, meetings about fishing, and trips to the local lakes for fishing.

Peter May

Index

Index

Index